Since Socrates

SINCE SOCRATES
Studies in the history of Western educational thought

HENRY J. PERKINSON
NEW YORK UNIVERSITY

LONGMAN
NEW YORK AND LONDON

SINCE SOCRATES
Studies in the History of Western Educational Thought

Longman Inc. New York
Associated companies, branches, and representatives throughout the world.

Developmental Editor: Nicole Benevento
Editorial and Design Supervisor: Judith Hirsch
Design: Angela Foote
Manufacturing and Production Supervisor: Kris Becker
Composition: Book Composition Services
Printing and Binding: Fairfield Graphics

Library of Congress Cataloging in Publication Data

Perkinson, Henry J
Since Socrates.

(Educational policy, planning, and theory)
Includes index.
1. Education—Philosophy—History. I. Title.
LA21.P45 370.1 79-9150
ISBN 0-582-28098-2

Manufactured in the United States of America

10 9 8 7 6 5 4 3 2 1

To Sir Karl Popper

Contents

Preface

These studies in the history of Western educational thought consist of interpretive essays on the thought of eleven philosophers from antiquity to the present. Here, I want to explain the method used in these studies and the purpose I hope they might serve.

The method is one I call intellectual biography. It focuses on educational theories—not on the personalities or acts of the theorists—and attempts to understand those theories by construing them as solutions to serious intellectual problems. With each theorist, I have tried to discover the initial problem that launched him on his intellectual career. The theorist's earliest writings reveal what intellectual problem he first grappled with and the original theories he used to solve his problem. They also disclose what new problems he uncovered, or perhaps created, with his fledgling intellectual efforts. By following the subsequent writings of each theorist in the same way—construing each work as a theory proposed to solve a recognized intellectual problem, and each theory as a source of new intellectual problems—I am led to interpret the philosopher's educational theory as an attempt to solve an intellectual problem generated by his previous intellectual efforts.

With this approach I assume that a serious philosopher will be self-critical—he will try to solve the problems generated by his own ideas and theories. My method consists of tracing the consequences—in a man's own thought—of his critical appraisals and refinements of his ideas. Tracing each philosopher's intellectual career in this way reveals, perhaps not surprisingly, their credentials as remarkably consistent and persistent thinkers.

As an educational historian, I find this approach rewarding insofar as it highlights the serious, often central, role that educational theories have played in the speculations of philosophers and intellectuals. Moreover, since these theorists have usually confronted the crucial political, social, and religious problems of their times, this book may help recall educational history from the peripheral regions it has too often occupied in studies of the Western intellectual tradition.

My purpose in writing this book inheres in the recurring theme in the essays—authoritarianism. I use authoritarianism as a broad, perhaps sweeping, term for any educational theory that purports to teach truth, or virtue, or wisdom; or that purports to teach how to attain truth, or virtue, or wisdom. For human beings, no matter how brilliant, are fallible; they do not possess truth, virtue, or wisdom; and they do not know how to achieve them. Thus, any educational theory based on such presumption is authoritarian. It becomes a warrant for imposition, a prescription to impose theories, values, and dispositions on others.

As I interpret them, almost all educational theorists since Socrates have developed authoritarian educational theories. These theories coalesce with, and are part of, the political, social, moral, economic, and epistemological theories the same philosophers created—and these theories, too, I find authoritarian. My thesis is that such authoritarianism emerges from attempts to transcend the human condition of fallibility. Since Socrates, most philosophers of the West have sought ways in which human beings, or some human beings, can grasp truth, become virtuous or wise, or create good societies or good political arrangements. This effort to escape from the human condition of fallibility has brought forth the authoritarian epistemological, moral, social, political, and educational theories that have dominated Western thought since Socrates.

Having inherited these authoritarian educational theories, we have, understandably, created educational institutions that are authoritarian. In recent years, many critics and commentators have identified and complained about the authoritarianism of our school policies, our school practices, and our school procedures. This authoritarianism, these critics have pointed out, prevents our schools from becoming what they could be: agencies to promote the growth of society and the individual growth of everyone in the society. The schemes these critics propose to combat educational authoritarianism usually focus on reforming the schools. Yet schemes to reform the schools, or to create new schools, or even to abolish schools, are all off the mark. For the authoritarianism we see in our schools stems from our authoritarian conceptions of education embedded in educational theories since Socrates.

As I see it, the initial step in combating the authoritarianism in our schools is to reconstruct a nonauthoritarian theory of education. This theory has lain dormant in our Western tradition since Socrates. But in the second half of the twentieth century, teachers in many schools, under many different conditions, have been trying to fashion a nonauthoritarian approach to education.

This book is addressed to those educators and others who share the hypothesis that a nonauthoritarian approach to education can better promote the growth of the society and the individual growth of everyone in the society. I think that educators can better go about their task of fashioning such an approach to education if they are aware of our Western tradition of educational theory. Moreover, I think they will find the theoretical base for a neo-Socratic, nonauthoritarian approach to education in the philosophy of Sir Karl Popper, to whom I have dedicated this book.

This book is also addressed to a wider group. I address it to all who want to articulate, clarify, and test their own theories about education—its nature and process, its function, and its worth. The best way to become clear about our own theories—to understand their meaning and their value—is through critical encounters with the theories of others. For this reason, I have tried to present the educational theories in this book fully but concisely, so that readers may grasp them and critically discuss them. I have restricted my own evaluations of these theories to brief comments at the end of each chapter. I present my evaluations to provoke teachers to do the same and to engender criticism and refutations by the reader. For my main purpose in writing this book is to promote a dialogue—a dialogue about educational theory.

ACKNOWLEDGMENTS

Earlier versions of some of these studies appeared elsewhere: *Journal of Educational Thought, Et cetera Paedagogica Historica,* and *History of Educational Quarterly;* and in *History and Education,* edited by Paul Nash.

A number of people have read one or more of these studies and made comments helpful to me. It is a pleasure to thank them: Robert Wellman, Lee Belford, Giorgio Tagliacozzo, Paul Nash, the late Stanley Ballinger, Hiram McClendon, Neil Postman, Don Adams, Thomas Collwell, Berenice Fisher, Sir Karl Popper, and especially, Stephenie Edgerton.

I want to express my gratitude to Marilyn Coppinger for typing the manuscript with patience, intelligence, and good humor—over and over.

Socrates's *Apology*

In the year 399 B.C. the Athenians killed Socrates. They found the seventy-one-year-old philosopher guilty of "corrupting the youth by his teaching." They also accused him of refusing to honor the gods of the city and introducing new divinities, but this was the lesser charge. In his defense speech during the trial Socrates paid little attention to the second charge, stating flatly that he did believe there are gods (Plato, *Apology* 36).

What bothered him was the charge that he was a corruptor of youth. He exclaimed to the jury that his accusers—Anytus, Meletus, and Lysias—almost made him forget who he was. They, of course, "hardly uttered a word of truth." For his part he promised to tell "the whole truth: not however delivered after their manner in a set oration duly ornamented with words and phrases.'' He would eschew the art of eloquence, he promised, and use the plain language he was accustomed to, since, he added, ''I am confident in the justice of my cause'' (*Apology* 17).

In his ''apology'' for himself Socrates tried to explain to his fellow Athenians that the charge against him rested on a misconception of him and a misunderstanding of the mission he had pursued throughout his adult life. He tried to tell them that he was a teacher unlike any they had ever known, a teacher whose mission was to improve men, improve them in a way strange to the Athenians.

I

Socrates' trial took place in the wake of a series of catastrophes that had rocked the Athenian people. In 404 B.C. the walls of Athens were destroyed by the Spartans, ending the great Peloponnesian War that had begun in 431 B.C. Many attributed the defeat to the traitorous behavior of the oligarchs who had conspired with Sparta. The most prominent of these were three former disciples of Socrates: Alcibiades, Critias, and Charmides. The latter two became leaders of the so-called Thirty Tyrants, a puppet government set up by the Spartans. The Athenian democrats overthrew the tyrants in 401 B.C., restored the democracy, and reestablished normal legal conditions. In 399 B.C. a case was brought against Socrates, who had his hand in the education of the most pernicious enemies of the state. Because of an amnesty for all political crimes, the charges against Socrates could not openly refer to the notorious three: Alcibiades, Critias, and Charmides. Thus the charge took the vague form that Socrates had corrupted the youth of Athens. Yet Socrates was not on trial only because he had been the teacher of three men who had become traitors. The Athenians really believed he had been, and still was, a corruptor of youth. Therefore, in his courtroom ''apology'' it was to this general charge that Socrates spoke.

At the outset of his speech, Socrates insists that the Athenians have never understood him or what he was trying to do. Some forty years earlier, he informs the jury, the comic playwright Aristophanes had maligned him in a play, *The Clouds*. He had painted Socrates as ''an evildoer, and a curious person who searches into things under the earth and in heaven, and . . . makes the worse appear the better cause; and . . . teaches the aforesaid doctrine to others.''

In that play, Aristophanes presented Socrates as a natural philosopher and a Sophist. Socrates protests to the jury that he is not now, nor ever was, either of these. Why did Aristophanes write these things? Socrates does not answer this important question, although analysis of the play goes a long way toward explaining Aristophanes' characterization of Socrates.

The Clouds is fundamentally a satirical criticism of the educational transformation that had taken place in Athens during the fifth century. In the play Strepsiades, deep in debt because of the extravagant "horsey" tastes of his young son, Pheidippides, decides to consult the "Sophist," Socrates, who will teach him the wrong or unjust logic so that he may use it to argue his creditors out of their due. Strepsiades proves to be too dense to learn the wrong logic, but he gets Socrates to teach it to his son, who then quickly disposes, by argument, of the creditors' claims. Later, the father and son have a violent argument—over the worth of Euripides as a playwright—that ends with the son soundly thrashing the father and then using the wrong logic to justify the act. At this point Strepsiades finally realizes the great danger inherent in this wrong logic, and he goes to smite Socrates and burn down his school. The play ends with Strepsiades shouting:

> For with what aim die ye insult the Gods,
> And pry around the dwellings of the moon?
> Strike, smite them, spare them not, for many reasons,
> But most because they have blasphemed the gods.

Within the play, the central scene is a contest between right logic, who represents the "old" education, and wrong logic, who represents the "new." Right logic pleads with Pheidippides to follow the old education, promising, "You will be as bright and fresh as a flower, spending your time in the gymnasium . . . you will go down to the Academy, and there, under the sacred olive trees, crowned with light reeds, you will run a race with a friend of your own age, to the scent of the yew tree and the white poplar that loses its leaves, enjoying all the delights of spring when the plane tree whispers to the elm. If you do what I tell you, and apply your whole mind to it, you will always have a powerful chest, a good complexion, broad shoulders, a short tongue, massive buttocks and a little rod. . . . But, if you follow present-day practices"—and here Aristophanes explicitly attacks Socrates' teaching—"you will have a pale complexion, narrow shoulders, a pigeon-chest, a long tongue, bony buttocks, and a big rod . . ." (*The Clouds* 1002).

The "old" education praised by Aristophanes consisted simply of gymnastics and music. Yet, he reminds his audience, it was this education that taught the "heroes of old to be hearty and bold," including those Athenians who had fought at Marathon (*The Clouds* 986). In the old days, Aristophanes says, the children marched in crocodile fashion to the gymnastics teacher and the music teacher "even if the snow fell thick as flour"—singing some manly old air like "O the dread shout of War how it peals from afar," or "Pallas the Stormer adore" (*The Clouds* 960–64). As a result of this education, Aristophanes claims that "Honor and Truth were in fashion with youth and Sobriety bloomed on our shore" (*The Clouds* 958). What the playwright ignores is the political context in which this educational program was embedded, a context that had altered drastically during the preceding century. Thus, to understand the *Apology*, we must understand Aristophanes' *The Clouds,* then to understand *The Clouds* we must understand something about the political-cultural changes in Athens during the fifth century B.C.

II

According to Thucydides, the Athenians were the first to put away their weapons and walk about the streets unarmed. This occurred sometime during the sixth century, and it marked the end of the heroic, or military, age. The warrior society had passed, giving way to a civil society. In the earlier society, the Greeks had educated men to a certain kind of excellence, or virtue (*arete*). In order to perpetuate their warrior society, they had to develop or train men who possessed the virtue of courage; their cultural hero was Achilles, the embodiment of the perfect knight. But once the warrior society had disappeared, a new education was needed. For now, instead of rule by the most courageous, the Athenians wanted a government guided by the idea of justice.[1]

Written law is the foundation of justice, and so during the sixth century the Athenians wrote down their laws. But these laws had to be administered, and this required a certain kind of human character, men with a special excellence or virtue: the rulers had to be righteous or just men. The Athenians saw the creation of just men as an educational problem, much as they earlier had viewed the creation of courageous men as an educational problem.

Rarely does a society create anew an educational program. As new needs arise, the old educational program is usually altered and made to serve new functions. So we find the old education of the knight, which consisted of learning how to fight and how to speak, becoming civilized and ritualized to serve a new function. Now the young man's education consisted of learning how to wrestle and how to box, how to throw the javelin and the discus, how to jump and how to run. Physical training replaced military training. At the same time he learned music—how

1. Donald Kagan, *The Great Dialogue: History of Greek Political Thought from Homer to Polybius* (New York: Free Press, 1965), p. 16. See also Werner Jaeger, *Paideia: The Ideals of Greek Culture,* 2nd ed. (New York: Oxford University Press, 1965), vol. I, chap. 6, "The City-State and Its Ideal of Justice."

to sing, dance, and play a lyre or flute. The aim of this training was to prepare the child for athletic and musical contests.[2]

By civilizing and ritualizing the old military education and by using it to prepare youths for competitive contests, the Athenians aimed to teach them to be honest, truthful, sober, and just. Young men of Athens now learned that life itself was a contest, a competition. They learned that one should strive to win, but also, and most important, that one must abide by the rules of the game; one must play fair, one must be just, honest, and truthful.

This education was originally for the aristocracy, the descendants of knights of the earlier period—landed proprietors who had wealth and a good deal of leisure, to be spent in playing sports and running the government. But gradually, during the next century, Athens became a democracy as political privileges, rights, and powers were extended to shopkeepers, craftsmen, and peasants.

Once again, political change brought about educational change. As political power became democratized, the whole system of what had been aristocratic education spread, becoming the standard education for every child in Greece.[3] The increased number of students made the old tutor-pupil system unfeasible. In the fifth century new educational institutions developed: the music school and the *palestra,* or physical training school. The aristocrats lamented this democratization of education as much as they did the democratization of politics. They argued that virtue (i.e., justice) could not be *taught*. The poet Pindar (522–443 B.C.), the most articulate spokesman for this point of view, held that one had to be a "good man," an aristocrat, in order to profit from education. As he saw it and expressed it, education makes sense only if it is given to a nobleman, who has to become "what he is." Pindar had nothing but contempt for the self-educated, "those who know only because they have lessons." [4] Throughout the fifth and fourth centuries, the Athenians continued to debate whether virtue could be taught. The arguments over this question led some to confront an even more fundamental question, a question about the nature of virtue itself: "What is virtue?"

Traditionally, the Greeks had viewed virtue as a character trait, a habit, a habitual mark of behavior. Moreover, they had always believed that education could help develop character traits: through education one became courageous or just. But now that the democratization of Athenian society had precipitated disagreement on the power of education to develop virtue, some men put forth a new and different concept of virtue.

---

2. H. I. Marrou, *A History of Education in Antiquity* (New York: Sheed and Ward, 1956), p. 40.

3. Ibid., p. 39.

4. Jaeger, *Paideia,* chap. 10, "The Aristocracy: Conflict and Transformation."

This revolutionary conception had first been enunciated by Xenophanes, a natural philosopher of the late sixth century. Xenophanes, an Ionian, spent his life traveling about the city-states of Greece as a minstrel, or poet. He was the first natural philosopher to move beyond the confines of his own disciples to preach the practical or political worth of philosophy.[5] Through his long philosophical poems, he informed his listeners that virtue was wisdom (*sophia*). Virtue, according to him, had to do with the intellect or the mind. Xenophanes looked scornfully upon the athletes, products of the traditional education in music and gymnastics. They, he argued, were of no value to the city-state; they were not fit to be its rulers. Instead, the city needed men of wisdom.

Xenophanes made little immediate impact on Athenians. He did not alter their conception of the nature of virtue, but he did sow the seed. And in the second half of the fifth century a group of itinerant teachers called Sophists appeared, who declared that virtue is knowledge; they claimed to be able to teach political virtue to anyone who would attend them. They wandered from city to city, and through panegyrics and harangues, as well as straightforward lectures on various questions of learning and life, they displayed their skills and attracted pupils. They instructed their pupils in the various doctrines of the natural philosophers but devoted most of their attention to the art of rhetoric. For at this time in Athens, the very time when Aristophanes was composing *The Clouds,* the ability to speak well was the prime requisite for a political leader. In this participant democracy, as Gomperz has noted, the chief instrument of government was the power of the tongue. Not just in the political arena—the assembly, the council, and so on—but in the law courts as well, words were the universal weapons. "The gift and faculty of speech was the sole road to honor and power." [6] Once the young Athenian had learned how to speak effectively he was ready to enter public life, anxious to influence and direct the course of public decisions.

Like the natural philosophers, the Sophists were intellectuals.[7] But whereas intellectuals had heretofore been isolated, exerting little or no influence on the political life of the city-state, they now, in the guise of Sophists, became a powerful force. What made the Sophists so dangerous was that in addition to insisting that virtue was knowledge and that it could be taught, they also insisted that virtue was conventonal or manmade. They taught that all values were manmade. And from this they concluded that all norms (i.e., all values and conceptions of virtue) were

---

5. Ibid., chap. 9, "Philosophical Speculation: The Discovery of the World Order." See also Arthur W. H. Adkins, *Merit and Responsibility: A Study in Greek Values* (Oxford: Oxford University Press, 1960), pp. 74, 75.

6. Theodor Gomperz, *Greek Thinkers* (New York: Humanities Press, 1964, vol. 1 first published 1901).

7. Gomperz uses this term to describe the sophists. Ibid., vol. 1, p. 305.

"merely arbitrary." This had, as Field has noted, "a dissolvent effect" on the traditional moral standards of the Athenians.[8]

We are now in a position to begin to see why Aristophanes misunderstood and misrepresented Socrates in *The Clouds*. Aristophanes was an antiintellectual, distressed by the increased power the intellectuals enjoyed in Athens, a power that seemed to him to be corroding the traditional values, beliefs, and attitudes of his native land. Without these traditions, he believed, Athens would decline. In opposing the intellectuals he made no distinctions, lumping together the natural philosophers, the Sophists, and Socrates. Socrates indeed was an intellectual, but he was neither a natural philosopher nor a Sophist.

In his "apology" Socrates explains patiently that he was not a natural philosopher—he had "nothing to do with physical speculations"; furthermore, he declares that many Athenians among those present could be brought forward to bear witness to this claim. As to the notion that he was a Sophist, this too was false, but here the matter is more complex and subtle. For, like the Sophists, he believes that virtue is knowledge, but he differs from them on the fundamental question whether or not virtue can be taught. He denies that he taught virtue to anyone, since he did not know what virtue was. And like the Sophists he accepts norms as being manmade, but he denies that they are merely arbitrary—he believes it is man's duty to improve them.

III

Many people called Socrates a wise man. How could this be, if, as he claimed, he neither taught virtue nor knew what virtue was? In order to explain how he got the reputation of a wise man, Socrates in the *Apology* recounts the story of Chaerephon and the oracle of Delphi. Chaerephon, an old friend of Socrates, went one time to Delphi to ask the oracle if anyone was wiser than Socrates. According to the story, the oracle answered that there was no man wiser.

When he heard what the oracle had said, Socrates could not believe it, since he knew that he had "no wisdom; small or great." Then, he says, he thought of a method of testing the claim. He would find someone who was wiser and thereby refute the oracle. Accordingly, he sought out those who claimed to be wise: the politicians, the poets, even the artisans. But when he talked to them and questioned them, he discovered that they were not really wise, even though others so regarded them and they so regarded themselves. At last, he concluded that, yes, perhaps he was

8. G. C. Field, *Plato and His Contemporaries*, 2nd ed. (London: Methuen, 1948), p. 82.

wiser than they, because they knew nothing but thought that they knew; whereas he, Socrates, neither knew nor thought that he knew.

Socrates' claim to wisdom is a negative one: he is wise because he is aware of his ignorance. Moreover, he insists that no man has wisdom; God alone is wise. So, he explains, when the oracle said that no man was wiser than Socrates, this was a case of God using him merely as an illustration, as if he said, "He, O men, is the wisest, who, like Socrates, knows that his wisdom is in truth worth nothing." And thus it came about that Socrates was given a mission, a "divine mission," to go about the world "obedient to the God," to search out those who claim wisdom and to question them. Upon discovering that they were not wise, he revealed their ignorance to them.

This inquisitorial mission won him many enemies, enemies of the worst and most dangerous kind. For those whose wisdom he refuted became angry, not with themselves, but with him. It is these enemies, he declares, that now bring him to trial. And because they cannot identify any evil that he practices or teaches, they merely repeat the ready-made antiintellectual charges traditionally made against philosophers: they corrupt youth and blaspheme the gods.[9]

These charges against him are, he repeats, false. At this point, he proceeds to refute them in a way that displays the inquisitorial method he has just described. Addressing himself to Meletus, one of his accusers, Socrates quickly reveals that Meletus had no interest at all in the youth of Athens. He shows that Meletus did not understand such matters as the improvement or corruption of people. Socrates exposes him, first by forcing him to accept the outlandish position that everyone in Athens, except Socrates, helps to improve the youth, and then by getting him to admit that he is claiming that Socrates is intentionally harming himself if he is in fact corrupting the youth of Athens.

In this interchange with Meletus, Socrates forcefully exposes what Brehier [10] calls his fundamental doctrine: that no man is voluntarily wicked; evil springs from ignorance. Through Meletus, he makes his point: the evil that Meletus is doing by accusing Socrates of corrupting the youth is the result of Meletus's ignorance—his ignorance of what Socrates does and of such matters as the improvement and corruption of people. But in the act of exposing Meletus and at the same time demonstrating his method of revealing ignorance, Socrates has made abundantly clear why he had so many enemies. He has treated Meletus harshly.

Socrates knows this. He admits that it is this behavior that now threatens to bring him to an untimely end. But he has no regrets. "A

---

9. E. Zeller, *Socrates and the Socratic Schools* (New York: Russell and Russell, 1962), chap. 3.

10. Emile Brehier, *The Hellenic Age* (Chicago: University of Chicago Press, 1963), p. 85.

man,'' he says, ''who is good for anything ought not to calculate the chance of living and dying; he ought only to consider whether in doing anything, he is doing right or wrong—acting the part of a good man, or of a bad'' (*Apology* 28). He is, he repeats, a philosopher—a philosopher with a divine mission. It would be wrong for him, because of fear of death, to desert the practice and teaching of philosophy. Even if the jury frees him, he promises that he will continue to probe and question his fellow Athenians, continue to reveal their ignorance to them. Furthermore, Socrates now makes the startling claim that in obeying the command of God he has conferred upon the state the greatest good it has ever received. So, quite simply, and in direct contradiction to his accusers, Socrates insists that he has done more than anyone else ever has to improve the city-state of Athens. ''I do nothing,'' he says, ''but go about persuading you all, old and young alike, not to take thought for your person or your properties, but first and chiefly to care about the greatest improvement of the soul'' (*Apology* 30).

What does Socrates mean by claiming that he has done more for Athens than anyone else? The answer lies in understanding, first, what Socrates means by the ''improvement of the soul,'' and, second, of the way he tries to bring about his ''improvement.''

For Socrates, ''the improvement of the soul'' consisted of an increase in knowledge. Like the Sophists and other intellectuals, Socrates held that virtue is knowledge; thus, to increase knowledge, to approach closer to wisdom, was to become more virtuous. Since no mortal man has complete wisdom, however, no mortal man is virtuous. All men, Socrates believed, do what they consider to be good; no man voluntarily does evil. But that which man considers to be good is never *the good;* it is never absolutely and completely good. There is always some residue of evil inherent in our conceptions of what is good, simply because we are not wise or infallible.

Socrates' role as a teacher is based on this conviction that man is fallible: man intends to be good, but he fails because he is ignorant of what the good really is. What Socrates tries to do, through questioning, is to get people to recognize that what they thought was good is, in fact, not good, or not so good as they thought. He tries to remind people that they are fallible.

At first blush, one might suppose that this negative approach to teaching would lead to skepticism. After all, if Socrates, or any teacher, continually revealed our ignorance to us so that we finally admitted that wisdom was not for us, then what other alternative do we have except skepticism and nihilism? This, I think, is exactly how the Athenians responded to the negative approach of Socrates. They could not believe that what he did could ever lead to the improvement of the soul. But—and this is the tragedy of Socrates' death—this was because, like Meletus, they did not understand the meaning of human improvement nor how it takes place.

First, human improvement can take place only if man is fallible; infallibility leaves no room for improvement. And if man is fallible, then he can never know what the good is, so the *only* way he can improve is by discovering or uncovering his own mistakes, his own errors, and then eliminating them. Therefore, rather than skepticism and nihilism, Socrates' negative approach leads to optimism *and* progress.

The Athenians (and many like them down to the present) argue that one can accept the fallibility of man but reject the negative approach to teaching. What is needed, according to this argument, is a teacher who transmits to youth the virtues, values, rules, norms, and so forth that have so far been accepted by the society. These values, of course, are to be transmitted as tentative, since they are not infallible absolutes and will probably change in time, to be replaced by others. According to this position, a teacher can improve youth by teaching them the values or virtues accepted by the society. This is precisely what Socrates denies. He denies that virtues can be taught, denies that the teacher can improve youth. Socrates' position is that improvement comes about only from within. No man can improve another; one is improved only through one's own efforts. All that a teacher can do is to help a student become aware of his errors, his mistakes, his limitations. It is up to the student to bring about the improvement. He does this by trying again; he makes a new conjecture or a new attempt.

In the *Meno,* Socrates demonstrates how this works. The central scene in this dialogue is that between Socrates and Meno's slave boy. Drawing the figure of a square in the sand, Socrates proceeds to ask this slave boy a series of questions about it. The boy eventually "discovers" the solution to the problem of doubling the square. At a certain point in the questioning, Socrates administers what Meno calls the "torpedo shock." This is the conclusive revelation of one's own ignorance. Yet this torpedo's shock is a stimulus to the growth of knowledge. For once the slave boy admits that one of his guesses or conjectures is wrong, he proceeds to make another, better conjecture. The new conjecture is better because it avoids the error of the previous one.[11]

---

11. The motion of making the slave boy aware of his ignorance I take to be socratic; but the notion of recollection of ideas (the theory of innate ideas), I take to be platonic. In this connection, see K. R. Popper, *The Open Society and its Enemies* (4th ed.; London: Routledge and Kegan Paul, 1962), chap. 3, esp. note 8; and Alexander Sesonske, "Knowing and Saying: The Structure of Plato's Meno," in *Plato's Meno,* ed. Alexander Sesonske and Noel Fleming (Belmont, Calif.: Wadsworth, 1965). Here I should express my great indebtedness to Karl Popper's interpretation of Plato. My analysis of Socrates grew out of my reading of the work of Popper.

SOC. Do you see, Meno, what advances he has made in his power of recollection? He did not know at first, and he does not know now what is the side of a figure of eight feet: but then he thought that he knew and answered confidently as if he knew and had no difficulty; now he has a difficulty, and neither knows nor fancies that he knows.

MEN. True.

SOC. Is he not better off in knowing his ignorance?

MEN. I think that he is.

SOC. If we have made him doubt, and given him the "torpedo's shock," have we done him any harm?

MEN. I think not.

SOC. We have certainly, as would seem, assisted him in some degree to the discovery of the truth; and now he will wish to remedy his ignorance, but then he would have been ready to tell all the world again and again that the double space should have a double side.

MEN. True.

SOC. But, do you suppose that he would ever have enquired into or learned what he fancied that he knew though he was really ignorant of it, until he had fallen into perplexity under the idea that he did not know and had desired to know?

MEN. I think not, Socrates.

SOC. Then he was the better for the torpedo's touch?

MEN. I think so.

(*Meno* 81)

The Athenians had never known a teacher like Socrates: a teacher who did not teach, a teacher who did not tell his students what was good, nor what was true, nor even what was better or more desirable. They could not understand a teacher who only told his students what was bad and what was false, what was evil and what was wrong. Nor could the Athenians accept Socrates' explanation that this was the way to persuade people to tend the improvement of their souls.

Summary and Evaluation

The trouble with the Athenians was that they were all like Meletus; they were not really concerned with human improvement. For if man is fallible, then the *only* way to improvement is through criticism of the accepted values, criticism of what people think is right or good. What people hold to be good or right can never be absolutely good or right (since man is fallible), but these accepted values and norms can serve as the starting point for future improvement. Through criticism, people can uncover the limitations of these values and be stimulated to create better ones.

A society that permits the comprehensive criticism of its values is an open society. An open society doesn't just happen; it comes about slowly, through the establishment of a critical tradition. The critical tradition is usually embodied in institutions that encourage criticism and protect critics. Frequent, free elections, together with two or more political parties and secret balloting, are all institutions that encourage criticism and protect critics. A bill of rights, as well as the separation of government powers, together with a system of checks and balances, are additional institutions that protect critics. Athens had some of these institutions, but not enough to protect Socrates.

He was well aware of his vulnerability, as is evident from his remarks on why he avoided any public service to the state. Quite bluntly, he admits that if he had engaged in politics, he would "have perished long ago and done no good, either to you or to myself" (*Apology* 31). Again, in the *Crito,* he discusses the responsibility the critic of the state takes on and the danger he faces. The critic of the state is an expert; he has an understanding of what is just and unjust, good and evil, honorable and dishonorable (*Crito* 48).[12] But unlike other experts (e.g., the physical trainer), the critic of the state is unprotected. The physical trainer is protected by traditions and institutions connected with the art of physical training so that when the physical trainer criticizes his pupils, they accept his censure, admit their errors and try to improve.

For Socrates, the role of the physical trainer was like that of the critic of the state. The physical trainer did not know what a perfect athlete was. His job was not to tell or show his students how to be athletes. His job was to criticize them, to make them aware of their mistakes. From him, the students learned what errors they had made, what evils to avoid. The critic of the state functioned in the same way: he did not know what the perfect state was; he merely uncovered the evils of the existing state. But, unlike the physical trainer, the critic of the state was unprotected by a critical tradition. Socrates, in fact, was as much the victim of this absence of a critical tradition in Athens as he was of the accusations of Meletus and the others. Indeed, the *Crito* may be read as an account of how Socrates attempted to teach the Athenians that they must establish institutions to protect the critics of the state.

In this dialogue, which took place in jail two days before his death, Socrates patiently explains to Crito why he cannot escape and flee Athens. It would be wrong for him to leave, he says, for by such an act he would renounce and deny his divine mission. That mission was to help his

---

12. This notion that the expert knows what is just and good, as well as what is unjust and evil, is more platonic than socratic. See page 16.

fellow Athenians improve themselves and their state by serving as a gadfly, a critic who made them aware of their mistakes and their errors.

He admits that the Athenians' condemnation of him has been a mistake, an act of injustice. Moreover, he realizes that his death will be an even greater injustice. But to make them aware of their mistake, to show them the injustice of their ways, Socrates must accept the fate they decreed for him. In effect then, in the *Crito* Socrates is agreeing to become a martyr, not for any ideology or belief, but as his last act of teaching, the final fulfillment of his divine mission.

By refusing to flee from Athens, by allowing his fellow citizens to kill him, Socrates makes them aware that it is wrong to silence critics. A free society, an open society, must have critics and must protect them. Socrates' death remains one of the most poignant and at the same time most significant acts of teaching in the history of Western civilization.

Plato's *Republic*

The execution of Socrates dramatically exposed how vulnerable intellectuals were in Athens. Without the critical tradition of an open society, the critic played a precarious role. No one perceived this more clearly than Plato, Socrates' most famous pupil. Plato proposed to eliminate the vulnerability of the intellectuals by having them control the whole of political life in the city-state. As Plato saw it, "there will be no cessation of the evils for the sons of men till either those who are pursuing a right and true philosophy receive sovereign power in the states, or those in power in the states by dispensation of providence become true philosophers" (*Seventh Letter* 326B).

Plato would have the intellectual avoid a vulnerable position in society by completely abandoning the Socratic role of critic, to become instead, an authority—a political authority, an infallible political authority. But this means that Plato must reject democracy and Socrates' dream of an open society. Plato does this, and presents as an alternative his own blueprint for a new kind of society, a closed society.[1] Moreover, since he proposes to use education, or the educational system, as *the* institution to create and sustain this new society, Plato has to abandon Socrates' conception of the role of the teacher; indeed, he will abandon Socrates' conception of the function of education. One can trace this almost total transformation of the political and educational ideas of Socrates in the Platonic dialogues that precede and culminate in the *Republic*.

I

There is no evidence to indicate that the Athenians regretted or renounced the murder of Socrates, and so we can assume that they continued to look with suspicion upon his disciples.[2] Thus Plato, conscious of his own precarious position, attempts in the *Crito* to convince his fellow Athenians that the *real* Socrates had entertained no revolutionary ideas.[3] He is able to do this in part because Socrates at his public trial had argued that the Athenians had never understood him nor his "divine mission." Socrates had even declared that "no greater good has ever happened in the state than my services to the God" (*Apology 30*). This gives Plato the opportunity to concoct a dialogue, the *Crito,* that portrays Socrates as an upright citizen, faithful and loyal to his native city.

In the *Crito,* Plato purports to report a private conversation between Socrates and one of his disciples that took place in jail while the old man awaited his execution. Crito, the disciple, urges his master to escape and flee from certain death. Socrates refuses. Running away, he explains, would stamp him as an enemy of Athens, which indeed he is not. Socrates' arguments against the advice of his disciple clearly reveal his deep loyalty to Athens and to its constitution, laws, and institutions. True, he admits that his fellow citizens have unjustly convicted him; but this makes him a victim of men, not of laws.

In this attempt to establish the loyalty and patriotism of his old teacher, Plato goes too far. By this I mean that he has Socrates say things about his duty to the state that sound quite unsocratic and in fact tend to portray Socrates as a proponent of the closed society Plato will later depict in the *Republic*.

---

1. K. R. Popper, *The Open Society and its Enemies,* 4th ed. (London: Routledge and Kegan Paul, 1962), vol. 1, passim.
2. T. Gomperz, *Greek Thinkers: A History of Ancient Philosophy*, 2 vols. (New York: Humanities Press, 1964 first pub. 1901), 2:118.
3. Of the *Crito,* Gomperz says it is Plato's attempt to defend himself and his group "against the suspicion of harboring revolutionary views."

The Socrates presented in the preceding chapter did believe that he had a duty to the state, a duty not unlike that of a teacher to his pupil. As he saw it, his duty lay in helping Athens to improve, to become a better, more open society. But in the *Crito* we find Plato's "Socrates" describing himself as a child and slave of the state, attesting that it had the right to destroy him, but not he, it; and averring that he must do what his city and his country order him to do (*Crito* 50, 51). Plato here does not have Socrates proclaim the subservience of the individual to the state, although in later dialogues he will do this. In the *Crito* he remains partially faithful to the tradition of Socrates by allowing for the possibility that the individual might persuade or change the state (*Crito* 51). Nor does he here base the notion of the individual's duty to the state on a conception of natural law, as he will later do in the *Republic*. In the *Crito* this duty stems from an agreement or contract that the individual freely enters into with his state. Plato's "Socrates" explains that he cannot escape from prison and flee Athens, since this act would break his agreement, destroy the contract.

To allay the suspicions of his fellow Athenians about his own loyalty to Athens, Plato had to convince them that they had an erroneous opinion of his teacher, Socrates. He does this in the *Crito* by casting doubt on the veracity of *all* public opinion. In the dialogue, Crito expresses misgivings about the opinion people will have of him and the other disciples if they do not help Socrates to escape. Plato then takes this opportunity to comment at length on the topic of public opinion. He insists that in questions of "just and unjust, fair and foul, good and evil," we ought to follow not the opinion of the many but that of the man who has understanding (*Crito* 47).

Once again, Plato goes too far. For here he is intimating that the wise man knows what is true and false, just and unjust, good and bad. This is different from the fallibilistic notion Socrates held, which is that the wise man possesses only negative knowledge, that he does not know the truth, that he knows only that some claims are not true. This fallibilistic approach holds for man's knowledge of justice and goodness as well. According to Socrates, the wise man does not know what the good is, nor what justice is; but he can identify evil, he can perceive injustice. The socratic wise man, or intellectual, is a critic, not an authority.

In the *Crito*, therefore, we see the beginnings of Plato's attempt to abandon the socratic notion of the intellectual as critic in order to replace it with the notion of the intellectual as authority. One of the ways Plato does this is to make a sharp distinction between ("mere") opinion and knowledge. One can find this distinction in Socrates insofar as he maintains that no man has certain knowledge. According to Socrates, all men merely conjecture. (Criticizing conjectures will improve them.) But in the *Crito*, Plato implies that the wise man does more than conjecture; the wise man has certain knowledge. It is to him that we should turn, not the masses. He is an authority.

If the wise man has intellectual authority (i.e., if he has certain knowledge of good and evil, justice and injustice, fair and foul) whence this knowledge? Plato has to explain how the wise man came to be wise. At this juncture, Plato takes up the role of the teacher, drastically altering the conceptions of his own teacher, Socrates. This transformation can be followed in the dialogues *Protagoras, Meno* and *Gorgias*.

II

In *Protagoras* we find a young, disputatious Socrates confronting a venerated teacher, Protagoras, the Sophist. The brash young man openly challenges the Sophist's claim that he, or anyone, can teach the art of politics to others, or that he or anyone can make men into good citizens (*Protagoras* 319). No one, Socrates insists, can teach another to be virtuous. But as Plato presents this position in the *Protagoras,* he makes a subtle transformation of Socrates' original position, as recorded in the *Apology*. In the *Apology,* as we saw, Socrates' denial that virtue can be taught came out of his theory of instruction. That is, he denied that anyone could teach anybody anything, and this included virtue. Teachers, he thought, can do naught but identify, and help their students themselves see the errors they make. But in the *Protagoras* Plato ignores this socratic theory of instruction and rests the case for the denial that virtue can be taught on a theory of curriculum. He has Socrates admit that some things can be taught; some, like virtue, cannot. Moreover, he has Socrates enlist the Athenian people in support for his theory of curriculum. His "Socrates" says:

> And I ought to tell you why I am of opinion that this art cannot be taught or communicated by man to man. I say that the Athenians are an understanding people, and indeed they are esteemed to be such by the other Hellenes. Now I observe that when we are met together in the assembly, and the matter in hand relates to building, the builders are summoned as advisers; when the question is one of ship-building, then the shipwrights; and the like of other arts which they think capable of being taught and learned. And if some person offers to give them advice who is not supposed by them to have any skill in the art, even though he be good-looking, and rich, and noble, they will not listen to him, but laugh and hoot at him, until he is clamoured down and retires of himself; or if he persists, he is dragged away or put out by the constables at the command of the prytanes. This is their way of behaving about professors of the arts. But when the question is an affair of state, then everybody is free to have a say—carpenter, tinker, cobbler, sailor, passenger; rich and poor, high and low—any one who likes gets up, and no one reproaches

> him, as in the former case, with not having learned, and having no teacher, and yet giving advice; evidently because they are under the impression that this sort of knowledge can not be taught (*Protagoras* 319).

In response to this argument from his youthful critic, Protagoras declares that virtue is taught to us by our parents, our masters, and our fellow citizens. He contends that all members of the city-state possess virtue, for unless this was the case, the city could not exist. All teach virtue, and this explains why specialists in virtue are unnecessary. Virtue is learned like a mother tongue that no one specifically teaches to children because in point of fact everyone that children come in contact with teaches them. It is nonetheless true, Protagoras adds, that some people, like himself, are particularly apt at such teaching.

Socrates confesses to be convinced by the argument. "I used to imagine," he says, "that no human can make men good; but I know better now" (*Protagoras* 328). He has only one small difficulty with what Protagoras has said; this concerns the nature of virtue. He wants to know "whether virtue is one whole of which justice and temperance and holiness are parts; or whether all these are only the names of one and the same thing" (*Protagoras* 329).

The question totally confounds Protagoras, who at first takes the position that these qualities are all parts of virtue but then, under the relentless criticism of Socrates, grudgingly admits his error. Socrates shows him that all these qualities are knowledge, which means that they are all one. But now Socrates announces that although he has won this second round of the argument, what he has in fact done is to provide an argument in support of the position Protagoras had taken earlier in the discussion. For, if virtue *is* knowledge, Socrates points out, it must be teachable.

If virtue can be taught, as Plato has argued in the *Protagoras,* how does this occur? He takes up this question in the *Meno*.

III

The *Meno* begins abruptly. Meno, the Thessalian, asks: "Can you tell me, Socrates, whether virtue is acquired by teaching or by practice; or if neither by teaching nor practice, then whether it comes to man by nature, or in what other way?" Socrates replies that none of the Athenians, himself included, know what virtue is, so how can they answer questions about how it is acquired? Meno is incredulous. Can this be the wise Socrates he has heard so much about? Socrates assures him that he is in fact Socrates, but he urges Meno to explain what virtue is, more particularly what Gorgias the Sophist said it is. Under Socrates' critical questioning, Meno soon flounders in helpless confusion. He good-humoredly confesses that Socrates' critical attacks have left his soul and tongue "torpid." For, in spite of the fact that he once could give speeches on the topic, he cannot now "even say what virtue is." He accuses Socrates of being like the "torpedo fish, who torpifies those who come near him and touch him" (*Meno* 80).

Having recognized his own ignorance, Meno is ready to learn. "Let us together inquire into the nature of virtue," Socrates suggests. But at this point, Meno raises an eristic objection that sets the stage for the central theme of the dialogue and at the same time provides Plato an opportunity to alter and radically transform Socrates' original theory of instruction as presented in the *Apology*.

Meno asks: "And how will you enquire, Socrates, into that which you do not know? . . . And if you find what you want, how will you ever know that this is the thing which you did not know?" (*Meno* 80). Before answering this objection, Plato ensures that the reader realizes its force by having Socrates repeat it: "You argue that a man cannot enquire either about that which he knows, or about that which he does not know, for if he knows, he has no need to enquire; and if not, he cannot, for he does not know the very subject about which he is to enquire?"

Before presenting Plato's complex solution to this paradox, it would be well to recall Socrates' theory of knowledge as presented in the *Apology* to see how he would deal with it. There, Socrates admitted that we have no criterion for truth, and so we can never know anything with certainty; all our knowledge is conjectural. The best we can do is uncover and eliminate the errors our conjectures contain. This conception of knowledge as conjecture would mute Meno's objection that one can never inquire into anything, for his objection has force only if one conceives of knowledge as absolute or certain. But this is precisely how Plato in the *Meno* does construe knowledge. For, in this dialogue, he ignores completely the socratic solution to the paradox, introducing instead—through the mouth of Socrates himself—the new (platonic) notion of innate ideas.

In decidedly unsocratic fashion, Plato appeals to the authority of certain "wise men"—jurists, priestesses, and poets like Pindar—who believed in the doctrine of the transmigration of man's immortal soul. This doctrine, he explains, guarantees that man already possesses all knowledge within.

> The soul then, as being immortal, and having been born again many times, and having seen all things that exist, whether in this world or in the world below, has knowledge of them all; and it is no wonder that she should be able to call to remembrance all that she ever knew about virtue, and about everything; for as all nature is akin, and the soul has learned all things, there is no difficulty in her eliciting, or as men say, learning, out of a single recollection all the rest, if a man is strenuous and does not faint; for all enquiry and all learning is but recollection (*Meno* 81).

Having declared that all knowledge is innate and that learning is but recollection, Plato next has Socrates demonstrate how teaching takes place. Taking an illiterate slave boy, Socrates through a series of questions helps him discover, or "recollect," that the square of the area of a square is equal to the square of its diagonal. This demonstration is faithful to the traditional "socratic method" sketched in the *Apology* insofar as in it the teacher does not transmit knowledge to the pupil. Moreover, it has Socrates making the boy aware of his ignorance, administering the "torpedo shock." But it differs from the traditional socratic method in that as a result of the inquiry, the pupil (in this case the slave boy) arrives at certain, or true, knowledge. This is platonic, not socratic. For Socrates, the pursuit of truth was a never-ending critical endeavor. For Plato, the pursuit leads to the possession of truth.

After demonstrating how the teacher can guide inquiry so that the pupil can "recollect" the true knowledge he has within, Plato goes on to explain that this is why inquiry can improve us, can make us better men. Yet, for Socrates in the *Apology,* improvement came about through the discovery and elimination of our errors and mistakes. Now, according to Plato, improvement results from the recollection of true knowledge. Plato has replaced Socrates' negative conception of improvement with a positive conception.

Through his doctrine of innate idea and the teaching demonstration, Plato has given his answer to Meno's original question: virtue can be taught—by a teacher who can educe from the pupil a recollection of the true idea of virtue innate within the recesses of the pupil's own soul. Meno fails to realize this and asks Socrates again whether or not virtue can be taught. Not bothering to explain to the uneducable Meno [4] that he has already answered the question, Plato takes it up anew and proceeds to propound an argument to show that virtue cannot be taught! He argues that virtue is not teachable because there are no known teachers of it.

At this point of the dialogue, Anytus, the future accuser of Socrates, appears. He maintains that there *are* teachers of virtue. But who are they, Plato asks, the Sophists? Anytus vehemently denies that they teach virtue. Who then? The great leaders—Themistocles, Aristides, Pericles, Thucydides? Great as these men were, Plato insists that they cannot be called teachers of virtue. Anytus, after being embarrassed by his lack of success, departs with a dire threat to Socrates and his "socratic" questioning. But Anytus departs before Plato has Socrates explain why these great leaders were unable to teach virtue. First, virtue can be taught because it is knowledge. Those great leaders did *not* teach it because they did not really have knowledge of virtue. They merely had right opinions.

---

4. Jacob Klein, *A Commentary on Plato's Meno* (Chapel Hill: University of North Carolina Press, 1965), pp. 184 et seq.

In practical affairs, Plato admits that "mere" right opinions suffice. These statesmen had governed the city successfully by means of right opinion, but lacking true knowledge of virtue, they had been incapable of transmitting their virtue to their offspring.

After revealing to the reader that so far no one, not even the greatest statesmen, had attained a knowledge of virtue, Plato declares that if such a person could be found "he and his virtue . . . will be a reality among shadows" (*Meno* 100). The import of this is obvious: he who has knowledge of virtue should be the unquestioned ruler of his people. In the *Gorgias,* Plato makes this clear.

IV

"Who should rule?" Plato asks. "The teachers, the teachers of virtue," he answers. He argues his case in the *Gorgias,* where he impugns the credentials of all others to rule.

He starts the dialogue by having Socrates illmanneredly ridicule the authority of the rhetoricians. Socrates informs Gorgias and the other rhetoricians gathered at the home of Callicles that what they practice is a form of flattery, a counterfeit of justice; something that aims at pleasure, not at that which is good. The orator, he declares, does not possess knowledge; he merely appears to possess it. Grounded on experience and not on knowledge, rhetoric is not even an art; it is a pseudoart, like cooking.

This fiery "Socrates" takes on one after the other the great Gorgias, his pupil Polus, and the host Callicles—decimating each one in turn. First, he forces Gorgias to admit that the rhetorician does not teach his students justice because they sometimes are themselves unjust. If the rhetoricians *really* taught them justice, they could not be unjust. Next, he confounds Polus by proving that the rhetorician is neither happy nor able to do what he wills. All men, Socrates insists, will happiness, and happiness consists in knowing the good. But since the rhetorician does not know the good, it follows that he is neither happy nor able to do what he wills. Finally, Socrates attacks his host, forcing him to admit that only the philosopher is a superior man. After starting out by insisting that those men of noble birth ought to be rulers, Callicles is forced to admit that the truly superior men are those who are just, courageous, and temperate. And since all these virtues are knowledge, he is thus forced to concede that the superior man *is* the wise man—he who pursues philosophy (*Gorgias* 500).

After arguing that philosophers ought to rule because they alone possess knowledge of those virtues demanded of a ruler, Plato reminds his readers that the primary duty of the ruler is to "improve citizens" for the benefit of his own state (*Gorgias* 515). Of course, none of the present statesmen, nor any of those great ones of the past, have improved the citizens. How could they teach the citizens to be virtuous when they themselves had no knowledge of virtue? Toward the end of the dialogue, Plato declares (through the mouth of Socrates): "I think that I am the only, or almost the only, Athenian living who practices the true art of politics; I am the only politician of my time" (*Gorgias* 521).

Through these three dialogues, Plato has constructed a rationale for his conception of the role of the teacher. The teacher teaches his pupils what is true and what false, what is just and what unjust, what is good and what evil. How does the teacher come to possess the authority to do this? Plato has argued that this authority is justified by the teacher's political authority. That is, the teacher is a public man, an official of the state, so he must pay heed to the good of the state; as such he must tell the young what is true, what is just, and what is good. This political authority of the teacher is in turn justified by his intellectual authority, for as a philosopher, he possesses true knowledge.

Through these dialogues, Plato has completely transformed the socratic role of the teacher as originally presented in the *Apology*. There, Socrates had actually denied that he was a teacher. Not being an authority on justice or temperance or virtue or any kind of knowledge, he never tried to *justify* himself as a teacher. True, he claimed to have a divine mission to help his fellow Athenians improve themselves. But he did not try to *justify* his work by declaring that it had been decreed by the gods. The work could not be justified; it could only be criticized. His "apology" was not an attempt to justify what he did, but rather an attempt to make clear to his critics just what his role was.

Socrates did not try to justify his work because he saw that all attempts to justify involved an appeal to some authority and that every authority in turn had to be justified by an appeal to another authority, and so on into infinity. The only way to escape this regress is to set up some final or absolute authority. Thus, attempts to justify lead either to an infinite regress or to authoritarianism. Plato, we just saw, has justified the authority of his teacher by appealing to his political authority, which in turn he justified by appealing to his intellectual authority. In the *Phaedo,* he goes on to acknowledge that this intellectual authority of the philosopher is an absolute authority. This dialogue ushers in Plato's authoritarianism.

VI

In the *Phaedo* Plato reaffirms his theory of learning. Recall that earlier, in the *Meno,* he had claimed that man acquired true knowledge—the forms or ideas—through recollection (*anamnesis*). Now he supports it with fresh arguments. Our knowledge of concepts, he declares, must have come to us before birth. Take, for example, the concept of absolute equality. This idea cannot come from sense perception because our senses never show us perfectly equal things. He concludes that the sight of *approximately* equal things revives the thought or idea of perfect equality—an ideal standard of which the approximately equal things we perceive through our sense of sight always fall short.

In this dialogue Plato fully develops his theory of ideas into a metaphysical theory of the nature of things. Earlier, when he had talked about moral matters—about justice, or courage, or temperance—Plato had argued that we must try to discover the idea or the essential characteristic that resides in all acts of justice, in all acts of courage, in all acts of temperance. This idea or essence, he declared, could be discovered and "separated" only through critical examination. In the *Phaedo* he insists that there is a "world of ideas," an objective "real" world, beyond the material world. Unlike the material world, which is accessible to us through our senses, the "real" world of ideas is accessible to us only through the intellect.

The ideas, Plato says, explain what exists (*Phaedo* 100). The ideas do what the natural philosophers promise to do but never accomplish. The so-called explanations of the natural philosophers actually explain nothing, he declares. In explaining, say, how two things form a pair, they tell us either that two things originally at some distance from each other have come close together, or else that one and the same thing was divided in two. But this does not explain how two things form a pair. No physical operation can explain the genesis of the dyad, Plato insists, for the dyad exists in itself, independent of all physical operations, like an object of mathematics: it is by participation in this dyad in itself that every pair of two things arises. Thus, ideas exist, and other things participate in them and derive their names from them (*Phaedo* 102).

How can one determine that he has certain or correct knowledge of these ideas? Earlier, in the *Meno,* Plato had shown how our knowledge comes to us through recollection but that it must be verified through criticism. In the *Phaedo* he shifts away totally from criticism. He explains it this way: "I first assumed some principle (idea) which I judged to be the strongest, and then I affirmed as true whatever seemed to agree with this, whether relating to the cause or to anything else; and that which disagreed I regarded as untrue" (*Phaedo* 100). This principle or idea must itself be derived from further hypotheses which justify or verify it. But they too must be justified or verified by further hypothesis from which they can be derived. Is there no end to this regress? For, if not, none of the ideas in the chain is ever justified or verified. Plato insists that there is a terminal point to which one can come, a point that is "enough in itself" (*Phaedo* 101). In the *Republic* Plato calls this terminal point the *Good,* or "the idea of the Good.'' In other words, the only final justification one can give of one's ideas is that they participate in the Good. As Brehier puts it, ''The Good is like a sun in whose light other things are known in their reason for being and by whose warmth they exist.'' [5]

How do we know when we have reached the Good? How can we know that it is not itself a hypothesis? Plato's answer to this crucial question comes later in the *Republic*: we can recognize the Good only by a direct intellectual intuition (*moesis*) and a sort of vision; it cannot justify itself in any other way (*Republic* 511).

Plato has now completely departed from the fallibilism of Socrates. Once we have attained knowledge of the Good, our knowledge is no longer conjectural; it is certain. Knowing the Good enables us to justify all the ideas in the entire chain of hypotheses we originally used to arrive there.

This theory of ideas, with its terminal idea of the Good, supplies Plato with his ultimate authority. Now he can justify the intellectual authority of his philosopher, which will in turn justify his political authority, which will finally justify his authority as a teacher. Plato pulls together all these threads and presents his entire scheme in the *Republic*.

VII

In the dialogues that led to the *Republic,* Plato had taken the socratic notion that virtue is knowledge and inferred from it the un-socratic notion that virtue can be taught. Moreover, he had argued that the teachers of virtue, the philosophers, ought rightfully to be the rulers of the state. This would necessitate a radically new society, one different from any heretofore known to the Greeks. Plato claims that this new society would not be just another utopian scheme; it would be the perfect society, the only society that participates fully in the idea of the state, the one that embodies the essence of the state. His theory about the world of ideas thus becomes the foundation for his *Republic,* placing it beyond all criticism.

What is the idea or the essence of the state? According to Plato, the state is an arrangement for satisfying the needs of men; thus the essence of the state consists of the best means of satisfying them. He tells us that the best or ideal method is through a strict division of labor. As the three basic or essential functions of a state are production, defense, and internal administration, the ideal state will contain three distinct classes of men: (1) artisans or workers who supply the material needs of all, (2) soldiers or warriors who defend the state against its neighbors, and (3) rulers or

5. Emile Brehier, *The Hellenic Age* (Chicago: University of Chicago Press, 1963), p. 104.

guardians who make the laws and enforce obedience to them. Plato insists that all men, by their very nature, fall into one or the other of these three categories. Some men, possessed of strong appetites, have as their primary concern the pursuit of the pleasures of this world. They are the artisans, the traders, the merchants, and so on, all of whom supply vital goods and services in return for wealth and the bodily pleasures it brings. These men, designed by nature to be workers, Plato identifies as men of brass and iron. A second group of men do not seek bodily pleasures so much as honor and glory. Possessed of an excess of spirit in comparison with their fellows, these men are designed by nature to become the soldiers or warriors of society. Plato identifies them as men of silver. The last group, the men of gold, are the guardians. Possessing mighty intellects, these guardians are little concerned with the pleasures of the world or the pursuit of honor and glory, but they do devote themselves to the pursuit of true knowledge.

The ideal state is a harmonious state. Its essence lies in having every man in his appropriate category or class. Here we can see that at root, Plato's theory or idea of the state is a biological or metabiological one. The three classes within the state correspond to the three parts of man: the guardians correspond to reason, the warriors to spirit (energy), and the workers to appetite. The state, like man, is an organism whose parts must function properly in themselves and in harmony with one another. Every man must be in his appropriate class, and each class must perform its appropriate function. The ideal harmonious state, Plato insists, is a just state: "when the trader (worker), the auxiliary (warrior), and the guardian each do their own business, this is justice, and will make the city just" (*Republic* 434).

After describing the perfect state as it was in the beginning in books 2 to 4 of the *Republic,* Plato turns in book 8 to the problem of accounting for its decline and fall. How could this perfect state decay? A state under the guardianship of the most noble and wisest of men? Plato answers that those wise men of the past were not so wise as he. They did not, like him, have a pure and rational knowledge of eugenics. Lacking this knowledge, they blundered and begat children in the wrong way. Plato then adumbrates a kind of numerology that, he claims, controls "the good and evil of births." When the guardians are ignorant of the law of births, "and unite bride and bridegroom out of season, the children will not be goodly or fortunate" (*Republic* 546). Thus the perfect state declines when the original men of gold produce offspring who are of baser metal. These "inferior" guardians generate opposition and hostility, especially among the warrior class, who in time wrest the reigns of power to themselves, creating what Plato calls a timocracy—rule by the military.

This timocracy represents for Plato a degeneration from aristocracy, the best or ideal state. It also degenerates in time. For the dominance of these men of spirit breeds ambition and contention within the state. The warrior type is a "lover of power" and a "lover of honor," a despiser of riches when young, but more and more attracted to them as he gets older "because he has a piece of the avaricious nature in him." The accumulation of gold in the treasury of private individuals leads, Plato says, to "the ruin of timocracy." As the ambitious timocrats vie with one another in wealth, "the great mass of citizens become lovers of money." Gradually, the timocracy transforms into an oligarchy ruled by the rich. The change is completed when they "make a law which fixes a sum of money as the qualifications of citizenship," "allowing no one whose property falls below the amount fixed to have any share in the government."

With the establishment of the oligarchy, we reach a state of potential civil war between the rich and the poor. The rich, desirous of becoming richer, pass laws to protect different modes of acquiring excessive wealth. As their anxiety for gain subverts all other interests, they become extravagant and soft and flabby. Moreover, they pay no attention to the poor, who, sunburnt and sinewy, come to despise and loathe the plutocrats who rule over them. Ultimately, a contest is kindled from which the poor emerge victorious to set up a democracy—the third stage of decay.

Plato's description of democracy is vivid but intensely hostile. With supreme irony, he describes democracy as "a charming form of government, full of variety and disorder, and dispensing a sort of equality to equals and unequals alike." It is true that a man is free in a democracy; a democracy, Plato says, is "full of freedom and frankness—a man may say and do what he likes," but this freedom, this supposed "glory of the state," contains the seeds of its own dissolution. For in a democracy, no one—no man, no group—will accept any restraints, any bonds, any limitations.

"Now in such a state," Plato rhetorically asks, "can liberty have any limits?" None at all. And this insatiable desire for freedom leads ultimately to anarchy. Now the citizens become hypersensitive, chafing impatiently at the least touch of authority, ceasing to care for the laws, written or unwritten: "they will have no one over them." This excess of liberty finally creates a demand for some protector, a strong man who will restore order. And so it happens that from the evils of the excess of liberty, men pass into the last stage of governmental decay: tyranny, "the harshest and bitterest form of slavery." With tyranny, we reach the last and most abject form of government, the most debased copy of the idea of the state.

Through this analysis of the decay and decline of the state, Plato has uncovered the driving force of political change. He has revealed that political changes come about through the overthrow of the ruling class by those they are supposed to rule. Class war, in short, is the key to historical change. Therefore, if the ideal, perfect state is to be restored, class war must be eliminated. One way to do this would be to abolish classes. But this, of course, cannot be Plato's way; his ideal society requires, in fact is based on, class divisions. Thus the only way open to Plato is to abolish or prevent class warfare.

One of the principal causes of class warfare is the internal weakening of the ruling class brought about when dissension or division develops within. To preserve the internal unity of this master class, Plato suggests abolishing private property and the private family. This total communism will prevent the jealousy and envy that cause dissension. No man will envy the property or the offspring of another, for no member of the ruling class will own property; nor will he be able to identify his own children or his own parents. They will all look on one another as belonging to one family.

In addition to using communism to prevent the weakening of the ruling class, Plato saps the strength of the workers by prohibiting them from carrying weapons and by depriving them of all political rights. The workers will work; the rulers, rule.

Besides these negative measures, Plato prescribes positive measures to inhibit class warfare. These amount to an attempt to establish beyond all doubt the superiority of the ruling class and thus their absolute right to rule. He will create a ruling class that will be racially, intellectually, and morally superior to all others, thereby making them invulnerable.

Infanticide and eugenics will guarantee the racial purity and racial superiority of the guardians; and to ensure their moral and intellectual superiority, Plato turns to education. Through the appropriate education, the future guardians will develop their intellects so that they will come to know (and hence practice) true virtue.

What shall be their education? "Can we find a better sort," Plato replies, "than the traditional sort?" The traditional sort included gymnastics and music, the one supposedly for the training of the body, the other for the soul. But here Plato departs from tradition, claiming that both "have in view chiefly the improvement of the soul." He explains that music alone produces students who are soft and effeminate, but music tempered with gymnastics produces students who are "gentle and moderate." In other words, through music tempered with gymnastics, students acquire the habit of temperance. Moreover, gymnastics, which alone turns out students who are hard and brutal, contributes to the development of the habit of courage when it is moderated by the study of music. Music and gymnastics will not develop real courage and temperance, which come only with the knowledge of the ideas of courage and temperance. This knowledge comes later.

After acquiring the habits of temperance and courage, the children of the ruling class take up studies that will lead, for some, to the habit of wisdom. The first stage of this second cycle of studies consists of mathematics: arithmetic, harmonics, geometry, and astronomy. At the age of seventeen or eighteen, they leave off from their studies for two or three years of compulsory military service. At the end of this period of service, most of the young men remain in the military as warriors; they will be the auxiliaries to the guardians. By means of careful observation throughout their entire educational career and through the use of severe tests, only those of the highest merit will be selected to continue their education to the point of actually possessing the virtue of wisdom and the other virtues as well. They alone will hold the position of guardians of the state.

Back in school once again, the future guardians resume the study of mathematics. During the earlier stage of mathematics instruction, Plato had insisted that the warriors needed to know practical mathematics. "Clearly," he had then said, "we are concerned with that part of geometry which relates to war; for in pitching a camp, or taking up a position, or closing or extending the lines of an army, or any other military manoeuvre, whether in actual battle or on a march, it will make all the difference whether a general is or is not a geometrician." Now, however, these best and brightest students no longer look to the practical applications of mathematics. Destined to become guardians, they now study mathematics in order to discipline their intellects. Through the study of pure mathematics, the intellect is lifted beyond the sense world, beyond the levels of being associated with music and gymnastics; it is raised to the realm of number and form. Colors, sounds, smells, tastes, and feelings play no part in a mathematical perception of the universe. All now becomes form and number.

They continue their mathematical studies until the age of thirty, when they begin dialectics, the coping stone of their education. Mathematics had raised the mind above the physical world, but it could not move higher into the realm of pure ideas. Mathematics could not go beyond its own assumptions, its own hypothesis; dialectics can. Dialectics questions all assumptions and hypotheses, doing away with them to lead the intellect directly to the ideas themselves. The dialectician alone "attains a conception of the essence of each thing." Through dialectics, one "attains at last to the absolute good by intellectual vision and therein reaches the limit of the intellectual world."

Nowhere does Plato more clearly reveal how far he has traveled from Socrates' notion of education than in his discussion of dialectics. Unlike Socrates, who directed himself to the youth of Athens, Plato warns that the students must not be allowed to taste the delight of dialectic too early. The young, he observes, "when they first get the taste in their mouths argue for amusement and are always contradicting and refuting others in imitation of those who refute them; like puppy dogs, they rejoice in pulling and tearing at all who come near them." The upshot of this critical attitude is that "they violently and speedily get into a way of not believing anything which they believed before, and hence, not only they, but philosophy and all that relates to it, is apt to have a bad name with the rest of the world."

Here Plato renounces the very principles Socrates had died for! Socrates had urged his students to approach accepted ideas and beliefs for the very purpose of criticizing them, of trying to refute them. Ideas or beliefs that could not withstand criticism ought to be abandoned. But, as Plato knew only too well, this negative approach to knowledge led to uncertainty, and uncertainty could undermine the harmony and stability of society. Plato's philosopher-king was not to undermine the society; he was to supply certitude, not doubt. Through the mysteries of dialectic, Plato sought to transcend the humanistic fallibilism of Socrates. He impugned the critical approach by identifying it as eristics and defined an eristic as one "who is contradicting for the sake of amusement." The dialectician, on the other hand, is "seeking for the truth."

In point of fact, Plato's dialectician or guardian is not merely a seeker of truth; he is its proud possessor. He alone has the requisite training to know the essence of things. And after five years of studying dialectics and another fifteen years of holding various public offices, "those who still survive and have distinguished themselves in every action of their lives and in every branch of knowledge come at last to their consummation." Now, at the age of fifty,

> [T]he time has arrived at which they must raise the eye of the soul to the universal light which lightens all things, and behold the absolute good, for that is the pattern according to which they are to order the State and the lives of individuals and the remainder of their own lives also, making philosophy their chief pursuit, but, when their turn comes, toiling also at politics and ruling for the public good, not as though they were performing some heroic action, but simply as a matter of duty; and when they have brought up in each generation others like themselves and left them in their place to be governors of the State, then they will depart to the islands of the blest and dwell there; and the city will give them public memorials and sacrifices and honor them if the Pythian oracle consent, as demigods, but if not, as in any case blessed and divine.

Summary and Evaluation

Plato solved the problem bequeathed him by his teacher Socrates: the vulnerability of the intellectuals. He did it by insisting that intellectuals abandon the socratic role of social and political critic and take up instead the role of social and political authority. The intellectual, the philosopher, he claims, is entitled to this role of authority because he alone has real knowledge; he alone knows what is good, what is true. As rulers, or guardians, the intellectuals are invulnerable.

The vulnerability of the socratic intellectual stemmed in great part from his role as teacher. Teaching or education, as Socrates saw it, is the process of making people critical, of making them aware of their ignorance. Plato's intellectuals were to be teachers too; but education, as Plato saw it, is the process of guiding (some) people to the truth. This educational authoritarianism parallels, in fact emerges from, Plato's political authoritarianism. Plato's solution to the problem of vulnerability of the intellectual has bequeathed to us the legacy of political and educational authoritarianism and completely obscured the fallibilism of Socrates.

Augustine's Teacher

I desire to have knowledge of God and the soul. Of nothing else? No, of nothing else whatever.'' Augustine wrote these words shortly after becoming a Christian in A.D. 387. To our ears they sound parochial, mystical, perhaps irrelevant. Yet they signal the emergence of a new conceptual framework in Western civilization. It is a framework that replaced the one fashioned by the Greeks and Romans; a framework that dominated Western civilization for a thousand years—a framework that transformed the educational theory of the West.

I

Born in 354 in the northern African town of Tagaste, Augustine had a Christian mother and a pagan father. His studies in Latin literature and grammar led to his becoming a teacher of rhetoric in Carthage. The unruly students there forced him to quit and go to Rome, where he opened a school of his own. Here the students behaved better, but they reneged on the payment of his fees. As a result, Augustine applied for, and got, a position as municipal professor of rhetoric in Milan. At this point his life changed dramatically.

Until this time, Augustine, in spite of his mother's entreaties and prayers, was not a Christian. Moreover, he had lived a dissolute life: he had a mistress, an illegitimate son, and was, he tells us in his *Confessions,* thoroughly licentious. But in Milan Augustine came under the influence of the bishop, Saint Ambrose, who converted him to Christianity. The intellectual conversion came first, the moral conversion he found more difficult, for Augustine had trouble resisting the temptations of the flesh. ("Give me chastity and continence," he prayed, "only not yet.")

Ultimately, Augustine triumphed. He gave up his professorship—and his mistress—returning with his son, Adeodatus, his mother, and some friends to Cassiciacum, a town near Milan, where he conducted seminars, attempting to work out Christian answers to philosophical questions about happiness, truth, and good and evil. Later, Augustine published the record of his seminars: *The Happy Life* (*De beata vita*), *Against Skepticism* (*Contra academicos*), and *Divine Providence and the Problem of Evil* (*De ordine*).

In 388 Augustine went back to Africa to his home town of Tagaste, where he established a monastery. In 392 he was ordained a priest and set up a second monastery in Hippo, a seaport town about 150 miles west of Carthage. Augustine became bishop of Hippo in 396, serving there for over thirty years. He died in 430 while the Vandals were sacking the city.

As bishop, Augustine spent much of his time combating heresies: the Pelagians, who taught that human beings could attain salvation through their own efforts; the Manicheans, who taught that two equal gods (one good and one evil) ruled the world; the Arians, who taught that God had created a son who was neither eternal nor equal with the Father; and the Donatists, who taught that only the pure and holy could be members of the church. In his battle against these heresies Augustine composed countless polemical sermons, tracts, letters, and books. (The one against the Manicheans comprised thirty-three books or chapters.)

In addition to his polemics, Augustine wrote books and monographs on matters of Christian doctrine, on free will, and on the Trinity. Of his writings, 113 books, 218 letters, and over 500 sermons have survived. His most famous book, *The City of God* (*De civitate Dei*), he composed to explain why Rome fell to the Goths in 410.

Augustine, his contemporaries Ambrose and Jerome, and Pope Gregory the Great (who came later) are called Doctors of the Church in recognition of their great influence on Christianity. The influence of Ambrose and Gregory came from their skill as statesmen; they established the independence of the church and its hegemony over secular rulers. Jerome's contribution was to translate the Bible into Latin. But it was Augustine who had the greatest intellectual influence on Christianity. It was he who fashioned the Christian framework.

II

The life of Christ had gone largely unnoticed by the great world. The great world was the Roman Empire, of which Judea had become a part only in A.D. 6. There, among the simple peasants and fishermen of Galilee, Christ spent his life preaching to a devout population of Jews hardly touched by the influence of the dominant Graeco-Roman civilization.

When Christ came to Jerusalem, his preaching aroused the opposition of both priests and pharisees. They handed him over to the Roman procurator, who put him to death as an agitator who endangered the political authority of Rome and the religious authority of the Sanhedrin and the priesthood.

What did Christ preach? What was his message? The message of Jesus was simple: "The kingdom of God is at hand." The early Christian Jews, convinced that Jesus was the "Messiah," had no thought of embracing a new religion. They simply believed that only righteous, law-abiding Jews who accepted Jesus as the Messiah would share in the kingdom he would set up at his Second Coming.

In the meantime, Jesus counseled moral behavior. Like all the prophets, he appealed to the spirit of the Hebrew law: to righteousness, to justice. To the insuperable injustice of Rome, he advocated nonviolent resistance, transmitting the "righteousness" of the prophets into something inward: purity of heart. Meet triumphant evil, he preached, by casting it out of your own heart; meet prejudice with tolerance, arrogance with humility, and hatred with love.

In the teachings of Jesus we find little sense of sin, little sense of moral struggle, and no sense that men need supernatural help to do right. All this came into Christianity with Paul. Unable personally to keep the Jewish law, Paul drew the conclusion that all men are wicked and evil by nature. To secure release from the desires of the flesh, he believed, man needed supernatural help. Thus the message of Christianity in the hands of Paul became one of salvation from sin. Christ became the mystical redeemer: Christ is a Divine Spirit who took on flesh, died, and was released from the flesh. By accepting and believing in Christ, man can be identified with him in a mystical union—dying to the flesh and rising transformed into a "life of the Spirit." This "rebirth" brings the moral freedom to do good, to love and serve one's fellows.

In becoming otherworldly, a system of mystical salvation, Christianity now emerged as a universal religion, a religion for Gentiles as well as Jews. Gradually, Christianity spread throughout the Roman Empire. As its members grew in numbers, the state came to recognize it as an enemy and persecuted it as a subversive force that undermined civil responsibility and civil obligations.[1]

The Christian cared little about this world. He was a stranger to it, a pilgrim in it, a sojourner on his way to his true home. Tertullian (160–230) wrote: "We have no concern with this life except to part from it as speedily as possible." The Christian had no time to spend working for the state or civil society. "Your citizenship," wrote Paul to the Philippians, "is in heaven." Paul even advised the Corinthians to abstain from marriage because "the time is short."

Of course, most Christians, Paul included, did not withdraw completely from the world. When the Thessalonians became so impressed with the transitoriness of life that they abandoned all their ordinary activities, Paul counseled them to tend to their business. But most Christians drew the line when it came to performing the business of the state. The Synod of Elvira (Illiberis) decided that a Christian municipal magistrate must absent himself from church during his years in office, and the Synod of Arles (Arlate) excluded from communion those who took up "political life."

Sometimes, Christian indifference to this world grew into outright hostility. "This world and the next are two enemies," wrote Clement in his second epistle. "The one urges to adultery and corruption, avarice and deceit; the other bids farewell to these things. We cannot, therefore, be the friends of both; and it behooves us by renouncing the one to make sure of the other." Christians sometimes directed this hostility toward the state, construing it as positively diabolical: in the pages of the Apocalypse, written in the first century, Christians found Rome pictured as Babylon the Great, the mother of harlots, drunken with the blood of saints and martyrs; the Roman Empire appeared as the Kingdom of the Beast, which sought to destroy the church. Later, antistate attitudes of the Christians reappeared in the Montanists of the second century and the Donatists of the fourth century (and also in the English Puritans of the seventeenth century).

While it is true that the church denounced Montanism and Donatism, both as heresies, it is nevertheless the case that all Christians—the orthodox as well as the heretics—looked at the world differently from the "pagans." Whereas pagans sought happiness in the form of wisdom, or honor, or glory in this world, Christians looked for it in the next. For them, true happiness was salvation.

---

1. John H. Randall, Jr., *Hellenistic Ways of Deliverance and the Making of the Christian Synthesis* (New York: Columbia University Press, 1970), passim; and Christopher Dawson, *The Making of Europe* (New York: Meridian, 1958), part 1.

In addition to this otherworldliness, Christianity presented a second threat to the perpetuation of the Roman Empire: its antipathy to "pagan" culture. Culture was the foundation of the empire; only his culture distinguished the Roman from the barbarian. Being a Roman was not a matter of blood or race or geographic location; one became a Roman through the acquisition of Roman (actually Graeco-Roman) culture. Education was the way. Through the study of the liberal arts and the humanities, and perhaps philosophy, one achieved *humanitas,* one became human and *free*. The Roman policy was to take as hostages the children from all the best families in the newly conquered lands and bring them up in Roman schools. Schools were everywhere—in Italy, Spain, Gaul, Britain, Africa. According to Marrou, "the whole of the Empire was covered with a fairly dense network of academic institutions: elementary school teachers were found more or less everywhere, grammarians and rhetors in places of any importance." [2]

Christians sent their children to Roman (pagan) schools so that they might learn to read and write, but they rejected the pagan culture. The Christian was to have nothing to do with pagan books; he had his Bible, which contained all he needed of history, poetry, philosophy, eloquence, and law. The "pagan" books came from the devil and should be thrown away, said a canon law on this matter. Saint Jerome followed this law when he censured priests for reading profane authors. It is sinful for them to do voluntarily, he wrote, what children *have* to do in school.

In accepting the necessity of learning how to read and write, but at the same time rejecting the pagan, or classical, culture, the Christian revealed that he had no need for education. Education initiates one into membership in a culture—in this case Graeco-Roman culture. But the Christian did not seek or need this. The Christian belonged to a mystical, universal brotherhood. One became a Christian not through education but through conversion—and conversion was an act of God.

The outline of this emergent Christian framework becomes clear: (1) in place of happiness in this world, the Christian seeks salvation in the next world; (2) the Christian foreswears induction into the classical, pagan culture for membership in a mystical universal brotherhood; and (3) he replaces education with a process called conversion. These become the core of the new Christian framework: salvation, universal brotherhood, and conversion.

In spite of his rejection of the ideals, culture, and education of the Romans, the Christian wanted to be a Roman too. What other alternatives were there? To be Roman was to be civilized—all the rest were barbarians. How to be a Roman and a Christian? Could there be a synthesis

2. H. I. Marrou, *A History of Education in Antiquity* (New York: Sheed and Ward, 1956), p. 296.

between classical culture and Christianity? Or would Christianity create a culture of its own?

By the end of the fourth century, this problem became acute. Until that time, emperors still construed Christians as the enemy of the state. Periodically they conducted massive campaigns of persecution against them. But the numbers of Christians within the empire had continued to grow. And by the second decade of the fourth century, the Emperor Constantine, recognizing the futility of eliminating them, granted religious toleration to Christians. By the end of the fourth century, Emperor Theodosius—in great part due to the influence of Ambrose, bishop of Milan—made Christianity the official state religion.

This union of church and state (really the triumph of the church) meant that the future of pagan classical culture was in the hands of the Christians. What was to become of it?

Enter Augustine.

III

The two pillars of classical culture, to use the metaphor of Marrou, were literary studies (usually called *rhetoric*) and philosophy. The fate of each pillar the Christians decided differently.

First, the literary studies: Almost all Christians opposed the pagan literary studies. The *Teaching of the Apostles* (*Disascalia Apostolorum*), a third-century document, made the prohibition quite explicit: "Avoid all books of the heathens." Christians saw these books of the pagans as subversive documents. Here is how the orator Aristides put the case:

> The Greeks then, because they are wiser than the barbarians, have erred even more than the barbarians, in that they have introduced many gods that are made; and some of them they have represented as male, and some of them as female; and in such a way that some of their gods were found to be adulterers and murderers of fathers, and thieves and plunderers. And they say that some of them were lame and maimed, and some of them wizards, and some of them utterly mad; and some of them played on harps; and some of them wandered on mountains; and some of them died outright; and some were struck by lightning, and some were made subject to men, and some of them were wept and bewailed by men; and some, they say, went down to Hades.
>
> And some of their goddesses they say that they contended about beauty, and came for judgment before men. The Greeks then, O King, have brought forward what is wicked, ridiculous and foolish concerning their gods and themselves; in that they have called such like persons gods who are no gods; hence men have taken occasion to commit adultery and fornication, and to plunder and do everything that is wicked and hateful and abominable. For if those who are called gods have done all these things that are written above, how much more shall men do them who believe in those who have done these things! [3]

3. Aristides, *Apology* 8.

Tertullian expressed the Christian animosity toward classical literature with malicious glee when he promised that one of the joys that awaited Christians in heaven would be the sight of the poets (and the philosophers) burning in hell.

Although the common and official Christian attitude toward classical literature was negative, some cherished and prized that learning. These, usually highly educated Romans who became converts to Christianity late in life, prized the classics for their literary and artistic merits. Saint Jerome, for example, was a literary scholar and artist, in love with language. He cherished the classics for their style, beauty, and grace—characteristics totally absent from the documents of Christianity. But Jerome, too, regarded the classics as fare unfit for devout Christians. Here is his famous story:

> Many years ago, when for the Kingdom of Heaven's sake, I had cut myself off from home, parents, sister, relations, and—harder still—from the dainty goods to which I had been accustomed; and when I was on my way to Jerusalem to wage my warfare, I still could not bring myself to forego the library which I had formed for myself at Rome with great care and toil. And so, miserable man that I was, I would fast only that I might afterwards read Cicero. After many nights spent in vigil, after floods of tears called from my inmost heart, after the recollection of my past sins, I would once more take up Plautus. And when at times I returned to my right mind and began to read the prophets, their style seemed rude and repellent. I failed to see the light with my blinded eyes, but I attributed the fault not to them but to the sun. While the old serpent was thus making me his plaything, about the middle of Lent, a deep-seated fever fell upon my weakened body, and while it destroyed my rest completely—the story seems hardly credible—it so wasted my unhappy frame that scarcely anything was left on me but skin and bone. Meantime, preparations for my funeral went on; my body grew gradually colder, and the warmth of it still lingered only in my throbbing breast. Suddenly, I was caught up in the spirit and dragged before the judgment seat of the Judge; and the light was so bright there, and those who stood around were so radiant that I cast myself upon the ground and did not dare to look up. Asked who and what I was, I replied, "I am a Christian." But he who presided said: "You lie; you are a Ciceronian and not a Christian." [4]

Jerome subsequently swore off the classics. "Lord, if ever again I possess worldly books, or if ever again I read such, I have denied thee." As a self-imposed penance, he set about translating the Bible into Latin—the first and most famous translation.

The Christian's final solution to the problem of pagan literary culture came from Saint Augustine. His solution, a pragmatic compromise, was to use pagan literary studies as a weapon in the battle against the pagans themselves. "All branches of heathen learning," he wrote, "con-

4. Jerome, *Epistle* 50.5.

tain . . . liberal instruction which is better adapted to use of truth. . . ." Christians should separate themselves from the "miserable fellowship" of the pagans, but take away with them their literary skills and devote them "to their proper use in the preaching of the gospel" (*De doctrina* 40).

Augustine called this "spoiling the Egyptians," likening the tactic he advocated to those the Jews used against the Egyptians, stealing from them their gold and silver, but not their beliefs. Augustine thought it possible to separate all that is useful in paganism from its impious, immoral, and undesirable elements so that Christians could take what is useful and disregard the rest. Here he suggested the compilation of summaries of the classic literary works so that Christians need not expose themselves to the corrosive influences of the original pagan contributions.

Augustine envisioned no sudden break with the pagan literary tradition. Christians were to borrow from that tradition, but the borrowing was to be limited to what was useful. His solution to the problem of the pagan literary culture was simple and straightforward. Others easily understood it and readily accepted it. As a result, one pillar of Graeco-Roman culture—literary studies—now became a handmaiden to the Christian religion.

As to the study of rhetoric itself, Augustine noted that eloquence itself was simply an instrument—either side could use it. Why not, he asked, "engage it on the side of truth?" To facilitate this, he advised Christians to compose their own technical treatises, based on the classical-style manuals, using the Scriptures to illustrate the rules and principles of rhetoric.

The consequences of the utilitarian approach to the classic heritage emerged during the next two hundred years. The most obvious, and expectable, result was the decline of interest in preserving the classical literature. Works heretofore conserved by Greek and Roman copyists disappeared; they were no longer useful to the Christians. Concomitant with this disappearance of the literary works was a decline in the quality of the Latin language. Christians saw no need to write or speak correct Latin (i.e., the Latin used by the ancient Romans). Christians worried solely about sharing the faith of their fathers, not their language. Gregory the Great, one of the Doctors of the Church who reigned as pope from 590 to 604, stated that he saw no reason for Christians to avoid barbarisms or solecisms.

There is another side to this decadence of the Latin language and the disappearance of the classical literary works. For there now emerged a new literature, a Christian literature. Of far less literary merit than that which it supplanted and often totally lacking in aesthetic qualities, this Christian literature became the sole diet of most literate Christians. It included (1) dogmatic works that interpreted Scripture and elucidated the doctrines of the church—here Augustine was a weighty contributor; (2) translations of sacred and traditional works, such as Jerome's translation of the Bible; and (3) the lives of the saints, a miscellany of writings about pious Christians that eschewed veracity, and often credibility, in order to inspire other Christians with accounts of saintly exploits.[5]

Even more noteworthy, perhaps, is the evolution of the Latin language itself. For with the changing attitudes toward language, Latin became a living language, no longer a language of the school. Out of it grew the family of different, but related, Romance languages.

IV

The second pillar of classical culture was philosophy. Here we find the same reaction patterns: some Christians condoned the study of philosophy; other Christians opposed such study; and there was Augustine's approach, the approach that prevailed.

The orator Aristides counted himself among those Christians who opposed studying the philosophers—"senseless wise men," he called them. The most famous Christian opponent of philosophy was Tertullian, who asked, "What has Athens to do with Jerusalem, the Academy with the Church?" He went on to assert that Christians had "no need for curiosity since Jesus Christ; nor for inquiry since the Evangel." The Christian, you see, possessed the truth, divine truth, and so had no need for the speculation of philosophers, those "patriarchs of the heretics." Tertullian put it in the form of a rhetorical question: "What is there in common between the philosopher and the Christian; the pupil of Hellas and the pupil of Heaven; the worker for reputation and for salvation; the manufacturer of words, and of deeds; the builder and the destroyer; the interpolator of error and the artificer of truth; the thief of truth and its custodian?" [6]

The philosophers (along with the poets) will burn in hell, a sight Tertullian eagerly looked forward to: "How vast the spectacle that day, how wide! What sight shall wake my wonder, what my laughter, my joy, my exultation as I see . . . those sages, the philosophers, blushing before their disciples as they blaze together, the disciples whom they taught that God was concerned with nothing, that men have no souls at all." [7]

We find Christians who had studied philosophy in the camp of those who now opposed it; some had even been philosophers themselves. For, by becoming Christians, they had found what they had searched for, and

5. M. L. W. Laistner, *Thought and Letters in Western Europe* (Ithaca: Cornell University Press, 1957).
6. Tertullian, *Apology* 46.
7. Tertullian, *De spectaculis,* 30.

had not found in philosophy. Clement of Alexandria (*c.* 215) for example, argued that it was not necessary to be a philosopher to grasp the truth of Christianity: "Almost all of us, without training in the arts and sciences and the Hellenic philosophy, and some even without learning at all, through the influence of a philosophy divine and barbarous, and by power, have, through faith, received the word concerning God, trained by self-operating wisdom." Another philosopher, Athenagoras, argued that Christians may not be able to explain their doctrine, but they can show the effects of it on their lives—unlike mere philosophers, whose intellectual wisdom cannot overcome their moral helplessness.

In the other camp, we find Christians who prized philosophy, who saw no conflict between the "Academy and Jerusalem." Lactantius (*c.* 260–340), for example, saw philosophers giving testimony to the belief "that there is one sovereignty over the world, one power, the origin of which cannot be discovered by thought, nor its might explained." Justin Martyr (100–165), who had come to Christianity only after studying all the different schools of philosophy, could not leave such a heritage behind: "When we [Christians] say that all things have been produced and arranged into a world by God, we shall seem to utter the doctrines of Plato. While we say that there will be burning up of all, we shall seem to utter the doctrines of the Stoics. While we affirm that the souls of the wicked, being enclosed with sensation even after death, are punished, and that those of the good are delivered from punishment and spend a blessed existence, we shall seem to say the same things as the poets and philosophers." [8]

The solution proposed by most Christians who prized philosophy was that philosophy could assist Christianity, that it could be the handmaiden to it. Perhaps Origen (185–254), who succeeded Clement as head of the school of philosophy at Alexandria, best expressed this approach. Here is an excerpt from one of his letters to his pupil Gregory:

> Thine ability is fit to make thee an accomplished Roman lawyer, or a Greek philosopher in some one of the schools esteemed reputable. But my desire has been that thou shouldst employ all the force of thine ability on Christianity as thine end, and to effect this, I would beseech thee to draw from Greek philosophy such things as are capable of being made encyclic or preparatory studies to Christianity; and from geometry and astronomy such things as will be useful for the exposition of Holy Scripture, in order that what the sons of the philosophers say about geometry and music and grammar and rhetoric and astronomy—that they are the handmaidens of philosophy—we may say of philosophy itself in relation to Christianity.[9]

8. Justin Martyr, 1.20.4.
9. Gregory Thaumaturgus, *Panegyric,* 8.

This belief that pagan philosophy could become the handmaiden to Christianity corresponded to Augustine's solution to the problem of what Christians should do with pagan literary culture. But here Augustine rejected the "handmaiden" approach in favor of a more audacious solution. His solution was nothing less than the creation of a total philosophy—a Christian philosophy.

V

In the act of "solving" the "problem" of the Christian attitude toward philosophy, Augustine elaborated and made more intellectually secure the new Christian framework. It was a framework that pitted salvation against worldly honor and glory, a framework that forsook initiation into Graeco-Roman culture for membership in a universal brotherhood, and a framework that eschewed education for conversion. Augustine's "solution" consisted of working through the final answers (the Christian answers) to the basic questions that had exercised philosophers for centuries.

There were three traditional questions that philosophers had tried to answer: (1) What is the world made of, and how did it come into existence? (2) Why do things happen as they do? And finally (3), what is man's purpose or goal? To each of these questions, the Christian had the same answer: God. Augustine's Christian philosophy begins with this answer and uses reason and arguments to demonstrate why it is the correct answer.

Let's look at the first question: What is the world made of, and how did it come into existence? So far as we can tell, Western philosophy began in ancient Ionia with this question. But philosophers had, thus far, not come up with a satisfactory answer to the origin of the world, in great part because, as Socrates noted, nobody was there at the time. But Christians, Augustine insisted, had the answer: God had created the world out of nothing.

"In the beginning, God created the heaven and the earth." In his commentary on this first sentence from the Book of Genesis (in the *Confessions,* bk. 12) Augustine argues that the world, as it is, confirms the fact of its creation: "Behold the heavens and the earth are; they proclaim that they were created; for they change and vary. Whereas whatever hath not been made, and yet is, hath nothing in it which before it had not, and this it is, to change and vary."

How did God make heaven and earth out of nothing? Not in the way a human being makes things—modifying something that exists into something else—because nothing existed prior to the world's creation. God created, Augustine says, through His Word: "Thou speakest, and they were made, and in Thy Word Thou madest them.'' But how did God speak? From on high? Out of a cloud? No, because the Word of God is the Eternal Word—''the Word of the Lord abideth forever . . . and whatever Thou sayest shall be made; nor dost thou make otherwise than by saying. . . .''

But why did God create the heaven and the earth? Why did He will it? Or, to ask the question another way, What was God doing before He created heaven and earth? Augustine relates that one answer to this is that before God created heaven and earth, He was busy creating hell for people who asked questions like ''What was God doing before he created heaven and earth?'' But, Augustine says he will refrain from making sport of questioners and, instead, will take the question seriously (*Confessions,* bk. 11).

The first thing to note, he points out, is that such a question about the will of God assumes that God exists in time. But this is false; God is, God is eternal. What then is time? And more importantly, does time exist coeval with God? Take the notions of the past, the present, and the future. Obviously, time past does not exist—it is gone; nor does time future exist—it is yet to be. Only the present exists. But does it? The present century does not exist—only this year is present. But of this year, only this month is present. But of this month, only this day is present . . . but of this day, only this hour . . . and so on. . . . In short, the present is naught but a passing moment, gone before it can be measured.

The solution to this puzzle about time, Augustine suggests, is to realize that time is a subjective phenomenon. It is the mind that measures time: time is in the human mind, which *expects* (time future), *considers* (time present) and *remembers* (time past). From this it follows that there can be no time without a created being. So to speak of time before the creation is meaningless: the question ''What was God doing before he created heaven and earth?'' is a meaningless question.

The second question that philosophers had puzzled over for centuries was Why do things happen as they do? Greek philosophy had moved beyond animism to construct elaborate answers to this question. Recognizing an order, a regularity, in the changes that occur in the world, Greek philosophers had construed change as a process. However, most Greek philosophers still retained the animistic notion that all that happened was teleological—every action resulted from an aim or purpose. Aristotle, for example, explained that stones fall to earth because they seek their proper resting place. To this teleological (final cause) explanation of why things happen as they do, Aristotle added the notion of the efficient cause, the material cause, and the formal cause.

Augustine's explanation of why things happen as they do appears in his *Literal Commentary on Genesis*. The orderliness of the universe, Augustine explains, is due to God, who created all things ''by measure and number and weight'' (Wisdom 11. 1:20). This order is universal and all-pervasive, even though to our limited human perceptions it may at times seem to be disorder. Human beings can never grasp this order in its entirety—only enough of it to recognize it as the work of a Divine Intelligence.

But if God created everything ''in the beginning,'' how can we account for the fact that many things have come into being since and are still to come into being? Augustine accepts the account in Genesis: God created everything in six days. But, he adds, everything that has appeared, or will appear, in the cosmos already existed in the original stuff of the universe. To explain this, Augustine uses the analogy of the development of a seed. (Today he might have used the analogy of the genetic code.) He argues that God created all things in the beginning but allowed some creatures to remain latent, seminal—seedlike—waiting for the right time and the right environment to actually appear. These tiny, invisible seeds (he calls them *rationes seminales*) are the originals of all trees, horses, human beings, and insects that grow and evolve into extended organisms each in its proper time.

Augustine then explains all the goings-on of living organisms as processes—interacting, functioning, and developing according to their own laws. But all such processes, he insists, were implanted by God: all are creatures of God and act in accordance with what He has determined.

> The elements of this bodily world have their own precise force and quality, what each of them can and cannot do, what can be made from what, or cannot. From these elements, as the original principles of things, all things that are generated take their origin and development, each in its proper time; and they receive their terminations and decreases, each according to its kind. Hence, it comes about that a bean does not grow from a grain of wheat, or wheat from a bean, or a man from a beast, or a beast from a man (*Literal Commentary on Genesis* 4. 17:32).

This theory of *rationes seminales* explains the actions of living creatures, but what about nonvital events in physical nature? the movement of winds? the flow of rivers? the rising of the sun? Augustine accounts for these goings-on by construing all as processes ordained by God: ''since the divine power governs the whole of creation, spiritual and corporal, the waters of the sea are summoned and poured out upon the face of the earth on certain days of every year.''

Augustine, who sought to have knowledge of but two things—God and the human soul—spent no great amount of time elaborating the Christian answer to the question, Why do things happen as they do? What he did say, however, sufficed for most Christians: God, in the guise of Divine Providence, ordains all that happens. As the Greek philosophers had noted, all that happens is reducible to a process; Augustine traces that process to God. "Like mothers heavy with their offspring, the world is heavy with the causes of things still to be; and they are created in the world by no one except that supreme being in whom there is no birth and no death, no beginning and no end."

The third question that had long troubled philosophers concerned the purpose of life. Since Socrates, most philosophers had proferred happiness as man's goal. What is happiness? Here philosophers differed among themselves, but by and large all construed happiness (or the highest happiness) as somehow related to the mind or intellect. For some, happiness consisted in the exercise of the intellect itself; for others, it consisted of understanding or knowledge; for still others, it consisted of using knowledge to control and guide one's life.

Augustine followed the Greek philosophers in proposing happiness as the goal of life. Happiness, he says, consists of satisfaction—complete satisfaction: "No one is happy unless he has all that he wants. . . ." But this is not totally true, for satisfaction of perverse and evil desires is not real and lasting satisfaction. Thus, Augustine adds an important qualification to his definition of happiness: "No one is happy unless he has all that he wants, *and wants nothing that is evil*" (*De Trinitate* 12. 5. 8; italics added).

In a radical departure from traditional Greek philosophy, Augustine relates happiness not to the mind but to the will—to the desires, to what he calls "love." Love is the dynamic force in human conduct: "My weight is my love: wherever I am carried, it is by it that I am carried." But what should man desire? What should he love, the possession of which will bring him happiness?

The answer, of course, is God. Happiness for human beings is the loving union or reunion with God, our heavenly Father. Man cannot, in this life, attain this loving union and possession of God; but he can move toward this final happiness by living rightly. And he can live rightly by choosing rightly (i.e., by choosing to love what he should love). This is clearly set forth in the Gospel According to Saint Matthew: "Thou shalt love the Lord thy God with thy whole heart, and with thy whole soul, and thy whole mind" and "thou shalt love thy neighbor as thyself." To lead a good and honest life, Augustine concludes, love as they should be loved those things which we ought to love: God and our neighbor.

Nevertheless, left to himself, Augustine declares, man will *not* love God nor his neighbor. For human beings have a multitude of loves (desires, impulses, drives), a bewildering variety of them, often in serious and sometimes agonizing conflict. It is not possible to satisfy all—the satisfaction of one desire inevitably means the frustration of another. This human predicament, Augustine believed, was the result of the Fall (of Adam). Prior to the Fall, man could attain happiness simply by following his natural desires. Now, however, he is no longer "upright." He is disordered and unable to see with facility what he should love, unable to discover the direction to take to attain happiness.

Augustine's *Confessions* is a personal account of his own attempts to find the way to happiness. Here is the famous sentence in the beginning of that book: "Thou (O God) has made us, and in making us, turned us toward thyself; and our hearts are restless until they come to rest in Thee." But Augustine did not come to love God through his own efforts nor through the efforts of his saintly mother nor even through the preaching of Saint Ambrose. Augustine came to love God only when God extended to him His divine help, called grace.

For man is a finite being and God is an infinite Being; therefore, the gulf between man and God cannot be bridged without divine aid, without grace. "The grace of God through Jesus Christ our Lord," Augustine wrote, "must be understood as that by which alone men are delivered from evil." Without grace, he continues, men can "do absolutely no good thing . . . in thought, or will, or affection, or in deed." Through grace, men come to know "what should be done" and come to do "with love what they know" (*On Admonition and Grace* 2. 3).

Man can do nothing to merit grace; it is a gratuitous gift from God. (Why God extends grace to some and not to others is a mystery to human beings, who can never fathom Divine Wisdom and Divine Goodness.) Once he receives the gift of grace, and only then, is man truly free. For man, since the Fall, is a creature of sin. To be truly free is to choose only what is good. And this can come only with God's grace. Here is how Augustine puts it: "To be able to do evil is a proof of free choice; to be able not to be evil is also a proof of free choice, but to be confirmed in grace to the point of no longer being able to do evil is the supreme degree of liberty."

As Augustine sees him, man, since the Fall, was sick. Divine grace was "the medicine of the soul working internally as drugs work externally on the body." With the help of grace, men are cured, and they become truly free (from sin) and therefore truly virtuous: grace so "diffuses love through their hearts that the soul being healed does good not from fear of punishment, but from love of justice."

To summarize Augustine's argument: Happiness is the goal or purpose of life. Happiness consists of loving union with God. To gain happiness, one must live rightly. To live rightly, one must will rightly. And to will rightly requires God's grace.

VI

In his Christian philosophy, Augustine has brought together the elements of Christian beliefs to synthesize a new world picture, a new Christian framework with God at the center. Here, all that exists is due to God—He created all. All that happens is due to God—to His Divine Providence. And man, too, is a creature of God, a creature whose final purpose is loving union with his heavenly Father, a union that can come about only through God's help, through Divine Grace.

In his monumental *City of God,* Augustine takes his theory that love is the divine force of human beings and expands it to explain the goings-on of society itself. Society, he says, is a community, a community characterized by a common desire or love. It comes into being when people who desire or seek a common object join together in common pursuit of that desired object. Thus it happens that the nature of the object, the end, the goal, determines the character of the society. Throughout history, Augustine claims, there have been two great communities or societies—the first made up of those who desire their proper end, God; the second made up of those who desire earthly goods. Thus, we have two societies or cities: the City of God and the city of man.

> And thus it has come to pass that though there are very many and great nations all over the earth whose rites and customs, speech, arms and dress, are distinguished by marked differences, yet there are no more than two kinds of human societies according to the language of our Scripture. The one consists of those who wish to live after the flesh, the other of those who wish to live after the spirit (*The City of God* 14. 1).

The City of God is composed of all those redeemed or saved—those who have lived, those still living, and those yet to live. The City of God is not the Christian church, but the church is the representative, the *only* representative, of the City of God here on earth. So, through the church, the City of God is made present to us in this life.

The city of man is the secular world. Augustine *de*nounced, but did not *re*nounce the secular city. Indeed, with Augustine we come to the end of the early Christian eschatology. Henceforth, Christians did not expect an imminent cataclysmic end to the world. The world goes on; and Christians must come to terms with it, live in it. Wars would be fought, money made, children begotten. But now, Augustine suggested, such things could be done, and should be done, in a more or less Christian spirit. Wars should be just, business should be honest, children should be legitimate. Thus, human beings can continue to live in the secular city but can recognize their true end in the City of God and so try to conduct their worldly affairs in ways that accord with the ways of that heavenly city.

Augustine's Christian philosophy made more intellectually secure the new Christian framework. The Christian's concern with salvation rather than worldly honor and glory was nothing more than a realization that man's final happiness lay in loving reunion with his Divine Father. And the Christian's repudiation of membership within the Graeco-Roman culture was simply a recognition that a far better brotherhood was that universal brotherhood of all those who were saved: the City of God was a society superior to the city of man. And the Christian recognized that initiation into this community of the saved was not the result of education but the result of conversion—something that came about solely through God's grace.

VII

Augustine was not content to replace education with conversion. He went further to argue that education, as the Romans and Greeks understood it, did not exist. No man, Augustine declared, can teach another. God is the only teacher.

In *Concerning the Teacher* (*De magistro*), a monograph composed at Cassiciacum in 387, Augustine takes up the question, "How does teaching take place?" The answer, obviously, is that teaching takes place through signs, written or spoken. Thus, the word *dog* is the sign for the real object, the dog. It would seem that teachers transmit knowledge of reality through signs. But, Augustine muses, is this really the case?

If we consider the matter more carefully, he suggests, we will discover that "there is nothing which is learned by means of signs." Here is his argument: "For when a sign is given me, if it finds me not knowing of what thing it is a sign, it can teach me nothing, but if it finds me knowing the thing of which it is a sign, what do I learn from the sign?" Take the sentence: "And their *saraballae* are not changed." If I do not know what the word *saraballae* means, I learn nothing from this sign. But if I know that the word *saraballae* means head coverings, I still learn nothing from this sign. How then does one learn? From direct experience, Augustine says. When one hears the word *saraballae* used repeatedly to refer to something already well known by sight, then one learns that this is a sign. Hence, the conclusion follows: "The sign is learned after the thing is recognized."

What this means, of course, is that teachers, since they deal in language, cannot transmit knowledge of reality. Teachers transmit only signs or labels. Knowledge of reality comes from direct experience with reality itself. Take another example: If a teacher says that water boils at 212° Fahrenheit, does the student *know* that the water boils at 212° Fahrenheit? Augustine would say that in this case the student merely *believes* that water boils at 212° Fahrenheit; he does not *know* it. All that he *knows* is that the teacher *said* water boils at 212° Fahrenheit.

Our knowledge of reality, therefore, comes not from teachers but from reality itself, from our perception or observation of the real world. But, and this is Augustine's main point, that reality is what it is because

God created it and ordained it to be such. (Water boils at 212° Fahrenheit because that is the way God made the world.) Hence, the conclusion: God is the only teacher.

In addition to this "sensible knowledge" we acquire from experience, there is another kind of knowledge that Augustine calls "intelligible knowledge." This consists of mathematical knowledge, like 5 + 5 = 10, or the sum of the angles of a triangle is 180°; it includes logical knowledge like "wise men are superior to fools." None of this kind of knowledge comes to us from the outside world, from reality. Not our senses but our minds perceive these things. If, for example, someone were repeatedly to measure the angles of a triangle and always come up with the sum of 178°, we would not then conclude that this triangle has 178°. We would conclude that this was not a triangle.

Intelligible knowledge is absolute and unchanging: the sum of the angles of a triangle is *always* 180°; wise men are *always* superior to fools. It is this absoluteness of intelligible knowledge that allows Augustine to hammer home his main point. It is impossible, he argues, for finite beings to comprehend absolute truth by themselves. They must, therefore, have some kind of help—Divine help. Augustine calls this Divine Illumination: "Indeed, when things are discussed which we perceive through the mind, that is, by means of intellect and reason, these are said to be things which we immediately, in that interior light of truth by virtue of which he himself who is called the interior man, is illumined." From this it follows, once again, that no man can teach another, for he is taught not through the teacher's words, but by means of the things themselves that God reveals within the soul. God is the only teacher, and as the Bible says, "we are not to call anyone on earth our master because there is only one master of all, who is in heaven."

Summary and Evaluation

Augustine became a Christian because he found in Christianity what he had searched for, but not found, in classical philosophy: certainty. Secure in the possession of revealed truth, he then used philosophy to demonstrate the certainty of that truth. When he turned his attention to education, it was not unexpected that he approached this human engagement with the same presumptions. He presumed that in such an activity, teachers possessed the truth and their task was to share that truth with their students. Inevitably then, Augustine construed education as an authoritarian process.

Yet Augustine's educational authoritarianism was mitigated by his Christian conception of human limitations. Teachers do not cause learning, he believed. They cannot make their students understand. Teachers can possess truth, but they do not transmit truth. Students grasp truth themselves—through direct experience and intellectual intuition. The teacher's task is to direct students, to guide them so that they discover the truth themselves—the same truth the teacher already possesses. Today many teachers, like Augustine, view their job as one of guiding and directing students so that they may discover those truths the teacher possesses and accept them. The upshot of such an approach, when it works (and it does work), is to make students dogmatic: they believe that they possess the truth about something—after all, it is "truth" shared with the teacher, and it is "truth" grasped by personal experience or personal insight.

What is lost with such an approach is the socratic concern with the continual advancement of knowledge. For a concern with advancement is not compatible with the presumption that the teacher possesses truths that are to be shared with the student. Education as an engagement to advance knowledge rests instead, as Socrates realized, on the presumption of human fallibility—of the student *and* the teacher.

Comenius's Didactic

In 1623 John Amos Comenius completed a book on education that had a rather long title: "The Great Didactic: Setting forth the whole Art of Teaching all Things to all Men, or, A certain Inducement to found such Schools in all the Parishes, Towns and Villages of every Christian Kingdom, that the entire Youth of both Sexes, none being excepted, shall *Quickly, Pleasantly,* and *Thoroughly* Become learned in the Sciences, pure in Morals, trained to Piety, and in this manner instructed in all things necessary for the present and for the future life, in which, with respect to everything that is suggested, its FUNDAMENTAL PRINCIPLES are set forth from the essential natures of the matter, Its TRUTH is proved by examples from the several mechanical arts, Its ORDER is clearly set forth in years, months, days, and hours, and finally, AN EASY AND SURE

METHOD is shown by which it can be pleasantly brought into existence.''

Who was Comenius? And why was he making such fantastic promises? What was he up to?

I

John Amos Comenius was born in 1592 in Bohemia (now Czechoslovakia). His family belonged to the Unity of Brethren, a Protestant religious group that traced its origins to the early reformer John Huss (1367–1415). From his earliest days, Comenius suffered from tragedies that followed him throughout his entire life. When he was twelve years old, plague killed his mother, father, and two of his sisters. Later, when Ferdinand of Austria took it upon himself to suppress Protestantism in Bohemia, Comenius, who by that time had become a minister in the Brethren, had to flee—leaving behind his two children and his wife, who was expecting their third child. He never again saw his native land or his family; all perished from plague. After seven years of wandering as a fugitive, he settled in Poland in a town called Lenzo, where he taught school and ministered to those of the Brethren who had also fled there.

Comenius's writings on spiritual and pedagogic reform brought him recognition and fame in many parts of Europe. Invited to England in 1641 as a consultant to reformers there, he left his second wife and family to spend a year in London. (On the voyage across the channel, Comenius almost lost his life when a storm all but capsized the ship carrying him.) He left England just a hairsbreadth before the outbreak of the Civil War. He next settled in Sweden, where his wife and family joined him. There, under the unceasing pressures to prepare textbooks for the Swedish schools, Comenius fell ill, as did his wife. Meanwhile, the Brethren remaining in Poland begged him to return—Comenius was now a bishop and secretary of the church. On their way back to Poland, his second wife died.

Comenius married again but the following year left his family to go to Hungary to establish a school in Sárospatak—a school to be based on his own pedagogical theories. About a year after Comenius arrived, his sponsor, Prince Rakoczi, died. Following this, the school began to fall apart when the teachers and the rector refused to cooperate with Comenius. He abandoned the project and returned to Leszno only just in time to gather his family and flee a Catholic army that burned the town to the ground. The fire destroyed a number of his manuscripts.

He finally settled in Amsterdam and set out to write his major work on the reform of human affairs. But, crippled by sciatica, saddened by the break up of the church, and grieved by the passing of his third wife, Comenius never completed his final book. On his deathbed in 1670, he pleaded with his son to publish his incomplete manuscripts. His son didn't do it, and it was not until almost three hundred years later that a Russian scholar discovered them in an orphanage library in Halle, Germany. They were published in 1966.

II

What was Comenius up to? What drove this tragic exile from country to country, seeking support from first one, then another, patron? We can get some inkling of his "mission" from his own explanation of why he wrote *The Great Didactic:*

> Let the object of this, our Didactic, be as follows: to seek and to find a method of instruction by which teachers may teach less, but humans may learn more; by which schools may be the scene of less noise, aversion and useless labor, but of more leisure, enjoyment and solid progress; and through which the Christian community may have less darkness, perplexity, and dissension; but on the other hand, more light, orderliness, peace and rest.

First and foremost then, Comenius wanted to bring about the reestablishment of the Christian community, a community torn to pieces by the horrible religious wars of his times. Setting Christian against Christian, these wars of the sixteenth and seventeenth centuries had decimated the population (Germany alone lost 40 percent of its people between 1618 and 1648); had brought plague, famine, and pillage to those still living; had led nations into bankruptcy; and had precipitated political revolutions in England, France, the Netherlands, and Portugal. Society, it seemed, was disintegrating. Many believed that the world was coming to an end. Comenius shared this belief.[1]

Yet, instead of the apathy and resignation we might expect, these apocalyptic visions of the sixteenth and seventeenth centuries sparked a flurry of intense activity. Christians associated the end of the world with the Second Coming of Christ: an occasion to be welcomed, an event to be prepared for. How does one prepare for the Second Coming? Here the Bible gave some guidelines. In the Book of Daniel (12:1–4) millenarian Christians found the following:

---

1. On seventeenth-century millennialism, see Charles Webster, *The Great Instauration: Science, Medicine, and Reform, 1626–1660* (London: Duckworth, 1975). Also see H. R. Trevor-Roper, *Religion, Reformation and Social Change,* 2nd ed. (London: Macmillan, 1972).

1. And at that time shall Michael stand up, the great prince which standeth for the children of thy people: and there shall be a time of trouble such as never was since there was a nation, *even* to that same time: and at that time, thy people shall be delivered, every one that shall be found written in the book.

2. And many of them that sleep in the dust of the earth shall awake, some to everlasting life, and some to shame and everlasting contempt.

3. And they that be wise shall shine as the brightness of the firmament; and they that turn many to righteousness as the stars forever and ever.

4. But thou, O Daniel, shut up the words and seal the book, even to the time of the end: many shall run to and fro, and knowledge shall be increased.

As they read it, many Christians of the seventeenth century believed that the Second Coming was to be heralded by a new era of enlightenment. This meant, to ardent believers like Comenius, that the time was ripe for universal education. What had learning and knowledge to do with the Second Coming? True knowledge led to piety. Through true knowledge, one could see, understand, and revere the greatness of God. And by disseminating true knowledge to all, Comenius and others believed it would be possible to restore a unified Christian community.

III

Piety had always been the hallmark of Christianity. The ancient Romans, of course, had also highly prized the virtue of *pietas*. Cicero had claimed that Rome surpassed all other people in piety: in faith, reverence, and obedience to the gods. Horace had written, "it is by obeying the gods, O Roman, that you rule the world."

Piety, as both the ancient Romans and the Christians understood it, meant to refer everything to God—all that existed, all that happened, and all that one thought, felt and did. With its conception of a personal deity, Christianity had the capacity for a more intense, more enveloping piety than the Romans. To the fundamental philosophical questions that had long troubled Western society, the Christian had a single answer. Saint Augustine elaborately developed that Christian answer: *Question:* "How did the world come into being?" *Answer:* "God the Creator brought it into being." *Question:* "Why do events happen as they do?" *Answer:* "God, as Divine Providence, so orders all that happens." *Question:* "What is man's purpose?" *Answer:* "To become reunited with God, his heavenly Father."

The philosophical basis for Christian piety informed the great outpouring of intellectual activity of thirteenth-century Christian thinkers like Albertus Magnus, Bonaventura, and Thomas Aquinas. Having rediscovered the works of Aristotle, these theologians composed vast treatises wherein they tried to fashion Christian answers to all the complex philosophical questions human curiosity could raise. But as these philosophical endeavors became more and more recondite, non-philosophers comprehended less and less. By the mid-fourteenth century, many, unable to fathom the subtle hair-splitting of the "scholastics," as they were called, accused them of subverting true Christian piety.

One of these leaders against the philosophers was Francesco Petrarch (1304–74), the father of Christian humanism. Petrarch argued that philosophy might help us understand virtue, but that this was not enough. "I have read," Petrarch wrote, "all of Aristotle's moral books, if I am not mistaken. Some of them I have also heard commented upon. . . . True virtue and all that is peculiar to vice, as well as to virtue, is egregiously defined and distinguished by him and treated with penetrating insight. When I learn all this, I know a little bit more than I knew before, but mind and will remain the same as they were, and I myself remain the same." A Christian, Petrarch insisted, needed not so much to know what virtue is, as he needed to *be* virtuous. Reading Aristotle does not make one more virtuous. Aristotle's lessons lack "the words that sting and set afire an urge toward love of virtue and hatred of vice." It is not Aristotle, not the study of philosophy, that will make Christians pious, Petrarch insisted, but the study of the humanities—the study of writers like Cicero, Seneca, and Horace.[2]

In the fifteenth century, Christian humanists like Thomas More of England and Erasmus of Rotterdam continued the attempt to make the humanities the source of Christian piety. The study of the classics, they argued, led men to live righteous lives. Here is what Erasmus said in his *Manual of the Christian Knight* (*Enchiridion militis christiani*):

> Make Christ the only goal of your life. Dedicate to Him all your enthusiasm, all your effort, your leisure as well as your business. . . . If you are interested in learning, certainly this is a fine quality, provided you turn your knowledge to Christ. If, on the other hand, you love letters only for the sake of knowledge, you have not gone far enough. You should go a step further. Let your study bring you to a clearer perception of Christ so that your love for Him will increase and you will in turn be able to communicate this knowledge of Him to others.

The humanists produced a revolution in the history of education: a new curriculum, new methods of instruction, a new clientele. This new learning was meant for all Christians, not just for the clergy. But it was meant especially for secular princes and their governors; these studies,

---

2. Francesco Petrarch, "On His Own Ignorance and That of Many Others," in *The Renaissance Philosophy of Man,* ed. E. Cassirer, P. O. Kristeller, and J. H. Randall, Jr. (Chicago: University of Chicago Press, 1948).

the humanists claimed, prepared men to be loyal, obedient, virtuous. "No one has ever claimed that a man needed Greek and Latin, or indeed any education, in order to be saved," Thomas More wrote. "Still," he added, "this education . . . does train the soul in virtue."

The Protestant Reformation of the sixteenth century helped institutionalize humanism as the established mode of education in Europe. Seeking to cultivate true piety in their followers, the Protestant reformers helped to found schools to teach the humanities. In England, in the years following the break from Rome, a number of new "grammar" schools were established to teach Christian piety through the study of Latin and Greek. In Germany, new schools called *gymnasiums* were opened. The one established by Johann Sturm in Strassburg became internationally famous. In Catholic countries, too, schools were established to teach piety through the humanities. In these countries a new institution called the *college* emerged under the aegis of the Society of Jesus. By 1600, the Jesuits had established two hundred colleges in the Catholic countries of Europe; and within the next fifty years, the number had doubled. The schools founded by the Catholics and the Protestants were remarkably similar. Students entered them at the age of six or seven and remained for about nine years. They studied some mathematics and some philosophy in their last years, but the rest of their school career they spent exclusively on Latin and Greek—learning first the grammar and then studying the classics, sacred and secular, of both languages.

The Protestant Reformation together with the invention of printing further institutionalized humanism through the publication of quasi-official grammar books. In England, Henry VIII requested all teachers to use John Lily's *Grammar Book* so that students "may the more readily and easily attain the rudiments of the Latin tongue, without the great hinderance which heretofore hath been, through the diversities of grammars and teachings." In Germany, Martin Luther's friend and assistant, Phillip Melancthon, prepared a grammar for use among their followers: "How many grievous errors," Melancthon wrote, "I might relate that have wrought great havoc in the Church, and that have arisen solely from ignorance of grammar."

By the seventeenth century, however, many Christians perceived difficulties. The problems inherent in humanistic education were both methodological and theoretical. First, there was the simple problem of the vast amount of time students devoted to learning Latin and Greek. This was especially so in countries like England and Germany where the Latin and Greek languages were so different from the vernacular. Numerous schemes emerged to expedite the teaching, but most of these were exceedingly laborious and cumbersome for the student. Here, for example, is the method of double translation prepared by Roger Ascham, one-time tutor to England's Queen Elizabeth I:

> Latin is to be taught as follows:—First, let the child learn the eight parts of speech, and then the right joining together of substantives with adjectives, the noun with the verb, the relative with the antecedent. After the concords are learned, let the master take Sturm's selection of Cicero's Epistles, and read them after this manner: "first, let him teach the child, cheerfully and plainly, the cause and matter of the letter; then, let him construe it into English so oft as the child may easily carry away the understanding of it; lastly, parse it over perfectly. This done, then let the child by and by both construe and parse it over again so that it may appear that the child doubteth in nothing that his master has taught him before. After this, the child must take a paper book, and, sitting in some place where no man shall prompt him, by himself, let him translate into English his former lesson. Then, showing it to his master, let the master take from him his Latin book, and pausing an hour at the least, then let the child translate his own English into Latin again in another paper book. When the child bringeth it turned into Latin, the master must compare it with Tully's book, and lay them both together, and where the child doth well, praise him; where amiss, point out why Tully's use is better.[3]

Even assuming that students finally learned—as some did—Latin and Greek and went on to study the classics, theoretical problems remained. The trouble lay with the content of the classical works. Most contained matter subversive of Christian beliefs. From the earliest, the Christian humanist had to reject certain classical authors as too risky for young Christian minds. Erasmus, for example, devoted much time and thought to selecting and expurgating the works of pagan authors for the use of Christian schoolboys. But censorship never works. Once someone learns how to read, it becomes impossible to control what he will read. So the continuous rediscovering and re-presenting of the classical works of antiquity did provide a vast array of non-Christian beliefs and life-styles that some erstwhile Christians could and did adopt and imitate. But, even if students resisted succumbing to a pagan way of life, did the study of the classics really make one a pious person? Many complained that such an education simply made one pedantic. Here is Montaigne's (1533–92) criticism of humanistic education:

> Men are apt presently to inquire, does such a one understand Greek or Latin? Is he a poet? or does he write in prose? But whether he grows better or more discreet, which are qualities of principle concern, these are never thought of. . . . We can say, Cicero says thus; these were the manners of Plato; these were the very words of Aristotle; but in what do we say ourselves? What do we judge? A parrot would say as much as that. . . . We suffer ourselves to learn and rely so strongly upon the arm of another that we destroy our own strength and vigor. Would I fortify

3. Quoted in R. H. Quick, *Essays on Educational Reformers* (New York: D. Appleton, 1904), p. 84.

> myself against the fear of death it must be at the expense of Seneca: would I extract consolation for myself or my friend, I borrow it from Cicero. I might have found it in myself had I been trained to make use of my own vision. I do not like this relative and mendicant understanding; for though we could become learned by other men's learning, a man can never be wise but by his own wisdom (*Of Pendantry*).

IV

If neither the study of philosophy nor the study of the humanities produced Christian piety, was there any study that would? Was there a source of knowledge that would lead Christians to understand and revere the greatness and grandeur of God? The millennium was drawing near; devout Christians had to prepare for the Second Coming. Where was such learning as they needed to be found?

No one had thought longer and deeper about the true source of knowledge than Francis Bacon (1561–1626). Morality and piety, he argued, are manifest in action, in behavior that *benefited mankind.* Such actions, he insisted, are based on knowledge of the world as it really is. We cannot get such practical knowledge from contemplation of abstract speculations of philosophy nor from books written by the ancients. Real knowledge can come only from the world itself. Man must read from the book of nature: "Man is but the servant and interpreter of nature," Bacon wrote, "what he does and what he knows is only what he has observed of nature's order in fact or in thought; beyond this he knows nothing and can do nothing."

His belief that the world itself was the source of this knowledge Bacon found reinforced in the prophecy of Daniel. Daniel had said that many shall run to and fro and science or knowledge shall be increased. As Bacon saw it, the recent developments in navigation and other mechanical arts (e.g., the compass, the sextant, the printing press) had brought increased commerce, exploration, and reading—resulting in many, literally and figuratively, "running to and fro." And these important developments in mechanical arts had not come about through the contemplation of philosophy, nor through the reading of the works of the ancients but from studying the real world of nature. Hence, science, true knowledge, must follow the path of the mechanical arts. Only by understanding nature will men have the power to do good, to better the human estate. Such knowledge, Bacon maintained, would restore true piety, for knowledge of the nature of things leads us to glorify the Creator.

Here is how Bacon expressed this in *The Advancement of Learning:*

> But farther, it is an assured truth and a conclusion of experience that a little or superficial knowledge of philosophy [science] may incline the mind of man to atheism, but a farther proceeding therein doth bring the mind back again to religion, for in the entrance of philosophy, when the

> second causes, which are next unto the senses, do offer themselves to the mind of man, if it dwell and stay there, it may induce some oblivion of the highest cause; but when a man passeth on farther, and seeth the dependence of causes and the works of Providence, then, according to the allegory of the poets, will easily believe that the highest link of nature's chain must needs be tied to the foot of Jupiter's chair.

Man must, Bacon added, read both the book of God's word *and* the book of God's *works,* endeavoring to progress in his understanding of each. Man must not, he cautioned, "unwisely mingle or confound these learnings together."

Bacon believed that the conscious and deliberate reading of the book of God's works would bring humanity back to the true path for advancing knowledge, a path abandoned since the time of Plato and Aristotle. Bacon planned, but never completed, a master plan for the great renewal. He called it the *Magna Instauratio.* The first part of this work, *Of the Professions and Advancement of Learning* (1605) is an inducement to the monarch, James I, to encourage and promote scientific learning. The second part, the *Novum Organum* (1620), presents the inductive method as the basis for the advancement of knowledge. The trouble with present knowledge about the world, Bacon said, is that it is based on generalizations that are "false, confused and over-hastily abstracted from the facts." Since these generalizations are the basic premises for making further deductions, it is obvious that errors accumulate and proliferate. Instead of floating in the air, science must rest on the solid foundation of experience "well-explained and weighed": "The syllogism consists of propositions; propositions consist of words; words are symbols of notions. Therefore, if the notions themselves (which are the root of the matter) are confused and over-hastily abstracted from the facts, there can be no firmness in the superstructure. Our only hope, therefore, lies in true induction."

V

During his student days at Heidelberg, Comenius read the two parts of Bacon's *Magna Instauratio.* To a devout follower of a persecuted religious sect, the promise of a great renewal was heady tonic indeed. Bacon had movingly expressed what Comenius longed for: "If, therefore, there be any humility toward the Creator, any reverence for a disposition to magnify his works, any charity for man and anxiety to relieve his sorrows and necessities, any love of truth in nature, any hatred of darkness, any desire for the purification of the understanding. . . . "Yes! Yes! All this was precisely what Comenius longed for. And how could this come to pass? Bacon pointed the way: ". . . We must entreat men again and again to discard, or at least set apart for a while their volatile and preposterous philosophies, which have preferred theses to hypotheses, held experiences captive, and triumphed over the works of God; and to approach with humility and veneration to unroll the volume of Creation, to linger and meditate thereon, and with minds washed clean from opinions, to study it in purity and integrity."

This notion that experience, or experientially based knowledge, should be the basis for true Christian piety became the theme of Comenius's first theological treatise, *The Labyrinth of the World and the Paradise of the Heart,* which he completed in 1623. Comenius's book, like its English counterpart, John Bunyan's *Pilgrim's Progress,* recounts the search of the author for the true calling of man. "When I had attained that age at which the differences between good and bad begin to appear to the human understanding," the book begins, "I saw how different are the ranks, conditions, occupations of men, the works and endeavors at which they toil; and it seemed most necessary to me to consider what group of men I should join and with what matters I should occupy my life."

Accompanied by his guide, "Searchall," the pilgrim sets off through the labyrinth of the world to behold "all earthly things that are under the sun" in order to choose a better way of life. One by one, he reviews the five conditions of man: the domestic life, the life of the marketplace, clerical life, military life, and the life of government. In each order of life the pilgrim discovers discord, disorder, and disarray. All who occupy these different conditions of life are hypocritical—they hide behind masks so that others cannot see them as they really are. And they really are, the pilgrim finds out, deformed creatures. Their callings have deformed them: they understand not what they do and occupy themselves with trivial and useless matters. He sees them to be fickle and unsteady. Yet, for all their faults, they are full of pride and presumption.

In reviewing the condition of the men of learning, Comenius gives us a glimpse of the educational enterprise of his times. First, he wrote, the only ones ever educated are those with health, talent, constancy, patience, and money. As to the process of education itself, it was quite painful: "for fists, canes, sticks, birch rods, struck them on their cheeks, heads, backs and posteriors till blood streamed forth, and they were almost entirely covered with stripes, scars, spots and weals." The content of their studies consisted solely of books. Some students, the pilgrim reports, chose the finest and most subtle morsels from the books and gently chewed and digested them. Others greedily crammed down everything that came to their hands. This simply swelled out their bellies, and what they stuffed down "crept out of them undigested, either above or below." Others merely collected books and displayed them ceremoniously.

This education, the pilgrim notes, actually deformed the students.

For when they completed their studies, Comenius observes allegorically: "Some . . . had eyes, but had no tongue; others had a tongue, but no eyes; others had only ears, but neither eyes nor tongue. . . . This bookish education had destroyed one or more of their senses so that they were incapable of perceiving the world as it really was.

Not unexpectedly, then, the so-called learned found nothing but discord and strife. These so-called wise men did nothing but quarrel (dispute) with one another. They "fought and hacked, threw and shouted . . . at one another . . . till it was fearful to behold." This discord and confusion infested not only philosophy but all branches of learning—grammar, rhetoric, even mathematics.

And what did these learned men know? What could they do? The pilgrim reveals that these educated men—possessing bachelors, masters and doctors degrees—had learned nothing:

> . . . I, who ever wished to see what would happen to these men, watched one of these masters of arts. . . . They asked him to count something together, but he knew not how to do so; they then told him to measure something, he knew not how to do so. They asked him to name the stars, he knew not how to do it; they asked him how to expound syllogisms, he knew not how to do it; they asked him to talk in strange tongues, he knew not how to do it; they asked him to speak in his own language, he knew not how to do it; at last, they asked him to read or write, he knew not how to do it.

What a sin this is! Comenius exclaims, "After spending a lifetime in schools, after laying out a fortune on this, after having received titles and such, it is at the end, still necessary to inquire if someone has learned anything. God help me against such mismanagement!"

In the other conditions of life, the pilgrim finds similar discord and disorder. In addition, each way of life has its own particular vices: businessmen are corrupt, the clergy are divided and dissolute, governors are unfit to rule and unjust to boot, and soldiers are cruel and licentious. All orders of life seem vain and unworthy. In each condition, men pursue the ephemeral goals of wealth, pleasure, and power.

Disillusioned and despairing of the ways of the world, the pilgrim finally enters the paradise of the heart, which, for Comenius, symbolizes the conversion to Christ. Christ, for Comenius, is the source of all wisdom. Christ speaks to the pilgrim: "Thou has seen in other conditions how the men who seek gain busy themselves with endless labours, what artifices they employ, what perils they risk. Those must now consider all this striving as vanity, knowing that one thing alone is necessary, the grace of God. Therefore, limit thyself to the calling which I have entrusted to thee, conduct they labors faithfully, conscientiously, quietly, entrusting to me the end and aim of all things."

Comenius then goes on to explain that such a conversion to Christ will help men to distinguish true from false wisdom, vanity from knowledge. Allegorically, he has God give the pilgrim a pair of spectacles through which he can behold all he could not see before. Equipped with these spectacles (the outward frame of which was the word of God, while the glass within was the Holy Ghost), Christians discover that "wherever they go in the world, whatever they see, hear, smell, taste, above them, under them, around them, everywhere they shall see the footsteps of God, and they know how to turn everything to piety."

The experience of the real world is the foundation for true Christian piety. It is through his senses that the Christian comes to perceive God: "The Christian in everything that he sees, hears, touches, smells, tastes—sees, hears, touches, smells, tastes, God." The real world, the wonder and splendor of the world, reveal the Glory of God, his omniscience, his omnipotence, his Divine Goodness.

True Christians, pious Christians, never despair or lose hope; they are "certain that whatever befalls them comes to them from God, according to his prescient consideration." And true Christians, Comenius assures us, recognize that they all belong to the same community: they are children of the one father, they partake of the same spiritual food and expect the same rewards. Learned Christians know not philosophy nor many languages but do know useful things—that is, "all God's works, and . . . arts [that] are of some use for the purpose of understanding him." If knowledge of the real world, God's works, will restore real Christian piety and re-create the true Christian community, then Christians require a new kind of education, not an education in speculative philosophy nor in the humanities, but an education that leads to a knowledge of the real world. This was to become Comenius's mission.

VI

While still a fugitive in his native land in the 1620s, Comenius began to compose educational works. His first education book, initially written in Czech, was *The Gate of Languages Unlocked*. A Latin translation, *Janua linguarum reserata,* appeared in 1631. The study of language, Comenius wrote, was the Adiran's thread to lead mankind out of the labyrinth. A universal language was a precondition for the looked-for great renewal, the restoration of a true Christian community. For a short time, he thought that Czech might become that universal language. Later, he toyed with the idea of creating a brand-new language, one that would be more onomatopoeic than any existing language and so better reflect the harmony between words and things. Finally, however, he realized that

Latin was the only practical answer to this quest for a universal language through which to unite all Christians.

Comenius had made a thorough study of the methods of teaching language. The main contention of the times was whether one should teach language by precept (grammar) or by the direct method. Comenius rejected both in favor of the textbook approach. The basic principle of his textbook was to use the vernacular as a means of learning a limited range of words together with their Latin equivalents. The most important aspect was the organization of the book. "I planned a book," Comenius explained, "in which all things, the property of things and actions and passions of things, should be presented, and to each should be assigned its own proper word, believing that in one and the same book the whole connected series of things might be surveyed historically, and the whole fabric of things and words reduced to one continuous context."

A copy of a textbook composed by three Jesuits had come into his hands in 1628. But this book, called *The Gate of Languages* (*Janua linguarum*), had not utilized the key of combining words and things. Hence Comenius set to work on his own book, *The Gate of Languages Unlocked.* His book contained 1,000 sentences divided into 100 chapters. Each chapter dealt with some aspect of the real world: Concerning the Elements, Fire, Water, Earth, Stones, Metals, Trees, and Forests, Herbs, Shrubs. Other chapters were on Animals, on Man (his body, his internal and external members), and so on. There were chapters on all the mechanical arts and on the Home, the Family, and various social institutions. Some chapters are about the several arts and sciences. The final chapters are on Games, Death, Burial, and the Providence of God. The *Janua* was published with parallel columns containing the vernacular and Latin sentences. Students first learned the vernacular ones and then the Latin. A minimum number of grammatical rules were appended to the book.

To supplement the *Janua,* Comenius in 1633 published a more elementary text, which he called the *Vestibule* (*Vestibulum*) to the *Gate of Languages.* This contained some four hundred sentences arranged into seven chapters. The first chapter was on the quality of things (*Deus est aeternas; mundus temporarius*); then the actions of things (*sol lucet; luna splendet*). Other chapters described things in school, things at home, things in the city, and the virtues.

In a third language textbook, not published until 1657, Comenius made the next logical extension of his method of teaching language: a picture book. One of the earliest examples of an illustrated textbook, he called it *The World Through Sense Pictures* (*Orbis sensualium pictus*). With the help of 150 copper woodcuts, this book presented "all the chief things that are in the world and of men's employments therein." The

Orbis pictus presented sense objects to the senses (with invisible objects, like God, depicted symbolically) so that the child could receive a "clear," "solid," "full," and "true" understanding of them. For nothing is in the understanding, Comenius wrote, which is not first in the senses. "And therefore, to exercise the senses well about the right perceiving of the differences of things, will be to lay the grounds for all wisdom, and all wise discourse, and all discreet actions in one's course of life."

The *Orbis pictus* covered the same material presented in the *Janua,* although it contained simpler sentences. There are the same parallel columns of the vernacular and the Latin, but this time the sentences are numbered to correspond to the numbered objects in the picture accompanying each chapter. Chapter 9, for example, has a picture of the earth containing High Mountains (1), Deep Valleys (2), Hills Rising (3), Hollow Caves (4), Plain Fields (5), and Shady Woods (6).

Both the *Janua* and *Orbis pictus* achieved worldwide success, becoming *the* textbooks of the West for over two centuries. The *Janua* went through 80 editions during Comenius's lifetime, and 26 more after his death. It was translated into all the European languages and into Oriental languages as well. The *Orbis pictus* gained even greater popularity with 21 editions in the seventeenth century, 53 in the eighteenth, 33 in the nineteenth, and 9 in the twentieth.

VII

Had Comenius written no other books than the *Janua* and the *Orbis pictus,* he would have become, as Pierre Bayle wrote, "immortal." But his language textbooks were only supplemental to his broader scheme of the total reformation of education and, ultimately, the total reformation of society. His initial book on the reformation of education was a tract called *The School of Infancy.* He dedicated it to the members of his own flock: "To Pious Christian Parents, Tutors, Guardians and All upon Whom the Charge of Children is Incumbent." This book explained the process of educating the child prior to its entering school.

The key to education for Comenius was that at each age, or at each level of schooling, the aims of education were always the same: piety, morality, and learning. In infancy, before the child goes to school, piety and morality are most to be stressed. Later, when the child enters school, the school will reinforce and deepen the piety and morality the child has already learned at home. During the first six years of life, the child must learn: "1. that there is a God; 2. Who, being everywhere present, He beholdeth us all; 3. that He bestows abundantly food, drink, clothing, and all things upon such as obey Him; 4. but punishes with death the stubborn and immoral; therefore, 5. that He ought to be feared, always be invoked and loved as a father; and 6. that all things ought to be done which He commands; 7. that if we be good and righteous, He will take us to the heavens."

Training in piety should begin, Comenius says, at the age of two. At that time, the child can know to be silent, fold his hands and sit quietly when others pray. He can learn that God is in heaven (up above); that He made all things and gives us all we have. At three, the child can begin to learn prayers—morning, evening, and before-meal prayers. Of greatest importance is to guard the child against "occasions of evil." Adults must see to it that the eyes and ears of the child come upon "nothing vile or impious," nothing that can contaminate the mind.

The teaching of moral virtue in the home is largely by example, although example should be accompanied by instruction that is prudent and timely: "Look, consider how I do . . . see how father and mother do it . . . do not do such things . . . be ashamed of yourself. . . . If you behave so, you will never become an excellent young man . . . street beggars, and bad people do so. . . ." When examples of virtue and admonition do not work, the child must be disciplined. The first step is to chide him, using fear and shame to move him "to a recollection of himself." If this fails, Comenius advises parents to use the rod or a slap to the head, "in order that the boy may recollect himself and become more attentive." Using these methods, Comenius promises, parents can accustom children to the following virtues "easily, prudently, and decorously": temperance, frugality, respect ("better to restrain children by discipline and fear than to reveal to them the overflowing of your love, and thus open, as it were, a window to forwardness and disobedience"); obedience, truthfulness, temperance, justice, benefice ("occasionally have children impart alms to others"); patience, services with alacrity ("my child, give that to me . . . carry this . . . place it upon the form . . . go call Johnny . . . tell Annie to come to me"); courtesy and civility of manners ("children must remember what is due to everyone"). Comenius's basic theory of instruction is that children can be as pious, moral, and learned as adults—in their fashion, and in accordance with their age.

Learning, Comenius says, consists of knowing, doing, and saying. And children should learn to know, to do, and to say *all* things, except such as are bad. By saying that the child should know all things, he meant the child should know them in his fashion, in accordance with his capacities. Thus the child, before the age of six, learns about nature, astronomy, geography, history, household affairs, and politics. About nature, the child should learn the names of the elements, the various natural phenomenon like rain, snow, ice, fog; the names of trees, plants, animals, and the outward members of his own body. In geography, the child should know where he lives and whether it is village, city, town, or citadel. He should know what a field is, a mountain, a forest, a meadow, a river. As to knowing how to do, the child in his first six years can learn dialectics, arithmetic, geometry, music, and manual arts. In arithmetic, for example, the child can learn that something is much or little, how to count to twenty ("or even all the way to sixty"), to understand what is an even and what an odd number; that three are more than two, that three and one make four, and so on. The child's music will be to sing some little verses from the psalms or hymns. As to the manual arts, the child can learn how to cut, split, carve, strew, arrange, tie, untie, roll up, unroll, and such. During infancy, the child can also learn to write and draw with chalk ("poorer persons may use a piece of charcoal"), making dots, lines, hooks, and round *O*s—either as an exercise or amusement. In learning how to say, children are actually learning grammar, rhetoric, and poetry. The grammar of the first six years consists of the child's learning how to express what it knows of things precisely, succinctly, and articulately.

The last task of the parents or guardians is to prepare the child to enter the school. They must avoid, Comenius cautions, telling children that at school they will not be able to play or that they will be beaten by rods. Instead, the parents should inspire children with pleasant anticipations, "as if fair days and the vintage were approaching." Parents should buy them new school clothes, a tablet, a book, and the like. Parents should praise learning and learned men and tell the future students that learning is not labor, but that amusement with books and a pen is "sweeter than honey." And the parents should incite in their offspring confidence in, and love of, their future teacher—calling him father's (or mother's) friend, or a good neighbor; praising his wisdom, kindness, and benignity; explaining that he never chastises obedient children.

Ultimately, however, sending the child to school is a religious act in which parents commend their children to God. Comenius holds out as a model the mother of the Bohemian martyr John Huss. While taking young John on his initial journey to school, she was so overcome with the importance of what she was doing that she frequently fell down on her knees with her son and poured out prayers. Comenius composed and recommended a long prayer for parents to recite on the first day of school, which includes the following:

> Fear of Thee, O Lord, is the beginning of wisdom; therefore, fill its heart with Thy fear, O Holy God, and enlighten it with the light of knowledge according to Thy will, so that its advanced age, if Thou shouldst deem fit, may be glorious for Thee, useful to its neighbors, and salutary to itself.

VIII

It is to the schools and their reformation that Comenius next turned. He wrote *Pansophia prodramus* (*Harbinger of All Wisdom*), which

Samuel Hartlib translated into English as *The Reformation of Schools* and published in 1642. In this work Comenius begins by pointing out that although these were the times foretold by Daniel (12:4), when "many run to and fro," when the rediscovery of the learning of the ancients and many recent inventions had greatly increased the store of wisdom, and when schools had been erected everywhere, there still remained the need to discover the easy way to teach all these things to all men. Once this is done, Comenius says, we can enjoy the great renewal: "I see not what should hinder us from a thankful acknowledgement and hearty embracing of that Golden Age of light and knowledge which hath been so long foretold and expected."

The learning found in the schools today is most inadequate, Comenius laments. It is prolix, too difficult for students, frequently in error, of no practical use, and not conducive to piety. There are many reasons for these inadequacies, but all boil down to the absence of a philosophy of education. He proposes such a philosophy, called *Pansophia,* which he promises will reduce school studies to "a solid breviary of universal learning," make learning easy and pleasant, purge it of error, make it useful to the affairs of our life and "a happy ladder leading us to God himself."

By the term pansophy, or universal wisdom, Comenius means that human beings can attain a kind of omniscience, a knowledge of God, of nature, and of art: "By art, we understand whatsoever is compassed by human industry, as our thoughts, works and actions; by nature, we mean whatsoever comes to pass of its own accord by those dispositions implanted in things; by God, all that power, wisdom, and goodness which, lying hid from eternity, hath hitherto displayed itself to us, either in divine words or works: He that knoweth these three, knows all things, for of these three the whole world consists."

All that exists, Comenius explains, is in accordance with its own idea. Art borrows the ideas of its works from nature, and nature borrows them from God; but God has them from Himself. "So, the ideas being first conceived in God, imprint their likeness in the creatures and likewise the reasonable creatures in things which they themselves affect." Since we cannot directly know Divine Ideas and since the idea of Art comes from Nature, it is nature we should study directly in order to obtain true knowledge—nature aided by Scripture: "Therefore, the rules whereby our Pansophy is to be enacted must be borrowed from these two; Nature and Scripture, whereby all things great and small, high and low, first and last, visible, created, and uncreated, may be reduced to such a harmony, (or Pan-harmony, rather) as which is true, perfect, and everyway compleat and satisfactory to itself, and to things themselves." Pansophy will, Comenius says, lead men away from the other books to the greatest book of all, the book of nature (and the Scriptures), so that they will begin to penetrate to knowledge of things themselves.

The basis for all things is harmony: "Nature is the image of Divine things, and Art of Nature." This means that the book of nature cannot contradict the book of Scriptures; nor can human art contradict nature or religion. True art, true philosophy of nature, must be in harmony with true religion. As he now construed it, pansophy would become the basis for the restoration of a pious community of Christians, the foundation for all research and inquiry, as well as the philosophy of education for the schools.

As a philosophy of education for the schools, pansophy will help children—"not yet filled with vain apprehensions of vain knowledge"—to draw in pure conceptions of things, thereby gaining a *real, solid,* and *well-grounded* wisdom: "Such as will serve for sound direction of the judgment, for multiplying of new ventures among men, and for a more perfect guide to lead us toward eternal bliss, the last end of our lives." In addition, pansophy will serve as the foundation for the research conducted by men of learning. The structure of knowledge, or Temple of Wisdom, as Comenius called it, erected by pansophy will wean researchers away from the study of transitory things and will clear their minds of conceits and vanities and invite them to discover truth and possess real goods.

But pansophy is not only for students and learned men; it is for all Christians of whatever rank, age, sex, or language. Pansophy will bring all Christians "to see and behold what admirable sights and pastimes, that ever to be adored wisdom of God exhibits unto all men in all times and places." Through rational contemplation and the comparing of God's words (Scripture) and works (nature) together, all will learn to observe the greatness of all the works of God and how wisely they are made. This restoration of learning will be the basis for the renewal of a true, universal, pious, Christian community.

Comenius never constructed his Temple of Wisdom—the complete pansophy that was to establish complete harmony among art, nature, and religion—although he did write numerous outlines of what needed doing and continually entreated others to take up the work to identify and explain the categories, structures, and laws that harmonized art, nature, and religion. In 1641 the English Parliament, largely through the urgings of Samuel Hartlib, invited Comenius to England, where he planned to establish a College of Light to complete the work of building a complete pansophy, or Temple of Wisdom. Nothing much came of this, save a few more outlines of pansophy. Later, when Charles II created the Royal Society in 1662, Comenius viewed himself as the "father" of that society, although most members traced its origin to Francis Bacon.

IX

Although he never completed his Temple of Wisdom, Comenius did apply the basic notion of harmony to the art of teaching. The result was *The Great Didactic: The Whole Art of Teaching All Things to All Men*. Comenius had mentioned his *Great Didactic* in *The Reformation of Schools* when he wrote in passing that he had "lighted upon" the art of readily and solidly teaching all things to all men by "reducing everything to the immovable laws and rules of nature." He had initially composed the *Didactic* in Czech between 1628 and 1632. Later, he translated it into Latin and published it in 1636 as an appeal to "all Christian kingdoms and states to found schools so that the entire youth of both sexes, none being excepted, shall *quickly, thoroughly,* and *pleasantly* become learned in the sciences, pure in morals and trained to piety."

Others, of course, had made suggestions of various kinds for the improvement of education, but none had ever attempted a plan so grand or bold as that of John Amos Comenius: how to teach *all* things to *all* men—pleasantly, quickly, and thoroughly. The boldness of the scheme rested on its scientific basis; it was rooted in the principle of pansophy: a true understanding of nature, art, and religion.

The universe, Comenius believed, is the school of mankind; through the study of the universe, one can become learned, moral, and pious. Universal learning was, therefore, possible for all, however much people differ in dispositions, simply because all have organs of sense and reason. Hitherto, Comenius explains, schools have failed to educate all because they lacked the proper methods of teaching. These methods are to be found inherent in the art of teaching, and this art is, must be, in harmony with the principles inherent in nature.

Comenius was highly conscious that his age had witnessed a number of significant mechanical inventions. For him and others, this flowering of creativity signaled the emergence of a golden age. Like others, he sought to understand why these mechanical inventions had occurred at this particular time. It was Francis Bacon—the philosopher of industrial sciences, as one recent interpreter has dubbed him—who supplied the best explanation: the mechanical inventions were the result of a better understanding of nature. Knowledge of nature confers power to shape, mold, bend, manipulate things to serve human needs—in Bacon's felicitous phrase, to improve the estate of man.

Bacon explained that all mechanical arts are simply technique. One sets forth an aim or a goal and then devises the appropriate means to attain that goal. And the appropriate means are always based on true knowledge of the nature of things, a knowledge born of sense observation. Comenius applied this construction of the mechanical arts to education, making teaching, for the first time, a conscious technique. In doing this he construed the student as an object, a thing to be worked on in order to produce a predetermined result. The teacher became an artisan, a technician, a producer. Comenius's favorite analogy for teaching was the newly invented *art* of printing: "How is it that the process of printing, by which books can be multiplied quickly, neatly, and correctly, are properly carried out? Assuredly, by means of order. The type must be cut, moulded and polished, placed suitably in the type-boxes and then arranged in the right order while the paper must be prepared, damped, stretched, and placed under the press." Likewise with teaching: as soon as we have succeeded in finding the proper method and order of teaching, we will be able to teach schoolboys, in any number desired—just as the printing press can cover a thousand sheets daily with the neatest writing. He even suggested the ugly word *didachography* (adapted from the term *typography*) as a label to describe his method (*the* method) of teaching: "Instead of paper, we have pupils whose minds have to be impressed with the symbols of knowledge. Instead of type, we have the class-books and the rest of the apparatus devised to facilitate the operation of teaching. The ink is replaced by the voice of the master since this it is that conveys information from the books to the minds of the listener; while the press is school discipline, which keeps the pupils up to their work and compels them to learn."

What is this method of teaching all things to all men? The art of teaching, according to Comenius, like all arts, is based on nature itself. So we must look to nature for a parallel to the art of teaching. Comenius finds this parallel in the process of a bird hatching out its young. Here is his first principle of teaching:

> Nature observes a suitable time. For example: a bird that wishes to multiply its species does not set about it in winter when everything is stiff with cold, nor in summer, when everything is parched and withered by the heat; nor yet in autumn, when the vital force of all creatures declines with the sun's declining rays, and a new winter with hostile mien is approaching; but in spring, when the sun brings back life and strength to all. Again, the process consists of several steps. While it is yet cold, the bird conceives the eggs and warms them inside its body, where they are protected from the cold; when the air grows warmer it lays them in its nest, but does not hatch them out until the warm season comes, that the tender chicks may grow accustomed to light and warmth by degrees.

We find, Comenius points out, that the gardener and the carpenter both imitate the ways of nature. They, like the bird hatching out its young, observe a suitable time: the gardener does not plant in winter, summer, or autumn, but in the spring of the year; the builder must choose the right time for cutting timber, burning bricks, laying foundations, and so forth.

But schools and teachers, Comenius goes on, deviate from the ways of nature. They do not select the right time for mental exercise, nor are the exercises properly divided so that students may advance through the necessary stages or steps. To rectify these errors of the schools and bring them into harmony with nature (and the other arts), Comenius recommends the following:

> The education of men should be commenced in the springtime of life, that is to say, in boyhood (for boyhood is the equivalent of spring, youth of summer, manhood of autumn, and old age of winter).
>
> The morning hours are the most suitable for study (for here again the morning is the equivalent of spring, midday of summer, the evening of autumn, and the night of winter).
>
> All the subjects that are to be learned should be arranged so as to suit the age of the students, that nothing which is beyond their comprehension be given them to learn.

To understand what Comenius is up to, we have to understand that he is *not* saying that gardeners, carpenters, and teachers learn or discover their various arts by observing how a bird lays an egg. He is merely pointing out the harmony that exists between nature and art in the case of gardening and carpentry, and suggesting that teaching—if it is to be a successful art—must also harmonize with the laws of nature.

Comenius merits the title of father of modern pedagogy because, following him, most educators have construed teaching as a technical process (like printing), where they, as intentional producers of a desired result, must have sufficient knowledge of the nature of the material (the students) they work on. The science of human nature today goes under the name of psychology, and it includes the principles of learning and the principles of human development. In his *Great Didactic,* Comenius was one of the first theorists to argue that the art of teaching must be based on the principles of learning and development. As an ardent pansophist, he tried to demonstrate the validity of his principles of learning and development by uncovering parallel principles in other arts, like gardening and carpentry, and uncovering parallels between these arts and the workings of nature.

Comenius established nine universal principles of instruction by this syncretic method and then went on to determine ten principles of facility in teaching and learning, ten principles of thoroughness, and eight principles of consciseness and rapidity.

Here are his ten principles of facility in instruction, principles that will enable students to learn quickly and pleasantly:

> Following in the footsteps of nature, we find that the process of education will be easy
>
> (i) If it begin early, before the mind is corrupted.
> (ii) If the mind be duly prepared to receive it.
> (iii) If it proceed from the general to the particular.
> (iv) And from what is easy to what is more difficult.
> (v) If the pupil be not overburdened by too many subjects.
> (vi) And if progress be slow in every case.
> (vii) If the intellect be forced to nothing to which its natural bent does not incline it, in accordance with its age and with the right method.
> (viii) If everything be taught through the medium of the senses.
> (ix) And if the use of everything taught be continually kept in view.
> (x) If everything be taught according to one and the same method.
>
> These, I say, are the principles to be adopted if education is to be easy and pleasant.

Of his ten principles of thoroughness, the most important is the fifth:

> Nature develops everything from its roots and from no other source. The wood, bark, leaves, flowers and fruit of a tree come from the roots and from no other source. . . .

The builder in his art imitates this principle, erecting a house in such a way that it can stand on its own foundations without the need of external props. But not the schools. They deviate terribly from this principle when, instead of showing students the objective world as it exists, they have them learn what this or that author wrote or thought about something in the world. To rectify this error, students must, as far as possible, "be taught to become wise by studying the heavens, the earth, oaks, and beeches, but not by studying books; that is to say, they must learn to know and investigate these things themselves and not the observations that other people have made about these things. We shall thus tread in the footsteps of the wise men of old if each of us obtains his knowledge from the originals, from things themselves, and from no other source."

Comenius's next list of principles—the eight principles of concise and rapid teaching and learning—all have to do with the proper organization and proper ordering of the process of instruction. Once we set forth well-formulated goals (Comenius's goals, you recall, were learning, morality, and piety), we then ascertain the means that infallibly lead to those goals. The parallel in nature, Comenius finds here, is the sun, which "sends forth its rays over the whole world and supplies all the elements, minerals, plants and animals with light, warmth, life and strength." Our schools should imitate the unifying and expeditious force of the sun. In teaching, we must be like the sun, Comenius counsels; we must eliminate the isolation of subjects and reveal to students the interconnections that exist among them. In addition, we should standardize both materials and methods in order to eliminate confusion and chaos. In the course of explaining how to render instruction rapid and concise, Comenius blithely lays bare the teacher-centered bias of his didactic approach:

> With a little skill, it will be possible to arrest the attention of the pupils, collectively and individually, and to imbue them with the notion that (as really is the case) the mouth of the teacher is a spring from which streams of knowledge issue and flow over them, and that, whenever they see this spring open, they should place their attention like a cistern beneath it, and thus allow nothing that flows forth to escape.

X

After having derived the principles of instruction, Comenius next turned to the methods of teaching. He based those methods on how people actually learn. Thus there are different methods of teaching for different kinds of learning: different methods for science and for art, for morality, and for piety.

Science, the understanding of the world of nature, we learn through observation, and so the golden rule is "Everything should, as far as possible, be placed before the senses." Arts we learn through practice; here we must provide students with models to imitate and methods and tools to work with. Morality we learn by doing what is right: "As boys learn to walk by walking, to talk by talking, and to write by writing, in the same way they will learn obedience by obeying, abstinence by abstaining, truth by speaking the truth, and constancy by being constant." Piety we learn through God's words and God's works. By meditation on the Scriptures and on the world itself, we come to see that all comes from God and each thing in the universe attains its end in accordance with his Divine Will. Piety, therefore, is the union of knowledge and morality—understanding and doing what God has willed.

Of the three aims of knowledge, morality, and piety, the most important for Comenius was piety. Piety he saw as the foundation stone for a restored Christian community that had shattered and divided. Knowledge and morality were merely instrumental to creating proper Christians—Christians who would know and understand the grandeur of the Creator and who would act in the ways He had ordained.

Summary and Evaluation

As a devout Christian (and the founder of pansophy), Comenius believed that science (the truth of nature) and art (appropriate actions) could never contradict or even conflict with revealed religion. This epistemological dogmatism was the soil out of which emerged his didactic approach to education. As I noted earlier, this didactic approach converts the educational process to a technique of instruction wherein teachers transmit to students predetermined ideas, skills, and dispositions (recall: "the mouth of the teacher is a spring from which streams of knowledge issue and flow over them").

The didactic approach is authoritarian. Yet it is a sensible way to construe the educational process as long as the teacher is, like Comenius, an epistemological dogmatist, convinced that he knows infallible truth. If the teacher is not an epistemological dogmatist (as most teachers today are not), the didactic approach is totally inappropriate. For its use transforms the education process into a charade and students who cannot be fooled into cynics.

Descartes's Method

Nourished on letters from childhood, René Descartes entered the Jesuit College of La Flèche with "an extreme desire to obtain instruction," believing that the study of the humanities would give him "a clear and certain knowledge . . . of all that is useful in life." Here, in one of the most celebrated schools in Europe, the young Descartes learned all that others learned and more, reading every book he could lay his hands on. But as soon as he had completed the entire course of study—"at the close of which one is usually admitted into the ranks of the learned"—he recorded his disappointment: "I found myself embarrassed with so many doubts and errors that it seemed to me that the effort to instruct myself had no effect other than the increasing discovery of my own ignorance."

Descartes had come to the Jesuits of La Flèche with "an excessive desire to learn to distinguish the true from the false.'' But they had failed to provide him with the criterion of truth. He had learned the languages and read the literature of the ancients, studying rhetoric and poetry, both of which he esteemed most highly. These books, he admitted, can, if ''read with discretion,'' assist in forming a sound judgment. But none of his studies satisfied his search for a criterion of truth. To be sure, he had studied the revealed truths of theology, but these, he noted, ''are quite above our intelligence . . . and I thought that in order to undertake to examine them and succeed in so doing, it was necessary to have some extraordinary assistance from above and to be more than mere man.'' Nor had his studies in philosophy satisfied him. He became disillusioned when he discovered that all the things discussed by philosophers were still subject to dispute. Moreover, since the sciences ''derive their principles from philosophy,'' he judged them to be dubious too. His quest for certainty unfulfilled, the young Descartes sadly concluded that ''there was no learning in the world such as I was formerly led to believe it to be.'' At this point he would have us believe that his schooling at La Flèche had turned him into a skeptic, a pyrrhonist. This confession of skepticism is the key to understanding what Descartes is trying to do in his *Discourse on the Method*.

I

As Richard Popkin has shown,[1] the intellectual conflict of seventeenth-century France was the battle between the skeptics and those they called dogmatists. At issue was the object of Descartes's quest: the criterion of truth. The skeptics denied that anyone had discovered such a criterion. They taught that one ought to suspend judgment on all questions concerning knowledge; the highest wisdom was awareness of one's own ignorance. Their opponents—all who claimed to possess the criterion of truth—the skeptics called dogmatists. There were old dogmatists—the scholastics who used Aristotle as the source and criterion for truth. And there were new dogmatists—the scientists and the mathematicians who used the senses as the criterion of truth.

Skepticism, or pyrrhonism, as it was called, had first appeared in the modern world as a means of defending Catholicism against the Calvinists. The Calvinists, like all Protestants, had rejected both the pope and the church councils as the criteria for religious truth. In place of these traditional (Catholic) criteria, the Protestants now substituted a new criterion: the Scriptures. In the ensuing battle over the criteria of religious truth,

1. Richard Popkin, *The History of Scepticism from Erasmus to Descartes* (Assen, Netherlands: Van Gorcum, 1960).

skepticism was reborn. It appeared first among some Catholic theologians, who, abandoning all rational grounds for religious certainty, tried to establish Catholic truths on purely fideistic grounds.[2]

At the same time, "secular" skeptics like Montaigne and Charron pushed skepticism even further, undermining the traditional grounds of all knowledge. For centuries, Aristotle had been accepted as the criterion of truth. Many schools, Montaigne quipped, make it "irreligious" to question any of the decrees of Aristotle. But why accept Aristotle or the other ancients?

> I do not know why I should not as willingly accept either the ideas of Plato, or the atoms of Epicurus, or the *plenum* and vacuum of Leucippus and Democritus, or the water of Thales, or the infinity of Diogenes, or the numbers and symmetry of Pythagoras, or the infinity of Parmenides, or the One of Musaeus, or the water and fire of Apollodorus, or the similar parts of Anaxagoras, or the discord and friendship of Empedocles, or the fire of Heraclitus, or any other opinion of that infinite confusion of opinions and determinations which this fine human reason produces by its certitude and clear-sightedness in everything it meddles withal, as I should the opinion of Aristotle upon the subject of the principles of material things. . . .[3]

The French skeptics, of course, were not alone in decrying the authority of Aristotle. Francis Bacon, for example, had ridiculed it, proposing instead that man's senses were the only reliable criteria of truth. Once he purged himself of all "idols," Bacon taught, man could read the book of nature as it lay before him—read it truly through his own senses. But the skeptics made short work of this. Montaigne wondered how naive sense realists like Bacon knew that man has all the requisite senses for obtaining knowledge. Moreover, even if humans do have all the necessary senses, there is the greater difficulty that our senses might deceive us. How can we tell that they are presenting us with a "true" reading of the book of nature?

Finally, the new scientific proposals made during this "age of genius" strengthened and broadened the skeptical attack. The theories of Copernicus, Kepler, Galileo, and Gassendi were not only an attack on Aristotelianism; they were at the same time an assault on the basis of all knowledge. Without a criterion of truth, how could one know what was true? By the third decade of the seventeenth century, a veritable skeptical crisis had developed. This crisis sets the stage for the *Discourse* of Descartes.

He starts out, as we have seen, by conceding that his schooling at La

---

2. Ibid., chap. 4.
3. *Apology for Raimond De Sebonde* in *Essays II*.

Flèche had not supplied him with the criterion of truth. But his desire for certainty was too great for him to remain a skeptic. Nor could he accept the awareness of his own ignorance as the end of education. If he could overcome skepticism by discovering the criterion of truth, Descartes could solve the most pressing intellectual problem of his age and, at the same time lay the foundation for an educational renaissance.

Convinced that the criterion was not to be found in the humanistic studies he had undertaken with the Jesuits, Descartes tells us he now "entirely quitted the study of letters." Several years spent in studying the "book of the world" delivered him from "many errors," he reports, but he still had not found the key to "certain knowledge." At last, he resolved to make himself the object of study. Here, within himself, he found his criterion of truth.

II

Years before he published his *Discourse,* Descartes had a vision. In it, the angel of truth came and bade him trust his intuition that the world is fundamentally mathematical in structure, that the laws of mathematics are the key to the mysteries of nature. This was in the year 1619, when Descartes was twenty years old. Inspired by this divine decree, this "pious physicist"—the term is John Herman Randall's—combined analysis and geometry in treating spatial relations, working out analystic geometry. His success encouraged him to see the world as pure geometry, pure extension. He went on to work out the details of a mathematical physics, completing in 1629 his *Traite du monde*. In this, he imagines how God might have created the world mathematically, using nothing but matter in motion. The world would be easily understood, perfectly knowable.

Then in 1633 Descartes heard about Galileo, who had been condemned for teaching doctrines contrary to the teachings of the church. At this point, Descartes decided to postpone publication of his treatise. (It did not appear in print until 1664, sixteen years after his death.) The first task was to prepare people to accept his ideas. So, between 1633 and 1637, he worked on the problem of providing a justification for his mathematical conception of the universe. It was this that led him to a controversy with the skeptics.

In order to prove his conception of the universe, he had to supply some standard by which it could be judged. The skeptics had to be refuted; the criterion of truth had to be found. In 1637 he finally published a book on meteors and geometry, together with a preface, "The Discourse on the Method of Rightly Conducting the Reason." Here, he unveiled his newly discovered criterion of truth by recounting the way in which he had discovered it. It was a dangerous way, Descartes admitted, and he cautioned others against repeating it. For what he did was to extend skepticism to the breaking point, using it to refute itself.

When he made himself or his own mind the object of study, Descartes laid down a basic rule "to accept nothing as true which I did not clearly recognize to be so: that is to say, carefully to avoid precipitation and prejudice in judgments, and to accept in them nothing more than what is presented to my mind so clearly and distinctly that I could have no occasion to doubt it." Then he showed how far this methodic doubt could be extended.

First, the fact that there are sense illusions supplies us with a warrant to doubt all knowledge obtained through sense experiences. Moreover, by supposing all our experience is part of a dream, we can doubt the reality of other objects we know of and even the reality of the world itself. Later, in his *Meditations on First Philosophy,* published in 1641, Descartes entertains a superskepticism by propounding the demon hypothesis. Here he supposes that there is an "evil genie," who is capable of distorting either the information we possess or the faculties we have for evaluating it. This raises skepticism to its highest level; now nothing could be certain, since our faculties themselves could be doubted. It transforms man from a repository of truth to, in Pascal's words, a "sink of uncertainty."

Only by carrying doubt to these depths could Descartes overcome the force of skepticism. For from this voyage into the abyss he returned with a new criterion of truth, a new jusification for human rationality. In the *Discourse,* he puts it this way: "I noticed that whilst I thus wished to think all things false, it was absolutely essential that the I who thought this should be somewhat, and remarking that this truth I think, therefore, I am was so certain and so assured that all the most extravagant suppositions brought forward by the skeptics were incapable of shaking it, I came to the conclusion that I could receive it without scruple as the first principle of the Philosophy for which I was searching."

Descartes had used skepticism to defeat itself: his method of doubt had discovered one indubitable truth—the *cogito.* This one indubitable truth overthrows the skeptical attitude; by analyzing this one truth, Descartes uncovered the criterion of truth itself. In his Third Meditation, he says: "Certainly in this first knowledge, there is nothing that assures me of its truth, excepting the clear and distinct perception of that which I state, which would not indeed suffice to assure me that what I say is true, if it could ever happen that a thing which I conceived so clearly and distinctly could be false; and accordingly, it seems to me that already I can establish as a general rule that all things which I perceive very clearly and very distinctly are true."

Descartes argued that whatever we discover to be clear and distinct, we accept as true. But does this mean that, in reality, whatever is clear and distinct *is* true? Descartes wanted to say so. But first he had to build a metaphysical bridge from his mind to reality, from subjective certainty to objective truth. God serves as this bridge. God, the perfect creator, would not have created man capable of being so deceived that clear and distinct ideas do not correspond to reality. The omnipotent, perfect, honest deity becomes the final basis for man's certitude. By the grace of God, then, whatever I clearly and distinctly perceive is actually true. But does God exist? Descartes offered two major proofs for the existence of God. First, the idea of perfection man possesses can be caused only by a perfect being, for there must be at least as much of reality of perfection in the cause as in the effect. Second, Descartes argues that the idea of a supremely perfect being must include existence as one of its perfections: God alone must necessarily exist because the power to exist is included in His essence.

Once Descartes had guaranteed his criterion of truth by God, he had justified his 1619 vision of the mathematical intelligibility of the world. Mathematical truths are clear and distinct. We are compelled to believe them, and they correspond to the physical world.

Physics, of course, he regarded as only a part of philosophy; he called it the trunk of philosophy, insisting that it should be derived from first causes or metaphysics, the roots of philosophy. In 1641 he published his *Meditations on First Philosophy,* which explained in greater detail the principles of knowledge he had sketched in the *Discourse on the Method.* A few years later, he published his *Principles of Philosophy* where he again explained his theory of knowledge and sketched a general introduction to the physics he had derived from the first principles he had discovered. He reminded his readers that the tree of philosophy included—as its branches—all the other sciences, principally those of medicine, mechanics, and morals. Descartes admitted that he did no more than adumbrate the whole of philosophy, lacking, he tells us, the financial means to pay for all the experiments necessary to support and justify his reasoning. But he had, he thought, set mankind on the proper path, providing it with the foundation of wisdom from which all truths could, in time, be deduced.

After confounding the skeptics and discovering "true philosophy," Descartes fully expected to supplant Aristotle in the schools. He dedicated his *Meditations* to the Jesuits of the Sorbonne—"To the Most Wise and Illustrious Dean and Doctors of the Sacred Faculty of Theology in Paris"—asking them to correct, add to and complete his work so that they might render public testimony to its truth and certainty. In a letter to Father Dinet, the French Provincial Head of the Society of Jesus, he explained that in the *Meditations* he had used a mode of writing "more suited to the usage of the schools." Again, in the same letter, he claims that his "true philosophy" will eliminate the perpetual warfare among philosophers rampant in the schools, establish peace and refute all heresies. In the *Principles of Philosophy,* which he tried to get the Jesuits to adopt as a textbook, he again repeated the charge that the philosophy taught in the schools was "the chief cause of heresies and dissension which now exercise the world."

All attempts to win Jesuit acceptance of his philosophy failed. During his lifetime, he was continually attacked by Jesuit philosophers, which included a scurrilous denunciation by Father Bourdin, professor of mathematics at the Sorbonne. The Jesuits suspected Descartes of Protestantism, so their opposition was both theological and philosophical.[4]

Descartes actually never abandoned the Catholic faith, but he was forced to spend much of his time showing how compatible his philosophy was with his religion. In fact, he claimed that his "true philosophy" supplied a perfect foundation for the Catholic religion. Unfortunately, the doctrine of the Holy Eucharist proved to be his undoing. He stated that the essence of body consists in extension in space; it is thus impossible for the same body to exist in different spaces or places, so that the real or bodily presence of Christ can in no way exist in the bread and wine. Father Valois, in a work published in 1683, epitomized the Society of Jesus' objections against him in the following title: "The Antagonism of the Doctrines of Descartes to the Church, and their harmony with Calvin."

By 1663, largely as a result of Jesuit insistence, the works of Descartes were placed on the Roman Index of prohibited books. In 1667 the French king—that most absolute of monarchs—at the urging of the Jesuits, refused to allow Descartes's remains to be buried in a church in Paris and permitted no funeral oration or monument. In the next few years, he forbade Cartesian ideas in the College Royal, in the University of Paris, and that of Angers. When four candidates competed, in 1669, for the chair of philosophy at the College Royal, they were required to discuss before a jury of thirteen on one of the following subjects: the immortality of the soul, motion, the superiority of the peripatetic (Aristotelian) philosophy—or they could give a refutation of the philosophy of Descartes.[5]

Denounced by the Roman church and the French king, prohibited from public institutions of learning, the philosophy of Descartes nevertheless exerted a profound influence on modern thought, precipitating at the same time an educational revolution. To understand how this happened, we must again return to that remarkable, brief treatise, the *Discourse on the Method*.

---

4. See F. Boullier, *Historie de la philosophie cartesienne* (Paris: Ch. Delgrave, 1868); also, Emile Boutroux, "Descartes and Cartesianism," in *Cambridge Modern History,* vol. 4 (Cambridge: Cambridge University Press, 1906); and Kuno Fischer, *History of Modern Philosophy: Descartes and His School* (New York: Scribners, 1887).

5. Lenora C. Rosenfeld, "Peripatetic Adversaries of Cartesianism in 17th Century France," in *Review of Religion,* November 1957.

III

Dissatisfaction with his education had led Descartes to search for the criterion of truth. Once he had found it he was faced with the educational problem: to teach men how to apply the criterion. As the full title of the *Discourse* reveals, he wanted to explain "the method of rightly conducting the reason and seeking for truth in the sciences." This work, then, is both a philosophical refutation of skepticism *and* a treatise in educational theory. In it, Descartes proposes a radically new foundation for education.

The initial paragraph presages this educational radicalism. Here Descartes declares his faith in the educability of *all* men.

> Good Sense [*bien sens*] is of all things in the world the most equally distributed, for everybody thinks himself so abundantly provided with it, that even those most difficult to please in all other matters do not commonly desire more of it than they already possess. It is unlikely that this is an error on their part; it seems rather to be evidence in support of the view that the power of forming a good judgment and of distinguishing the true from the false, which is properly speaking, what is called Good Sense or Reason, is, by nature, equal in all men. Hence, too, it will show that the diversity of our opinions does not proceed from some men being more rational than others, but solely from the fact that our thoughts pass through diverse channels and the same objects are not considered by all. For to be possessed of good mental powers is not sufficient; the principal matter is to apply them well.

Descartes supplies the method of rightly conducting the reason in four succinct rules, all of them rooted in his basic conviction of the mathematical nature of the universe. The first rule, mentioned above, was to accept only clear and distinct ideas. The second rule reveals the mathematician's assumption that all things are made up of discrete and separable units: "to divide each problem or difficulty into as many parts as possible." The third rule reveals a seventeenth-century mathematician's prejudice that small units are simpler and easier to understand than large units: "to commence my reflections with objects which were the simplest and easiest to understand, and rise, thence, little by little, to knowledge of the most complex." The last rule is based directly on the mathematician's axiom that the whole is equal to the sum of its parts: "to make enumerations so complete, and reviews so general, that I should be certain to have omitted nothing."

In spite of the fact that these rules for conducting the reason were rooted in the mathematical philosophy of nature, they soon took on a life of their own, shedding their mathematical roots as they became Descartes's most important contribution to modern thought. For his fame continued, not as a philosopher of nature, but as the one who taught men how to think, as the one who had raised men's reason as the ultimate authority. Fontenelle expressed it well: "He, in my opinion, it is to whom we are indebted for this new method of reasoning, a method far more valuable than his actual philosophy, a good deal of which, judged by his own rules, is either doubtful, or definitely unsound." [6]

At his death, Descartes, according to a contemporary, had disciples "as numerous as the stars in the firmament or the grains of sand by the sea." [7] The antagonism of the establishment had not dimmed his fame; in fact, the opposition of the primary agencies of formal education in Europe helped to generate experiments in informal education all over the Continent. In all the large cities, we find public lectures being given on the Cartesian philosophy; in all echelons of European society, circles and groups of people gathered for the purpose of studying and discussing the "true philosophy."

Descartes had popularized education. By proclaiming that all men can know, he broke the monopoly of the learned professions. All men, he wrote in his preface to *Principles of Philosophy,* no matter how dull or slow of understanding, can attain "to all the profoundest sciences" if they were trained in the right way. This widespread quest for wisdom among the people was not a desire for knowledge for its own sake. Knowledge was sought because it was useful. In the *Discourse,* Descartes had explained that true knowledge can procure the general good of all mankind. He confessed that he had felt obliged to reveal his *Discourse* to the world (published, significantly, in French and not the Latin of the schools and the learned professions) because through it he himself had come

> to see that it is possible to attain knowledge which is very useful in life, and that, instead of the speculative philosophy which is taught in the schools, we may find a practical philosophy by means of which, knowing the force and the action of fire, water, air, the stars, heavens and all other bodies that environ us, as distinctly as we know the different crafts of our artisans, we can in the same way employ them in all those uses to which they are adapted, and thus, render ourselves the masters and possessors of nature.

Years earlier, Francis Bacon had made a similar claim for the power of knowledge. But when Descartes combined this notion of usefulness with that of the educability of all men, he produced that greatest of all modern Western religions: faith in the power of education. All men could know; therefore, mankind could create a better world, an enlightened

---

6. Quoted in Paul Hazard, *The European Mind 1680–1715* (London: Hollis and Carter, 1953), p. 131.
7. Boutroux, "Descartes."

world. Descartes, as many have noted, is the true father of the so-called Age of Enlightenment. Descartes's epistemological optimism liberated man. Man can know; thus he can be free from ignorance and from all the evils that it spawns.

Cartesian optimism not only created a renaissance in informal education, but it also provided a new foundation for formal education. Schooling could be shorn of all dogmatism. Neither the teacher nor the student had need for any authorities. The student only required instruction in how to think, how to conduct his reason properly. This differed markedly from the traditional conception of instruction as the transmission of knowledge. It directly challenged the humanist educators who believed that the teacher's task was to transmit the wisdom of the ancients. Descartes himself did not deny the traditional goal of instruction, wisdom; but he refused to accept the ancients as the repository of wisdom. Most important, he offered a new way to attain wisdom, a new method of instruction. And this new method appeared at the very moment when the humanist educators were themselves preoccupied with a search for *the* method of instruction.

Believing that all wisdom lay in the ancient classics, the humanist educators, as we saw in the preceding chapter, had prescribed a long and laborious study of Greek and Latin authors, preceded by an equally laborious study of Latin and Greek vocabulary and grammar. The Protestant Reformation and the Catholic Counterreformation had strengthened educational humanism by generating schools (English grammar schools, German gymnasia, and Jesuit colleges) and semiofficial grammar textbooks (Lily's *Grammar* in England, Melanchthon's in Germany)

The triumph of humanism in the sixteenth century as the dominant educational movement in Europe led to a frantic search for appropriate methods of instruction, ways that would shorten and sweeten the laborious course of study that lasted as long as ten years in some schools. During the sixteenth and early seventeenth centuries, this quest for a pedagogical method occupied a great number of educators including Roger Ascham and Richard Mulcaster of England, Wolfgang Ratke of Germany, and, most famous of all, John Amos Comenius, the Moravian bishop from Bohemia, who, in his *Great Didactic* (1632) promised to set forth "The Whole Art of Teaching All Things to All Men."

All these educators saw the pedagogical problem in the traditional way: one of transmission (i.e., how best, quickly and thoroughly, "to get the material across"). Only after Descartes do we find the new conception of the role of the teacher: to teach students how to think (i.e., to teach them how to conduct their reason so that they end up with *true* ideas).

Descartes himself never encouraged the schools to adopt this new conception of instruction. He, as we have seen, wanted the schools to accept the *results* of his method, the "true philosophy." Anxious to refute skepticism, not encourage it, he cautioned in his *Discourse on the Method* that his design was "not . . . to teach the method which everyone should follow in order to promote the good conduct of reason, but only to show in what manner I have endeavored to conduct my own."

The task of developing the method into a full-fledged theory of instruction fell to one of Descartes's most famous disciples, Antoine Arnauld (1612–94). An implacable foe of the Jesuits, the Great Arnauld, as he was called, taught for a time at the Jansenists' community at Port-Royal. In 1662 he published *The Art of Thinking,* which came to be known as the "Port Royal Logic." During his lifetime this book went through six editions and twelve printings. The sixth edition, published in Amsterdam, was reprinted six more times. A seventh edition appeared in 1738, an eighth in 1750—with eight reprintings—the last one in 1855. A ninth edition came out in 1843, followed by three more in 1850, 1854, and 1869, with each one going through a number of reprintings. The last edition in France was published in 1877. The first English translation was printed in 1674, followed by other English versions in 1685, 1693, 1702, and 1717. In 1850 a new translation was made by Thomas Baynes that went through frequent reprintings. In 1964 the first American edition appeared, translated by James Dickoff and Patricia James.[8] Numerous translations appeared in other European countries. In Italy, six separate editions (three in Latin, three in Italian) appeared between 1722 and 1749.[9] The viability of this book—it was used as a textbook throughout Europe—gives ample support to the verdict of William Kneale in his monumental *The Development of Logic:* ". . . the general conception of logic . . . expounded in this book was widely accepted and continued to dominate the treatments of logic by most philosophers for the next 200 years." [10]

In the preface of his book Arnauld announced that he had "borrowed from the books of a celebrated philosopher of this century who is distinguished as much for his clarity of mind as others are for confusion." (The "celebrated philosopher" was, of course, Descartes.) In the first sentence of the book Arnauld displays his Cartesianism: "Nothing is more to be esteemed than aptness in discerning the true from the false." He then goes on to explain that philosophers in the past have given rules to distinguish good from bad reasoning. But these rules, he notes, do not help us to distinguish the true from the false. They apply only to the validity of arguments, not to the truth of propositions. "Most of man's errors," he points out, "derive not from his being misled by wrong inferences, but

8. Antoine Arnauld, *The Art of Thinking,* trans. James Dickoff and Patricia James (Indianapolis: Bobbs-Merrill, 1964).

9. G. Maugain, *Etude sur l'Evolution intellectualle de l'Italie de 1657 a 1750 environ* (Paris: Hachette, 1909), p. 199.

10. William Kneale and Martha Kneale, *The Development of Logic* (Oxford: Oxford University Press, 1962), p. 320.

rather from his making inferences from premises based on wrong judgments." The object of his book was to supply a remedy. The remedy turns out to be Descartes's criterion of truth. "The truth," he says, "needs no mark save the enveloping clarity that surrounds it and persuades the mind despite any objections." [11]

In the first part of the book, called Conceptions, Arnauld explains how man can determine the truth of ideas by applying the criterion of truth discovered by Descartes. The second part, Judgments, is devoted to ideas. The use of the syllogism, which Arnauld treats as a kind of judging, he deals with in the third part of the book, called Reasoning. In the last part, Ordering, he explains the three different ways man can obtain true knowledge. He quickly goes through the way of divine faith and that of intellectualization (immediate seeing), and focuses his attention on the third way: understanding. There are two methods of obtaining true knowledge through understanding: by instruction and by discovery. Instruction, which he calls synthesis or, more appropriately, demonstration, is used to make others understand a truth. To make someone understand through instruction, one must order thoughts sequentially "such that the first judgments—axioms—are immediately known as true to the person instructed, that all subsequent judgments follow deductively from prior judgments, and that the last judgment is the judgment to be established." [12]

Discovery, which he also calls analysis, is the method used to discover a truth of which we are already ignorant. Arnauld says little about the method of discovery "which, after all," he explains, "consists more of discernment and acumen than of particular procedures." [13] This lack of emphasis on discovery is misleading, as Dickoff and James admit,[14] for since one cannot demonstrate a truth without first discovering it, the method of discovery is of far greater importance than the method of instruction. After some general guiding precepts about the method of discovery—"the first thing to determine is the precise point of the question," "do not omit some condition essential to the question posed"—he ends by recommending and repeating the four rules of method Descartes had set forth in his *Discourse on the Method.* These rules are the best guides to the discovery of truth.

In his preface Arnauld says that the principal task of the teacher is "to train the judgment, making it as exact as we can." Then he adds: "to this end, the greatest part of our studies should be devoted."

---

11. Arnauld, *Art of Thinking,* p. 11.
12. Ibid., p. xliii.
13. Ibid., p. 308.
14. Ibid., p. xliii.

> We are accustomed to use reason as an instrument for acquiring the sciences, but we ought to use the sciences as an instrument for perfecting the reason: accuracy of mind is infinitely more important than any speculative knowledge acquired from the truest and most established sciences. A wise man engages in science not to employ his mind, but to exercise it. A scientist without this viewpoint fails to see that the study of the speculative sciences—geometry, astronomy, physics—is little better than ignorance. Ignorance at least is not painful to acquire and gives no excuse for that foolish vanity so often accompanying sterile and fruitless knowledge.
>
> Not only does science contain otiose and barren areas, but even as a whole science is useless. Man was not born to spend his days measuring lines, examining the relations between angles, or considering the many motions of matter. His mind is too large, his life is too short, his time too precious to be occupied with such trivia. Rather, man must be just, equitable, and discerning in all his speech, in all his actions, and in every piece of business he transacts. To these ends he ought to discipline himself. Such discipline is much needed, for precision is a rare quality of mind. On every side, we find defective minds, minds scarcely capable of any discernment of the truth.[15]

In emphasizing the training of the mind as the goal of instruction, Arnauld rejects the traditional instructional goal of wisdom or erudition. For him, the key educational term is "discipline"; man's mind must be disciplined so that he will be "just," "equitable," and "discerning." And the best subject for the purpose of disciplining the intellect was, of course, mathematics. Here Arnauld followed Descartes, although he ignored completely Descartes's view that mathematics was the key to understanding the mysteries of the universe. "Mathematics and all difficult things in general help to stretch the mind, to exercise its power of attention, and to give the mind a firm hold on what is known." [16]

The educational views of Arnauld are strikingly similar to those later expressed by John Locke, who also advocated mental discipline (especially through mathematics). Like Locke, Arnauld thought that the mind could be disciplined by habituating it to function—in Conceiving, Judging, Reasoning, and Ordering—according to certain procedures or principles. This concept of mental discipline soon triumphed in Europe and the United States as *the* primary function of the schools. One consequence of this was the almost total disappearance of utilitarian studies from the schools for the next two hundred years. The schools now existed to train people to think. Useful studies, those that help man improve his own

15. Ibid., pp. 7–8.
16. Ibid., p. 14.

condition and the general condition of mankind, were pursued outside the schools through informal educational agencies, as well as through various forms of private instruction.

Summary and Evaluation

I have tried to show how Descartes, convinced that his mathematical view of the universe was correct, sought and found a criterion of truth that would establish the veracity of his philosophy of nature. Proclaiming the utility of his "true philosophy" and the ease with which it could be acquired, Descartes hoped that it would usurp the Aristotelianism taught in the schools. Although he was unsuccessful in his attempt to have his "true philosophy" taught in the schools, his epistemological optimism about the possibility of universal enlightenment popularized education, generating many new agencies of informal education.

Descartes's influence on the schools (as distinct from his influence on informal education) came about indirectly through the work of Antoine Arnauld, who developed a theory of instruction on the basis of Descartes's criterion of truth. Rather than transmit knowledge to the student, as in traditional conceptions of instruction, the teacher's role was to discipline the student's mind so that he could distinguish the true from the false.

Today our teachers have abandoned their concern with mental discipline. But the spirit of Descartes lives on in the classrooms of the twentieth century. This spirit is nothing more than his epistemological optimism, which is rooted in his doctrine of manifest truth. According to this doctrine, once the truth is revealed to us, we have the power to distinguish it from falsehood and to know that it *is* truth. This doctrine of manifest truth encouraged men to think for themselves. It gave them hope that they could free themselves through knowledge—free themselves from servitude and misery. It became the basis for the fight for freedom of thought and speech and the dream of a free and enlightened society. Not least of all, it became the basis for demands for universal education.[17]

In spite of all the good that came from it, the doctrine of manifest truth is patently a myth. Truth is not manifest; in fact, truth is hard to come by and frequently lost. Descartes's own "true philosophy" was false. Moreover, the doctrine of manifest truth is authoritarian, even though it was born, as we have seen, out of the war against the authority

---

17. Karl Popper, "On the Sources of Knowledge and Ignorance," in *Conjecture and Refutations* (London: Routledge and Kegan Paul, 1963). I have relied heavily on this analysis by Popper in this section. In this connection, see also William W. Bartley III, "Rationality versus the Theory of Rationality," in *The Critical Approach to Science and Philosophy* (New York: Free Press of Glencoe, 1964), esp. pp. 20 et seq.

of Aristotle. Rejecting the dogmatism of the schools and refusing to fall into skepticism, Descartes proclaimed that man had no need of authorities, since he could perceive the truth for himself. Descartes did *not* succeed in freeing himself from authority. He merely replaced the authority of Aristotle with the authority of the intellect. Man's trained intellect became the authority for truth.

The authoritarianism of this theory of knowledge stems from Descartes's adoption of a justificatory approach to knowledge. Recall that Descartes went through his methodic doubting to discover the criterion of truth *in order to justify* his mathematical conception of the universe. Questions of justification—"How do you know?" "What supports your beliefs?"—all beg for authoritarian answers, whether the authority is the Bible, Aristotle, sense experience, or intellectual intuition. A demand for justification can be satisfied only by providing something authoritative, something that is unquestionable and does not itself need justification.

Most teachers today adopt a justificatory approach to teaching—they expect their students to be able to justify their claims to knowledge. And these teachers pride themselves on being able to do likewise when challenged by their students. This justificatory approach is rooted in the Cartesian faith in the authority of man's intellect, which in turn is based on the doctrine of manifest truth. Without this doctrine of manifest truth, attempts at justification lead to an infinite regress. Indeed, many teachers have experienced the shock of the ground disappearing beneath them when some persistent student continues, sequentially, to pose the question: "How do you know?" The doctrine that truth is manifest cuts off the regress. Thus, the teacher finally tells the student: "Well, the truth of this claim is obvious to all the other students in the class, so there must be something wrong with you." Or the student might be silenced with the curt reminder that rational men accept the veracity of such a claim, so too will he when he can use his reason, or open his mind, or think clearly. This is authoritarianism.

Vico's New Science

In 1706, Giambattista Vico, professor of rhetoric at the University of Naples, delivered his seventh annual oration. "Which," he asked, "are the better methods of study—ours or those of the Ancients?" In his six previous annual speeches Vico had developed the traditional theme that the aim of education was nothing less than the pursuit of wisdom. In this seventh and most famous oration Vico boldly declared that the methods of study of his time simply would not fulfill this aim.

He traced the inadequacy of the methods of study of his time to the then prevalent theory of education—a theory derived from, or inspired by, the philosophy of Descartes.

I

Vico's first oration, delivered in 1699, presents the following argument: "That the knowledge of self is for each of us the greatest incentive to the compendious study of every branch of knowledge." "Knowledge of the self" he equates with "knowledge of one's soul," and he argues that "just as we recognize the Divine Being through examination of the things in the created universe, so the soul is divined—through means of the reason . . . the emotions, and through means of the memory and the intellect." [1] How does this "knowledge of the self" incite us to the compendious study of every branch of knowledge?

Vico's answer at this point is obscure and difficult to understand: "The soul is in each one of us as a God, O listeners, and divine is the force that sees, divine that which hears, divine that which judges, divine that which concludes, divine that which remembers; seeing, hearing, inventing, comparing, deducing, recalling, are divine activities." (*Orazione inaugurali,* p. 73). To this hint, he adds a bit when he deals specifically with the study of *belle lettres*. We should study *belle lettres,* he claims, because man, through his very nature, tends to the truth. Moreover, man derives the greatest pleasure in finding what is noble and secure in the new things he discovers. These two aspects of the nature of man—that he tends toward truth and that he derives pleasure from the discovery of new truths—are variations on that haunting theme that Vico will develop, strengthen, and integrate in the philosophical composition that is to come.

In the second oration, Vico argues "that there is no enmity more dire and dangerous than that of the fool against himself." It relates to the first oration insofar as Vico describes the fool as someone who does not know himself. Wise men, he explains, see that the universe is ruled by divine wisdom that inhabits all parts of the world, vivifying everything, harmonizing the various parts, and conserving all. Man gains this wisdom through self-knowledge insofar as he who knows himself knows that "the law that God sanctions for mankind is wisdom." Whoever applies himself to the pursuit of wisdom follows his own nature (ibid., p. 83). In this oration, Vico seeks to convey the fool's alienation from himself, from his true nature as a man. The fool—not knowing himself, not following the pursuit of wisdom—is at war with himself. In alienating himself from his true nature, the fool violates "that law whose sanctions determine punishments that are immediate and ready." Vico describes these punishments: uneasiness and remorse, deprivation of a place in the world, unhappiness, and loss of freedom—becoming a slave to fortune and chance.

1. Giambattista Vico, *Orazione inaugurali,* prima traduzione dal latino, studio critico e note de Stefano Massilli (Firenze: Edizione Tempo Nuovo, 1935), p. 71. Here, as elsewhere in this chapter, unless stated otherwise, the English translations are mine.

Vico calls the third oration a practical appendix to the first two. In it, he argues "that the society of letters must be rid of every deceit if you would study to be adorned with true, not feigned; solid, not empty, erudition." It complements the first two orations by explaining how one attains wisdom: through "true erudition."

Vico begins the oration with a discussion of what became the major preoccupation of his life: the universal laws governing man. Of all things in the universe, he points out, man alone does what he wants, becomes what he pleases, makes what agrees to him. Unlike man, animals have no control over themselves: the lion is never a timid animal, nor the hare a courageous one. "Whoever, therefore, sees that all created things are slaves of nature, and observes that man is instead the moderator and arbiter of himself, would certainly realize that he, through his freedom from nature, is, if not its lord, almost its lord" (ibid., p. 96).

But, he continues, it is through this very freedom that man brings evil upon himself. And one of the greatest evils is false or feigned wisdom. To identify false wisdom, Vico suggests a criterion or rule, the rule of erudition: "As reason joins men; language, nations; public things, citizens; titles, nobles; blood, relations; economically productive things, merchants; so it is necessary that erudition work to unite those who profess the study of letters, the investigators of nature, and the philosophers" (ibid., pp. 98–99).

He then proceeds to ridicule those sham scholars who, on a comparatively short acquaintance, claim an intimate appreciation of ancient authors, about whom the greatest critics confess themselves on uncertain grounds. A second kind of feigned or empty wisdom exists when thinkers—ancient or modern—claim to know things of which they are ignorant. Vico concludes that man's finitude means that human knowledge will always be limited. Reminding his hearers of the prohibited curiosity of Adam, "our first father," he maintains that man is "condemned from the true cognizance of things" (ibid., p. 101).

In the fourth and fifth orations Vico turns to the results of wisdom for the community. The argument of the fourth oration is "he who would reap from the study of letters the greatest advantages combined with honor, let him be educated for the glory and good of the community." To the notion that the possession of truth is the highest good, Vico now adds that in the society of men, what is true is always useful to the community. Moreover, virtuous acts of the individual are always good for the community. He admits that this does not always seem to be the case, but that in time it is always found to be so. Turning to education, he concludes that since what is useful and good for the community is true and good for the individual, then children must be educated not for themselves alone, nor for truth or virtue, but for the "good and glory of the community" (ibid.).

The argument of the fifth oration is "that commonwealths have been most renowned for military glory and most powerful politically when letters have most flourished in them." In this oration he applies his notion of alienation to the nation. Just as the fool's alienation is alienation from himself, from his purpose (as a man) to pursue wisdom, so the alienation of a nation is the alienation of a people from its purpose of advancing humanity.

Vico explains this alienation of a nation as he did that of a fool—in terms of breaking a law. The law for nations he calls the "natural law of nations." This law serves as the basis for all treaties. When a nation disregards this natural law, it becomes alienated from itself, and war is the result. He sees in the history of wars a pattern or plan according to which, in the long run, those nations that pursue the study of letters—thereby attaining wisdom—will attain military and political greatness (ibid., p. 121).

To cap his argument that the great nations have been those that have cultivated the study of letters, Vico points out that great military leaders must have virtues of justice, clemency, moderation, temperance, and sincerity. These virtues one finds among people where wise men have founded the state with noble institutions, which learned men then conserve by means of letters. "Neither the institutions of peace, nor those of war are able to obtain the highest glory . . . without a diligent love for letters" (ibid., p. 134).

The argument of the sixth oration is "that the knowledge of the corrupt nature of man invites us to study the complete cycle of the liberal arts and sciences, and propounds and expounds the true, easy, and unvarying order in which they are to be acquired." Once again, Vico takes up the problem of alienation and the role of education in overcoming it.

Vico declares that because of the sin of Adam, man is divided from man by tongue, mind, and heart. To punish the sin of our first parents, God divided and scattered their progeny. As a result, man is corrupt: anyone who looks can perceive the "insufficiency of the tongue, the obfuscation of the intellect by opinions, and the spoilation of the soul by vice." The tongue divides man from man because it often fails and often betrays the ideas through which man would, but cannot, unite himself to man; the mind divides through the variety of opinions springing from the diversity of tastes in which men do not agree; finally, the corruption of the heart prevents even the conciliation of man with man by uniformity of vice (ibid., p. 143).[2]

Vico, however, finds that this condition of man, this alienation from his true nature or from what he could be, actually points the way to its own cure. "The insufficiency of the tongue, the variety of opinions of the

2. *Autobiografia,* in *Opere,* a cura de Fausto Nicolini (Milano: Riccardo Ricciardi, 1953), p. 37.

intellect, the passions of the soul, which are the punishments of the corrupted human nature, are correctable respectively with the following disciplines: Eloquence, Science, and Virtue, the three points around which move all letters and knowledge'' (ibid., p. 143). Vico views these three disciplines as the roots of wisdom: they enable man to know with certainty, to act with rectitude, and to speak in a worthy manner.

Turning to the second half of his argument—that the knowledge of our corrupt nature shows the *order* and the *way* of studies—Vico formulates a theory of human development. In childhood, the use of reason is weak, but memory is strong. Hence, educators ought to devote early education to the training of the memory. This, for Vico, means the learning of languages. Moreover, languages should come first because language is the most powerful means for setting up human society. Children should study both Latin and Greek—the first because it is more diffused and hence will bring the student in contact with what has been best in human society, the second because it is more difficult and hence will develop a concern for precision in language.

In the second period, or adolescence, Vico says that the imagination and fantasy dominate. Therefore he recommends the study of history—both fabulous and true. At this time the reason also begins to function. It is still weak, but mathematics will greatly aid its development through the great number of images one must form. But because in mathematics one considers things in demonstrations as points and lines, there is a loss of materiality. To rectify this, the pupil should study physics, which concerns the principles and causes of material being. Then, to purify the mind of dense and material thought, study should pass to metaphysics, the study of spiritual substance. Finally, the student should begin the study of God, or theology.

What is clear at this point is Vico's conviction of man's natural state of alienation from his ends: from truth, from goodness, and from God. What is equally clear is his belief that the pursuit of wisdom is the way to overcome this condition. Wisdom will direct man to these three ideals. These, then, are the goals of education.

In his seventh oration, his most famous, Vico examines contemporary practices and theories of education to see how well they promote the pursuit of wisdom.

II

Unlike the preceding orations, Vico's seventh presents not a thesis but a question: ''Which are the better methods of study; ours, or those of the ancients?'' [3] His main target is the ''theory'' of modern education, a theory derived from, or inspired by, the philosophy of Descartes.

3. Giambattista Vico, *Il Metodo Degli Studi Del Tempo Nostro* (hereinafter referred to as *Il Metodo*), in *Opere,* a cura di Fausto Nicolini (Milano: Riccardo Ricciardi, 1953), p. 172.

Vico saw Cartesian educational theory leading to an intensification of man's condition of alienation from truth and goodness. "Today, all studies," Vico says, "are initiated by *critica.*" He never defines *critica,* but by it he means a critical attitude toward all knowledge, an attitude encouraged by the Cartesian philosophy. He is not against *critica,* or the use of the critical attitude, but he is against teaching this attitude to children: on one level, he bases his opposition on the theory of human development he outlined in the sixth oration. He argues that if the order of education does not follow the order of human development, then we might impede the growth of the memory and the imagination, faculties of primary importance in the arts of poetry, oratory, and jurisprudence. And through these arts, man, in part, pursues wisdom (*Il Metodo,* p. 173).

First, by following *critica* alone, students accept only what is "certain" and thus neglect, or cut themselves off from, whatever is likely (*versimili*). Second, by following *critica* alone, they judge things before knowing them fully, so their judgments cannot be true or certain. Next, Vico extends his criticism of Cartesian education to claim that it alienates from truth not only the students but the rest of society as well. This happens because those taught only *critica* cannot communicate new truths to the rest of society. Not exercised in rhetoric, they "never have the experience of immediately seeing whatever is persuasive is implicit in every cause." Students of Cartesian education cannot persuade the masses to accept the truths they try to share with them or try to teach to them (ibid., pp. 178–80).

After criticizing Cartesian education because it intensified man's alienation from truth, Vico next attacks it because it intensified man's alienation from the good or from the performance of good acts. In fact, Vico thinks this is the gravest defect of Cartesian education. For, "while we occupy ourselves diligently with natural sciences, we neglect morality, especially that side that concerns itself with the character of our soul and of its tendencies to civil life" (ibid., p. 192).

"Today," he continues, "the [Cartesians say that the] single end of studies is truth." Accordingly, we study nature insofar as it seems certain to us, and we do not observe human nature because it is uncertain. But then, this method of study prevents the sufficient development of prudence in students so that they can conduct themselves in civil life. Civil life, Vico argues, cannot be conducted according to science because human affairs are dominated by occasion and choice, both of which are uncertain. Those taught to cultivate truth exclusively have difficulty in availing themselves of the means to act in civil life. "So, deluded in their very propositions, they frequently desert political action" (ibid., p. 193).

Then Vico extends his criticism to claim that the Cartesian education alienates not only the students from the pursuit of goodness but the rest of the community as well. The reasoning here is similar to that used in the earlier instance: this kind of education prevents the students from sharing their knowledge of the good with the masses; it prevents communication or instruction in what are good acts, what not. Wise men perform their duties because they understand them, but the masses must first love their duty by being allured to it through the corporal images of oratory. Once they love it, it is easy to induce them to believe and, finally, to will it (ibid., pp. 196–97).

In attacking the Cartesian education Vico has attacked the philosophy of Descartes, or at least the central tenet of that philosophy: all men can attain certain knowledge. Descartes based this tenet on the certainty of mathematics. Here is how Descartes put it in his *Rules for the Direction of the Mind:* "Arithmetic and Geometry alone are free from any taint of falsity or uncertainty . . . not, indeed, that Arithmetic and Geometry are the sole sciences to be studied, but only that in our search for the direct road towards truth we should busy ourselves with no object about which we cannot attain a certitude equal to that of the demonstrations of Arithmetic and Geometry." [4]

In the seventh oration Vico makes a rather remarkable comment on the Cartesian conception of mathematics as the model of perfect or absolute knowledge. Speaking of the use of mathematics in physics, he says: "We demonstrate geometrical things because we make them; if we were able to demonstrate physical things we would make them." This is not a criticism of the certainty of mathematics but an insight into the reason for its certainty. What it does is to deny that mathematical knowledge is knowledge of the real world. These rather cryptic remarks about mathematics are the first expressions of his famous and important epistemological formula: *verum est factum* (truth is made). In his next work, *Metaphysics,* Vico develops this epistemology (ibid., p. 184).

III

Vico published his *Metaphysics* in 1710. In this remarkably concise work, he lays the philosophical foundation for his attempt to demonstrate how man can, and does, pursue truth and goodness. It is necessary to distinguish two different metaphysical systems in this book. In the first, a cosmological metaphysics, Vico presents a metaphysics to support his own physical theories, demonstrating that God is immanent in the physical universe. The second metaphysical system is an epistemological one that Vico will later use in the *New Science.* Here he uses it to explain how it is possible for man to pursue truth and goodness. It is this metaphysics of the mind that I will discuss here.

4. René Descartes, "Rules for the Direction of the Mind" in *Philosophical Works,* trans. E. S. Haldane and G. R. T. Ross (New York: Dover Publications, 1931), 1:5.

The metaphysics of the mind Vico describes as "the modifications of the human mind." Baldly stated, the basic tenet is that man creates or makes his world; he makes the true and makes the good. The theory of knowledge is not completely worked out in the *Metaphysics,* and it is not until his next work, *The Universal Law,* that Vico arrived at a clear conception of what he had been groping for in the first inaugural orations and sketched somewhat clumsily in the dissertation *On the Method of Studies of Our Time,* and a little more distinctly in the Metaphysics (*Autobiografia,* p. 50).

The basic formula—"truth is made" (*verum est factum*)—Vico claimed to have derived from the Latin language in which, he says, "*verum and factum* have reciprocal rapport, or to use the language of the schools, they are convertible." This philological foundation is not the only support he offers for his epistemological formula. He also attempts to support it by an ingenious explanation of the nature of science. Science is the "knowledge of the genesis of things, that is, of the guise in which things come to be made." He translates this into somewhat plainer language when he says that science is knowledge of the causes of things. This knowledge of the causes of things is real or true knowledge.[5]

If knowledge of the causes of things gives us true knowledge of things, then what, Vico asks, gives us true knowledge of the sciences themselves? The answer, obviously, is knowledge of the cause or causes of sciences. In trying to go back to the origins or the causes of science, Vico is searching for a criterion of truth. That is, to answer the question, "Why do the sciences give us truth?" one must uncover the criterion for truth.

Vico includes both mathematics and physics under the label of science. Taking the mathematical sciences first, he declares that arithmetic originated with the unit, geometry with the point. In arithmetic, man started with the unit, multiplied it and so created a world of numbers. Further, by means of addition, subtraction, or calculations of the numbers in various ways, this world that man makes is, in a sense, an infinite world. In like manner, man started with the point in geometry, prolonged it into lines, and by the shortening and the configuration of these lines in various other ways, man has created a world of figures which, like the world of numbers, is in a certain sense infinite (*Il Metafisico,* pp. 248, 260).

These two bases of geometry and arithmetic—the point and the unit—are fictions, Vico explains, because as soon as the point is designated, it is no longer a point—since it then has dimensions. Second, as soon as the unit is multiplied, it is no longer a unit—it is then a number more than one. Vico's argument is that man has made the point and the

5. Vico, *Opere, Il Metafisico,* pp. 248, 260.

unit, or better, he has "feigned" them (they do not exist). And on these fictions, man built the sciences of arithmetic and geometry (ibid.).

Through these creations, though their foundations are fictitious, man proceeds to the infinite: "Through such a way, man has created a certain world of figures and numbers which he contains within himself, and by prolonging, shortening and configuring the lines in other modes, or by the addition, subtraction, or calculation of the numbers in other modes, man comes—as one who now knows within himself infinite truths—to give life to creations without end." From his examination of the origins or causes of the mathematical sciences, Vico concludes that man is their cause. Man has made these sciences.

Turning next to the physical sciences, Vico notes at once that man has not made the physical world as he has the world of numbers and figures. But he has made words and definitions about the physical world: "Being denied possession of the elements of things through means of which those things come to exist in a certain way, man is able to feign elements of vocabulary, instigators at their time [of creation] of ideas not susceptible to controversy" (ibid.).

The physical sciences rest upon words and definitions that express man's ideas about physical things. Ideas, in Vico's view, are metaphysical entities, whereas words are physical. Nevertheless, ideas and words appear, or are made, at the same time. The important point is that man has made this world of ideas, ideas about the physical universe. Thus, in both the physical and mathematical sciences, man is the maker, the cause of the "worlds" these sciences create (ibid., p. 254).[6]

So, if true knowledge is knowledge of the causes of things ("in the guise in which they come to be") and if our knowledge of causes is nothing more than the making of causes, then the criterion of truth is "to have made it." Vico has established his epistemological formula: "truth is made" (*verum est factum*).

Insofar as man's ideas are metaphysical entities, they embody or contain the highest or perfect truth in the way a seed contains the final or perfect plant it is to become. Because our ideas are metaphysical, they can, like a seed, day by day in their development become more perfect. Of course, man's ideas never become absolutely perfect since perfection is proper to God alone; but man's ideas can (in the sense of "possibility") tend toward perfection (ibid., p. 262).

How does this improvement take place? It occurs through what Vico calls the modifications of the mind: sensing, perceiving, judging, and reasoning. The first movement or modification is sensation. In keeping with his belief that man is active, not passive, Vico claims that man makes his sensations, ". . . seeing, we make the colors of things; tasting, the

6. See also *Opere, Scienza nuova,* par. 234.

tastes; listening, the sounds; touching, hot and cold." The objects of the external world—normally said to "produce" sensations in us—Vico calls the "occasions" for the acts of sensing. Sensations are the acts of the *animo* (soul). "The *animo* is a virtue, seeing an act, the sense of sight, a faculty" (ibid., pp. 292–93).

Unlike all the rest of the physical existence, man has his own force within. In his cosmological metaphysics, Vico already explained that there can be no force within the physical universe, only motion (force is metaphysical), and he maintained that all physical phenomena can be explained purely in terms of motion. But man, even though he is part of the physical universe, is an exception to the purely physical laws that rule the universe. Man has a metaphysical force, his *animo,* and man's behavior can be explained only in terms of his *animo* (ibid., p. 287).

The most significant consequence of Vico's claim that man has an *animo* is that man is the only thing in time. Vico defined time as "rapport between two places, one of which is still, the other moving." Therefore, since all of physical existence is in motion—every extended particle and every extended body is in reciprocal motion—then there can be no such thing as time in the physical universe. Time is a metaphysical conception: the only thing not moving is God; and man, or man's *animo,* is in rapport to God. Therefore, man alone is in time (ibid., p. 280).

Time began, says Vico, with the Fall of Adam, when man was sent out from God, who is perfect truth. Time, consequently, is nothing more than the movement of man, or of his *animo,* back toward truth, back toward the perfect truth of God.[7]

This movement of the *animo* takes the form of conversion from virtue to act, or presence. The first step, as we saw, is the conversion of the *animo* into sensation. For it is in his sensations that man's *animo* is first felt to be present. "Men first feel without paying attention, they pay attention with a troubled and agitated *animo,* finally they reflect with pure mind" (*Scienza nuovo,* par. 218).

Sensations are not knowledge. They can become knowledge, converted into knowledge by means of the intellect which makes ideas. But sensations themselves are not knowledge. The first movement of the mind—the having of ideas—Vico calls "perceiving." This is a conversion of the *animo* into act or presence. Initially, the *animo* is converted into sensation through the sense faculties; now, in perceiving, the *animo* is converted into idea or into mind or into thought. Thought, mind, idea—as Vico uses these terms here—all refer to the same thing: the *animo* present as mental act (*Il Metafisico,* pp. 297, 290).

This conversion of the *animo* into idea is accomplished by means of

---

7. Giambattista Vico, *Dell' Unico Principio E Fine Del Diritto Universale* (hereinafter referred to as *Diritto universale*), prima versione di Nicola Corcia (Napoli: [n.n.] 1839), p. 27.

the intellect, which "distinguishes similarities among things and makes them." This means that the intellect discovers the similarities among the sensations one has and makes ideas of them. The mind does not interact with the body nor with the external world. What happens is that on the occasion of having sensations, man makes ideas. The sensations are occasions for the making of ideas; they do not cause ideas (*Diritto universale,* p. 17).

Vico's occasionalism is not unlike that of Malebranche (1638–1750), but it differs in one important detail. Vico professed astonishment that Malebranche acceded to Descartes's *"Cogito, ergo sum."* "Since precisely because he admits that God creates in me an idea, Malebranche would have to reason thusly: 'Something thinks in me, therefore, is.' But, in my thought I do not meet with any idea of body, therefore, what thinks in me is pure mind, that is, God." According to Vico, the mind—with its first movement called perceiving—"presents itself to itself." But, in the very act of knowing itself, its own existence, the mind perceives God as the essence of that existence (*Il Metafisico,* pp. 290–91).

He explains this in his comments on Descartes's *Cogito.* Descartes confused essence (being) with existence. He should have said, "I think, therefore, I exist." Then he would have realized that something sustains existence; namely, substance. Vico concludes, ". . . substance carries with it the idea of sustaining, not of being sustained; therefore, it is by itself; therefore, it is eternal and infinite; therefore, my essence is God who sustains my thought." [8]

When he first proposed this conception in his *Metaphysics,* Vico did not explain how God thinks in man. Later, in *The Universal Law,* he makes quite clear that God thinks in man through His divine providence: "The wisdom of God in so far as it gives life to all things, each one in its own due time, is called Divine Providence." The ways of divine providence, Vico continues, are opportunities, occasions, and causes. That is, God provides the opportunities, occasions, or causes for man to make ideas (*Diritto universale,* chaps. 8 and 9).

In the next movement of the mind, judging, man makes his ideas certain. Once again, Vico did not fully explain this movement until *The Universal Law.* There he says that man's will dominates his mind. As mistress of the mind, man's will is moved by what he calls "utilities" of the body. These encompass all necessities and luxuries. Man's will accedes only to those ideas that are useful to him, useful in getting along in the physical universe. Consequently, man's ideas become certain when they are shown to be useful. The mind, or the faculty of the mind, the intellect, demonstrates this usefulness of the new ideas to the will. The will then accedes to them, thereby conferring certainty on them. Certainty is subjective.[9]

---

8. Vico, *Opere,* Risposta 2:326–27.
9. Vico, *Opere, Il Metafiscio,* p. 297; *Diritto universale,* chaps. 21, 31.

In the next movement of the mind, called reasoning, man makes new ideas. Vico maintains that man can actually make new ideas only through induction, and by combining this with experimental demonstration, he can make his new ideas certain. That is, just as a child makes his ideas certain by making words or models from his ideas and comparing these with the words and things made by the rest of society, so in a similar manner, man makes his new ideas certain. After making new ideas or theories about the physical universe through induction, man makes these ideas certain by making models from them and comparing these models with the actual physical universe. "Therefore, in physics, those theories come to be recognized good that present themselves to make us work [or operate] something to conform to them; and in the field of the natural sciences, a theory comes reputed to be excellent when one can validate it with an experiment, an experiment in which one makes a facsimile of the work of nature" (*Il Metafisico* pp. 255, 297).

An experiment makes evident the usefulness of our new ideas or theories. The intellect measures this usefulness by reference to the usefulness or certainty of previously held ideas. By making models based on the new idea, the intellect can ascertain if the new model is more useful than those models made from old ideas or theories. In the presence of demonstrated usefulness, the will accedes to the new idea or theory, making it certain.

Vico defines truth as "conformity to the eternal order of things." Therefore, if the new model is more useful than the old, then the new model must conform more closely to the eternal order of things. Hence the new idea—the source of the new model—corresponds more closely to the perfect idea of the actual physical universe. This perfect idea, of course, exists only in God (*Diritto universale,* chap. 17).

Man cannot have perfect ideas, Vico explains, simply because he is dominated by his will, not by his mind. This domination by the will has two important consequences. First, man makes new ideas only at the urging of his will. As long as man "gets along" with the ideas he has and with the things he has made from those ideas, man is contented. But when this well-being is upset, when his ideas and artifacts break down or prove not to be useful; when, that is, man suffers physical discomfiture—pain, shame, fear, and so on—then man's will agitates his *animo* (which is present as mind) in order to make new ideas from which man will derive utility or physical comfort: "Men at first feel without paying attention, then they pay attention with a troubled and agitated *animo,* finally, they reflect with pure mind." [10]

The second consequence of the dominion of the will over mind is that the will, moved as it is by corporal utility, accedes to, or makes certain, only those ideas that the intellect shows to be useful. And this usefulness

10. Vico, *Diritto universale,* chap. 21; *Opere, Scienza nuova,* p. 218.

of new ideas is known only in reference to useful or certain ideas already possessed.

These two results of the dominion of the will mean nothing more than that man is in time. To Vico, being in time, as noted above, means movement in relation to God, who is perfect truth. Vico sees this movement in terms of man's *animo*—the movement of the *animo* toward perfect truth. Were man dominated by his mind (the *animo* in act), then, Vico says, he would be able to know truth with facility. Such indeed was the nature of man as he was originally created by God: "Upright man, therefore, through the contemplation of eternal truth, that is, of God himself, with a pure mind, and through love of the eternal good, with a pure soul, and through the desire of all human kind towards the eternal good, manifested his upright nature to God" (ibid., chap. 42).

By "upright man," Vico means that the first man, Adam, was upright precisely because his mind or intellect dominated his will. But, as a result of the first sin, man lost this upright nature; his will became mistress over his mind. As a result of the first sin, time began. This means that although God through his providence "thinks in man," man, dominated by his will, moves toward perfect truth not readily or with facility but in time. Divine providence is "that wisdom of God insofar as it gives life to all things, each one in its own due time" (ibid., chap. 8).

In this guarantee of man's pursuit of truth, Vico has developed, strengthened, and integrated those themes introduced in his early orations. He has reached his "grand theme," his conception of man. "Man is a finite being, able to know, to will, who tends toward the infinite." [11]

IV

In 1719, nine years after the publication of his *Metaphysics,* Vico again delivered the inaugural oration at the University of Naples, lecturing on the "universal law." He proposed to show "that the origins of all things proceed from God, that all return to God by a circle, that all have their constancy in God, and that apart from God, they are all darkness and error." His listeners, Vico tells us, considered the argument "more magnificent than effectual." He never published this oration, but out of it grew his book *On the One Principle and the One End of Universal Law,* usually referred to as *The Universal Law,* first published in 1720 (*Autobiographia,* p. 50).

The Universal Law supplied the additional theory necessary to complete the epistemology he had first proposed in the *Metaphysics.* Moreover, in this work he used the two main theories of his epistemological metaphysics—the conception that man seeks utility, and the concep-

11. Vico, *Diritto universale,* chap. 10; *Opere, Autobiografia,* p. 39.

tion of divine providence—in his attempt to guarantee man's pursuit of the good.

The physical objects that man makes from his ideas constitute the "necessities, utilities, and luxuries of life." In *The Universal Law,* Vico usually refers to them as "utilities." These utilities have an order or distribution in the life of the individual, and in the society. Man pursues the good through ordering these utilities. Vico's basic dictum for this process is "When reason ponders and regulates utilities, it is justice" (*Diritto universale,* chap. 43).

Through his intellect, man knows what is wrong (unequal) in the actual order of utilities, and sees how to correct it by making an idea of what would be an equal order. Next, Vico says, "that which is equal when measured, the same is just when chosen." So, when reason knows, or makes, an equal order—an equal order that is only idea—and the will chooses this equal order, the will is choosing what is just, is making justice. This Vico calls the "equal good." Man makes the good by an equal ordering of utilities (ibid., chap. 44).

To explain why the reason makes an equal ordering of utilities and why the will accedes to that equal ordering, Vico relies on the "natural law." The natural law has two aspects or two parts, one pertaining to man's will, the other to his reason. As it pertains to man's will, the primary natural law is that man desires his own being, his own physical well-being, and physical utilities that pertain to his physical well-being. As it pertains to man's reason, the secondary natural law is that man is able to know and wants to know (ibid., chap. 85).

Since the Fall, man's will dominates his reason. Therefore, when man—who according to the primary natural law seeks his own well-being—is perturbed by the existing order of things, the will agitates the mind or intellect, which acts in accordance with the secondary natural law: it seeks knowledge. The intellect distinguishes the order that exists, the order that perturbs man's well-being, and then creates or makes an idea of a new, more equal order. Since there is but one eternal order of things, there can necessarily be only one useful order of utilities—in conformity with the eternal order of things. But since man does not know truth with facility, he only moves in time closer to knowledge of that eternal order. Thus, when the reason creates an idea of a new order of utilities that does more closely approximate the eternal order of things, it will be more useful. The will accedes to it. The usefulness of the new order, not knowledge of its truth, induces the will to accede, but the amount of usefulness recognized in any ordering of utilities is an indication of how true that order is. Thus, man pursues the good in accordance with the natural law—necessarily with his reason since there is but one eternal order of things, and voluntarily with his will since man accedes only to what is most useful (ibid., chaps. 72 and 63).

These laws come into being naturally, they follow the natural law:

"That which is just is known; that which is good is chosen; the law therefore naturally results from the choice of the good that will be known [as] equal" (ibid., chap. 47).

All law, all jurisprudence, Vico says, rests on reason and authority. The reason of the law comes from the necessity of nature; the authority of the law comes from the will of the legislator. By the necessity of nature, Vico means that the legislator is limited by the actual amount and actual distribution of utilities in a given society at a given time. Pondering these utilities and their distribution, the legislator, by means of the intellect, distinguishes the equality of the existing distribution, and makes an idea of a more equal distribution. The will accedes to this idea as being more useful. This gives the law authority (ibid., Preface).

Laws made through the reason and will of the legislator are true and certain. Laws are true when they "conform to the eternal order of things." Laws made through reason conform to the eternal order of things since they are intended to regulate the order of utilities that man has made from his ideas of the eternal order of things. Of course, no society possesses perfect truth, but all societies are in time, and in time they can more nearly approximate perfect truth. The amount of truth a society possesses at a given time determines the amount of utilities the society possesses, as well as their possible distribution. Consequently, as new truths come into existence, new utilities are made, and new possibilities for their distribution arise. Thus, the laws change in time. But this does not mean that the old laws were not true. For the old laws conformed to the eternal order of things insofar as that society at the time the laws were made had attained knowledge of the eternal order of things. The reason for the old law may cease, or "idle away," but it can never become false, never be refuted (ibid., chap. 61).

The certainty of the law is due to the will of the legislator. As with all men, only utility moves the will of the legislator; in this case, the public or common utility. The legislator chooses the most useful distribution of utilities in the society. In this way, the law is made certain, certain because it is useful; and because it is useful, the legislator authorizes it or gives it authority (ibid., chap. 82).

As man makes more truth or improves his truth, he makes more utilities, thereby increasing the utilities in the society. In this way, the legislator gets the opportunity or occasion to distribute them equally. So man makes both the true and the good in the same way: by means of occasions. Just as the physical objects of the external physical world serve as the occasions for making truths, so these truths give birth to utilities that in turn serve as occasions for man as legislator or make the equal good. The legislator converts the true into the good.

This equal good that the legislator creates is usually called justice. Therefore, since it is through divine providence that man attains truth—

truth that he converts into the equal good through establishing laws that are just—then God is the principle or beginning of all human law, all human justice, and it is possible for man's laws, in time, to approach the universal justice of God. Vico has completed the argument of his book: "We demonstrated God's cognition to be the beginning and end of all human and divine knowledge; jurisprudence to be the communication of divine and human things. The one beginning and end of universal law is therefore demonstrated" (ibid., chap. 123).

By claiming that God is the beginning and end of the universal law, Vico has enlarged his theory that man tends toward the infinite to include society itself. Society tends toward the infinite through its laws, following the universal law by which "all things proceed from God. All return to God by a circle. All things have their constancy in God" (ibid., Preface).

In addition to the legal or equal good of society, Vico discusses the ethical good of the individual. Good for the individual is nothing more than the conversion of truth into act or actions; or, as Vico puts it, "to live truly." To live truly means to live according to the truths known to the members of one's society; that is, to become a part of "the society of truth." This, Vico will point out in the *New Science,* occurs naturally—through education.[12]

The common sense a society possesses will never be able to be complete or perfect truth. All societies exist in time. But this means that they can move closer to truth. Man, therefore, is not just a passive member of society, absorbing its common sense. To the contrary, the individual can make new truths, truth from which new utilities—hence new occasions for making good—arise. It is the interaction between the common sense of the society and the new knowledge that individuals create that produces the movement of man toward the infinite.

Vico insists that if one knows the truth, one will "live truly." This follows from his "natural law" and his definition of truth as "conformation to the eternal order of things." Because there is an eternal order, the truth that men attain will better enable them to live in this eternal order of things. Consequently, man—when he exercises his reason—will recognize the utility of any given truth, and so, according to the natural law, will seek utility, thus making the good, which consists in living truly (ibid., chap. 55).

Of course, not all men live truly and no man does good all the time. Men do evil out of ignorance. Vico lists five different kinds of ignorance and the evils that naturally result from such ignorance. The first is ignorance of facts. We call these errors. The natural result of error is infelicity. The second kind of ignorance is ignorance of common sense. This is ignorance of the judgments commonly made by the members of the soci-

12. Vico, *Diritto universale,* chap. 55; *Opere, Scienza nuova,* pars. 458–59.

ety as to what is true, hence what is good. The natural result of this kind of ignorance is shame. Next, those who deliberately sin or do evil, do it from ignorance of general ideas (i.e., ignorance of reason, with which man makes general ideas). These people, guided solely by their sensations, are naturally inert or lifeless; without the life of reason, they cannot move toward the infinite. The fourth kind of ignorance is ignorance of self. This ignorance results in excessive delights and luxuries of life because "not knowing themselves, they look for themselves in the idleness and blandishments of living." The fifth and last is ignorance of one's own things. This ignorance leads naturally to negligence and incautiousness, since through this ignorance one maltreats the utilities man has made (ibid., chap. 67).

With the *Universal Law,* Vico completed his philosophical speculations. He believed he had accomplished his aim of uniting human and divine wisdom. Human wisdom was the conversion of truth into good. In acquiring knowledge of divine things, man conducts human things to the highest good. Divine things are those things made by God: the physical universe. Human things are those made by man: his ideas and the conversion of these ideas into actions and into laws. Since man makes human things on the occasions of having sensations of the physical universe—created and ruled by God—then human wisdom is joined to, and results from, divine wisdom through means of divine providence.

Consequently, it is divine providence—that wisdom of God insofar as He gives life to all things, each in its own due time—that is the basic principle underlying the universal law: ". . . from the three elements of knowing, willing, and being able, through a single force of mind towards truth, with the aid of divine light, or the inevitable assent to truth, all humanity originates from God, is supported by God, to God returns; and without God, there would be no laws in the world, no states, no society, but solitude, ferocity, turpitude, and injustice" (ibid., chap. 212).

Vico insists that the existence of society itself confirms his philosophical speculations about the universal law. For men, disassociated from one another through the sin of Adam—thereby losing their "upright" nature—could not on their own have created society. Without worship of God, all things must originate from man's *animo.* If men were still upright, they could contemplate and adore God with facility, and so with facility know truth and with the same facility conform to truth. Instead, society came about both naturally and through divine providence. It came about naturally according to the natural law of the development of man's *animo:* from sensation to idea, to certain idea, to truth, and finally to the conversion of the true to the good. It came about through divine providence supplying the occasions for man to make truth, hence to make the good. "Use and necessity," Vico says, "were the good occasions through which divine providence recovered men to make them sociable'' (ibid., chap. 46).

In the second half of *The Universal Law* Vico abruptly abandons his philosophical speculations about the workings of the universal law to supply empirical evidence for his theories, evidence from philology: ''Hereafter . . . we shall try to divine these things from the testimony of philology ordered to the examination [already made] by philosophy.'' [13]

For the remainder of *The Universal Law,* Vico gave ''historical evidence'' for his philosophical speculations. He continued to do this in two additional books of notes and replies to his critics published under the titles *On the Consistency of Philology* and *On the Consistency of Jurisprudence*.

But, he tells us in his *Autobiography,* these proofs were unsatisfactory to him because ''he tried therein to descend from the minds of Plato and other enlightened philosophers into the dull and simple minds of the founders of the gentile peoples, whereas he should have taken the opposite course.'' He took this ''opposite course'' in his last and greatest work, *The New Science* (*Autobiografia,* p. 87).

V

In 1725, Vico's masterpiece appeared with the title, *Principles of a New Science of the Nature of Nations, from which Are Derived New Principles of the Natural Law of Peoples*. This work he later referred to as *The First New Science,* to distinguish it from *The Second New Science,* published in 1730. In *The Second New Science,* he corrected the arrangement of material in the earlier work. In the first version, he had ''treated the origins of ideas apart from language, whereas they are by nature united.'' Vico continued to add corrections and notes to *The New Science* until his death in 1744. In the same year, shortly after his death, the ''third'' *New Science* appeared with all the notes and corrections he had added (*Autobiografia,* p. 87).

The New Science, Vico explains, is in its principal aspect ''a rational civil theology of divine providence.'' This type of civil theology has been lacking, he says, ''because until now philosophers have contemplated divine providence only through the natural order, and in this way they have shown only a part of it.'' But Vico will ''contemplate the providence of God in respect of that part of it that is most proper to men, whose nature has this principal property—that of being sociable.'' In providing men with this property,

---

13. Vico, *Diritto universale,* footnote to chap. 86, ''The Idea of This Work.''

> God has so ordained and disposed human things, that men, fallen from upright justice through original sin, always intending to do something quite different, quite to the contrary—so that to serve utility, would live in solitude like wild beasts—men instead have been led by this same utility through these very diverse and contrary ways to live with justice, and to conserve themselves in society, and indeed to celebrate their sociable nature, which in this work will be demonstrated to be the true civil nature of man, and thus that law exists in nature (*Scienza nuova,* pars. 2, 385).

Vico employs both philosophy and philology to show that the beginnings of society are due to divine providence and the natural law. "Philosophy," he says, "contemplates reason, whence comes science of the truth; philology considers the authority of human choice, whence comes recognition of the certain" (ibid., par. 138).

By "science of the truth," Vico means that philosophy provides the knowledge of causes—in this case, the knowledge of the cause of truth. So, by "philosophy," Vico means his own philosophy, presented in his earlier works, according to which, God, through His divine providence, causes men to have true knowledge.

In regard to philology, Vico tells us that he will consider as philologians all grammarians, historians, and critics who have occupied themselves with the study of the languages and deeds of people. These "philologians" are historians of words and deeds concerned with "the domestic affairs, such as customs and laws, and the external affairs, such as wars, peace, alliances, travels, and commerce" of the past. In saying that "philology considers the authority of human choice," Vico means that these words and deeds of the past were all voluntarily brought about by the people of the past themselves. In adding "philology gives recognition of the certain," he means that historians do not, as historians, know the causes of these past words and deeds; they know only that these did happen or did exist in the past (ibid., par. 139).

The contribution of the new science is to combine philology with philosophy, which "reduces philology to a science," supplying knowledge of the causes of man's past words and deeds: first, divine providence, which "gives life to all things, each one in its own due time," and second, the natural law, the law in nature, by which men choose that which is useful (ibid., par. 390).

Philology tells us what has happened in the past, philosophy tells us why it happened; this is true history. In all, the new science contains seven different aspects. The first, and principal one, is "the rational history of divine providence." The second is a philosophy of authority—it explains why certain ideas have been held in the past. From this follows the third aspect: a history of human ideas. Out of this grows the fourth: a philosophical criticism of the history of ideas (i.e., an understanding of why these ideas have changed in the way that they have). The fifth aspect is an eternal ideal history along which travel, in time, the histories of all nations. The sixth aspect is a system of the natural law of peoples, from the beginnings, showing how all the laws of all nations are conversions of truth into the good; this explains how the first laws of the first peoples came into being. The seventh and last aspect of *The New Science* is that it contains the principles of universal history: it shows how humanity did, in fact, come into being, and how all history is the movement of man back to the infinite, back to God (ibid., pars. 385–99).

All these aspects were already present, as postulations, in his earlier work. But now Vico seeks to confirm this philosophy, confirm it by history. This interpretation, he points out, is a metaphysical one, insofar as it emerges from a contemplation "of the world of minds and of God" (ibid., par. 42).

This attempt to confirm his philosophy will take Vico back to the beginnings of history: "In such dense night of darkness covering the early most remote antiquity shines the never-waning eternal light of this truth, which cannot on any terms be called into doubt: that this civil world has certainly been made by man. Therefore, the beginnings can be recovered, where they should be, in the modifications of our own human mind" (ibid., par. 331).

In *The New Science,* Vico tries to prove his earlier speculations that man has naturally—according to the law in nature by which he acts voluntarily and at the same time necessarily—followed the ideal eternal law by which all humanity returns to God through occasions provided by divine providence. Through history he shows that the world of nations had come from the mind of man, even though this mind has often been diverse and the results contrary to the intentions. He shows that the mind of men is always superior to the ends men propose to themselves: their narrow ends, in time, become means to serve wider ends. Indeed, the mind of man has so far preserved the human race on this earth (ibid., par. 108).

Summary and Evaluation

Through a chronological analysis of his writings, I have tried to present Vico's works in their intellectual wholeness as a philosophy of education. After claiming, in his seven inaugural orations, that the aim of education is the pursuit of wisdom, Vico attempted to provide a philosophical guarantee for this pursuit in his *Metafiscio,* and then in *The New Science,* he tried to "prove" or demonstrate this philosophical guarantee.

Although Vico made few references to education in his later works, he does make one rather significant observation in *The New Science* that reveals his awareness of the educational nature of his philosophy. Among the etymological axioms he lists for his new science he has the following: "The order of ideas must follow the order of things" (*Scienza nuova,* par. 238). This is a deduction from his notion that making and knowing are the same: those things that man makes and to which he gives names, are, when looked at historically, a history of ideas.

Vico follows this axiom with another: "This was the order of human things: first the forests, after that the huts, thence the villages, next the cities, and finally the academies" (ibid., par. 239).

Then Vico explains the axiom: [14]

> This axiom is a great principle of etymology, for this sequence of human things sets the pattern for the histories of words in the various native languages. Thus, we observe in the Latin language that almost the whole corpus of its words had sylvan or rustic origins. For example, *lex.* First, it must have meant "collection of acorns." Thence we believe is derived *ilex,* as were *illex,* "the oak" (as certainly *aquilex* is the "collector of waters"); for the oak produces the acorns by which the swine are drawn together. *Lex* was next "a collection of vegetables," from which the latter were called *legumina.* Later on, at a time when vulgar letters had not yet been invented for writing down the laws, *lex*, by a necessity of civil nature, must have meant "a collection of citizens" or the public parliament; so that the presence of the people was the law that solemnized the wills that were made *calatis comitiis,* in the presence of the assembled *comitia.* Finally, collecting letters, and making, as it were, a sheaf of them in each word, was called *legere,* "reading."

The "order of human things" are those things that have, in the past, held people together in society, or made them human: "first the forests, after that the huts, then the villages, next the cities, and finally the academies." The derivations from the word *lex* shows that people used the same words or derivations of them to refer to those things which did, in fact, hold them together.

The significant passage for us is "finally the academies." I interpret this as meaning that, today, it is education that civilizes or makes men human. In civil society, schools are the natural means to bring people to humanity. Vico's analysis of the evolutions from the word *lex* supports this: whereas people were once held together by a bunch of acorns (food), today, reading (*legere*) or the written word, holds them together. Moreover, education is now the natural means by which humanity continues in its ideal eternal history, its movement toward the infinite.

As mentioned earlier, Vico died a short time before the publication of the third, definitive, edition of *The New Science* in 1744. But before his death, he wrote two short appendices to this work. The second, entitled

14. Vico, *Opere, Scienza nuova,* par. 240, translated from the third edition (1744) by Thomas B. Bergin and Max H. Fisch (Ithaca: Cornell University Press, 1948), p. 70.

"The Practice of the New Science," makes quite clear that he saw the new science in its practical application as a guide for, and a guarantee of, education.

The practice or application of the new science will take place in the academies. There, in schools, the process used in order to discover the principles of the new science will be reversed. That is, by contemplation of the world of minds and of God, Vico discovered certain principles; now these principles will serve as the foundation for education (ibid., par. 1406).

Vico discovered these principles in what he called the common sense of mankind—in those certain ideas that men have made. Consequently, education should have as its criterion of truth (i.e., what should be taught) this common sense of mankind. Education should be founded on "that criterion of truth: that one should revere the common judgment of men, or what is the common sense of mankind."

Moreover, since he discovered three fundamental ideas that have always, at all times, existed in all societies, then, ". . . the academies with their sects of philosophers [should] not be founded on the corruption of the sects of these times, but on those three principles on which this science is founded: that is, that one gives one self to divine providence; that, because they can be, the human passions should be moderated; and that our souls are immortal" (ibid.).

Teachers, Vico continues, if they are wise, will teach youths "how from the world of minds and of God, one descends to the world of nature, in order to live honestly and justly in the world of nations." This world of nations is the matter, the mind of man is the form. This world of nations is defective, obscure, sluggardly, divisible, mobile, "other." But it is the matter to be in-formed by the mind of man—who makes it ordered, bright, living, harmonious, and beautiful (ibid., par. 1407).

Included in this world of nations are men themselves. Through education, their lives are ordered, made bright, harmonious, and beautiful (ibid., par. 1409). Thus, Vico depicts two levels for the practice of the New Science: first, the practice of educators who, through imparting to the young the common sense of humanity, bring them to share in and be a part of, that humanity; second, the practice of the educated, who, in time, bring order into the world of nations, an order that is the result of their active intelligence rooted in the common sense of humanity.

On the last page of his *Autobiography,* Giambattista Vico recorded some of the comments that had been made about him by friends and foes. Among these, he mentions that "some advanced to him a praise all the more grand as it was impetuous: that he was worthy to give good directions to teachers themselves." I have tried to suggest how appropriate this comment was by construing the corpus of Vico's thought as the deliberate creation of a coherent philosophy of education.

Locke's Thoughts

In 1660 John Locke, student at Oxford University, celebrated the restoration of Charles II to the throne of England with a poem:

As in the World's Creation, when this frame
Had neither parts, distinction, nor a name
But all confus'd did in the Chaos jarre
Th' embleme and produce of intestine warre,
Light first appears . . .
Beauty and Order follows, and display
This stately fabrick guided by that ray.
So now in this our new creation when
This isle begins to be a world again,
You first dawn on our Chaos, with designe
To give us Order . . .

> Till you upon us rose and made it day
> We in disorder all and darkness lay.[1]

For the twenty-eight-year-old Locke, the return of Charles signified that anarchy would give way to peace and order. After spending his entire life in a "storm," Locke welcomed the approach of a calm. Ten years old when the Civil War began, he was a student in his second year at Westminster when rebels beheaded Charles I nearby at Whitehall. The war, the regicide, and the purges by the victorious rebels had deeply affected him. Before the Restoration, young Locke had looked to Oliver Cromwell, the Great Protector, to restore peace to England. The death of Cromwell ended that hope. Now he looked to the restored monarch to establish peace and security. "I would be quiet and I would be safe," he wrote during this period, "but if I cannot enjoy them together the last must certainly be had at any rate." [2] John Locke's entire intellectual career can be seen as a quest for a secure society, a quest that led him from theology to epistemology, then to political theory, and finally to the theory of education.

I

Within a year of the Restoration, a crisis emerged that threatened to destroy the calm Locke had so long awaited. "To suppress, not begin a quarrel," Locke composed a manuscript on the hotly disputed question "Whether the Civil Magistrate may lawfully impose and determine the use of indifferent things in reference to religious worship." [3]

Although the controversy had begun long before, the Restoration exacerbated the question of indifferent things into a national, moral, and political crisis. "Indifferent things" were those actions considered neither bad nor good, but morally neutral: in Christian terms, the terms of the dispute, those actions neither required nor condemned by the Law of God. Indifferent things included bowing at the name of Jesus, making the sign of the cross at baptism, wearing the surplice while preaching, kneeling at the sacrament, having set forms of prayer, pictures in churches, and others.

The question "Should indifferent things be imposed in religious worship?" had begun in the late sixteenth century, becoming one of the issues of the Civil War in the mid-seventeeth century. With the Restoration, it

---

1. Philip Abrams, *John Locke's Two Tracts on Government* (Cambridge: University Press, 1967), pp. 51–52.
2. Ibid., p. 8.
3. Abrams (see note 1) edited and published Locke's manuscript under the label "Tracts on Government." Locke wrote two tracts; one, in Latin, possibly for delivering as a formal academic oration (p. 16).

flared up again. In the first six months of 1660, twelve contributions to the debate were published at Oxford alone. One of these, *The Great Question concerning Things Indifferent in Religious Worship,* by Edward Bagshaw, prompted Locke to prepare a rebuttal.

Bagshaw, while insisting on his support for the restored monarch, argued that the king, "the civil magistrate," was not empowered to fashion laws making indifferent things necessary for his subjects. He presented a theological argument, insisting that this attempt by the civil magistrate—or by any Christian, for that matter—would violate the spiritual conscience of others. Each Christian must be free to do or omit anything indifferent in the light of his beliefs about it.

Locke argued in favor of imposition. He claimed that the civil magistrate must have this power for political and sociological reasons. Christians, he points out, have freedom to *believe* that all indifferent things are unnecessary for their salvation. Yet the *use* of indifferent things presents a problem: this is not a matter of conscience; it is a matter of security. Men *do* actually have freedom as to the use of indifferent things, but the survival of society demands their imposition by the civil magistrate. Without this imposition, anarchy, leading to chaos and violence, would ensue.

But whence do civil magistrates get the authority to impose indifferent things in religious worship? Locke gives two answers. They may, he first argues, get this authority from God Himself. God's Divine Law, known through revelation and natural reason, is intrinsically binding on man. From this Divine Law, the civil magistrate derives the power to make laws about indifferent things. Locke argues that the civil magistrate must make laws explicitly stated to be necessary by God, or laws indispensable as means to achieve something explicitly stated by God to be necessary. Thus the Divine Law commands man to live in order; the magistrate exists to determine the forms of order for the society and to impose them. This first attempt to justify the power of the magistrate provides moral obligation to human law: men should obey human law because human law is but an extension or determination of Divine Law. But it fails to be rationally convincing simply because Divine Law lacks specificity: Divine Law is ambiguous and vague.

In his second argument to justify the authority of the civil magistrate, Locke presents a more rational but less morally persuasive argument. According to this argument, subjects *must* give up their freedom to use indifferent things as they choose so that society can avoid anarchy and chaos and gain order and security. Here the authority of the civil magistrates derives from the people; they give up their freedom to choose, conferring this power on him.

John Locke's quest for security led him, initially, to support a strong "civil magistrate." He justified the expansion of the powers of the civil authorities by two arguments, one deriving the authority of civil government from God and the other deriving it from the subjects themselves. He failed to make either argument morally and rationally convincing. His next move was to try to make the morally persuasive argument—that the civil magistrate derives his authority from Divine Law—rationally convincing by exploring the link between Divine Law and human law. That link is the mysterious domain of natural law.

II

In 1661 John Locke became a tutor at Oxford. His college duties included lecturing and conducting disputations with Bachelors of Arts. At least one of the subjects, perhaps the only subject of these disputations, was natural law. At any rate, Locke composed, but never published, seven essays in Latin on natural law.[4] In these essays he takes up the epistemological question "How we know the law of nature."

In the seventeenth century, most took it as axiomatic that God had endowed man with innate knowledge of good and evil.[5] But Locke rejects innate knowledge as an extremely weak defense for the Christian faith. How could the law of nature be inscribed in the minds of men, Locke asks, when we do not find it among the foolish, the insane, the primitive? Nor do we find universal obedience to it; nor even acknowledgment that such a law exists.

If knowledge of the law of nature is not innate, how do we know it? Locke maintains that we know it by the light of nature, and by this he means that "Reason can attain the knowledge of Natural Law through sense experience" (Essay IV).

The senses, Locke says, tell us of bodies and their properties, of motion, and of all the wonderful regularity in the orbits of the stars and the changes of the seasons. Then, using the argument from design, Locke infers the existence of an all-powerful and all-wise Deity who has made the whole universe and created mankind. From this notion of God, the Creator–Law Maker, Locke concludes that man's duty is to worship God, to contemplate His works, and to enter into and maintain a life in society with other men.

Here, Locke has not so much shown that the natural law can be known by the senses as he has shown that it can be deduced from the existence of a Divine Creator, whose existence can be known (by inference) through the order and design perceived by the senses. Hardly a convincing argument.

---

4. John Locke's *Essays on the Law of Nature,* ed. W. Von Leyden (Oxford: Oxford University Press, 1954).

5. See Richard Ashcraft, "Faith and Knowledge in Locke's Philosophy," in *John Locke: Problems and Perspectives,* ed. John Holton (Cambridge: University Press, 1969), p. 199.

In 1664 Locke completed his term of office as censor of moral philosophy at Christ Church. According to the tradition of the college, he delivered his own "funeral" oration. In it he paid tribute to his pupils, the Bachelors of Arts. They, he said, had vanquished him in the philosophical arena. "I took part this year in your disputations on such terms that I always went out at once beaten and enriched." Defeated by his own pupils, he remained undaunted, never doubting the existence of natural law. He now told them: "That law, about which was all our strife, had often eluded my fruitless quest, had not your way of life restored that very same law which your tongue had wrested from me."

The epistemological basis of natural law now became a serious philosophical question for the young tutor. To secure adequate support for his Christian ideology, he would have to move from theology to philosophy. By 1671 he had completed two drafts of his major work in epistemology, his epoch-making *Essay concerning Human Understanding*.

III

Locke completed the *Essay concerning Human Understanding* in 1686, publishing it in 1690. In the "Epistle to the Reader," he explains that he had written the *Essay* in "incoherent parcels, after long intervals of neglect, resumed again as humor and occasions permitted." He had never planned to write so much. But the problems with his first draft became clear to him after completion. To support the position he took there, he had to expand the *Essay* to almost three times its original length.

The *Essay* came out as a long, complex probe into the "origin, certainty, and extent of human knowledge." The initial, and crucial, matter for Locke was the question of man's knowledge of the "principles of morality and revealed religion." [6] Locke maintains that the truths conveyed through revelation must be believed, whereas the natural law or principles of morality can be known with certainty. The argument for this follows.

Using the first book of the *Essay* to demolish the notion of innate ideas, Locke then declares that all knowledge is founded on sense experience. Our sensations produce ideas in the mind. In the second book of the *Essay* he works out the rather devastating consequences of this account of the origin of knowledge. Man is in an egocentric predicament: he knows only his "ideas"; he has no knowledge of the essence of things, "no knowledge of the internal constitution and true notion of things" (*Essay* II. xxiii. 32). In the third book of the *Essay,* Locke explains that our

6. See notation of James Tyrell in Maurice Cranston, *John Locke* (London: Longmans, Green, 1957), p. 141. Also see Ashcraft, "Faith & Knowledge."

knowledge of morality or of moral propositions is of a different ontological order from our knowledge, or lack of it, of the natural world. Morality is a *product* of the mind, having no reference to any real existence or to any sensible standard provided by nature. He asks, rhetorically, "To know whether the idea of adultery or incest be right, will a man seek it anywhere amongst things existing?" (ibid., III. v. 3).

If man cannot obtain knowledge of true morality from observing the practices and customs of the world he lives in, how can he obtain it? Consistent with his notion that all knowledge comes from sense experience, Locke declares that whatever produces pleasure in us we call "good," whatever produces pain we call "evil." "Things then are good or evil only in reference to pleasure or pain" (ibid., II. xx. 2). Pleasures and pains serve as the rewards and punishments for complying with, or violating, the natural law. In an italicized passage, Locke declares: "*Moral good and evil then is only the conformity or disagreement of our voluntary actions to some law, whereby good or evil is drawn on us, from the will and power of the law-maker;* which good and evil, pleasure and pain, attending our observance or breach of the law by the decree of the lawmaker, is what we call *reward* and *punishment*" (ibid., II. xxviii. 5).

Locke has finally answered the epistemological question that has long plagued him. He has explained how man can attain knowledge of the natural law through sense experience. Those actions that bring us pleasure are good, those that bring us pain are evil.

Locke does not intend a hedonistic ethics; he does not abandon man to his immediate appetites or his passions. Man seeks pleasure and seeks to avoid pain, but he can make mistakes about future pain and pleasure because of "*the weak and narrow constitution of our minds*" (ibid., II. xxi. 64). To prevent this sort of error, man will not act before due "examination" (ibid., II. xxi. 47). Thus, reason comes to guide man's pursuit of pleasure and avoidance of pain. Through using his reason to attain the greatest happiness or pleasure, man will discover the law of nature; he will do what God commands. The natural law, as Locke has continuously maintained, follows from the Divine Law. The Divine Law comes to man through the use of his natural faculties, by sensation and reflection (ibid., IV. xviii. 2).

In the fourth and final book of the *Essay,* Locke returns to the matter of the limitation of man's knowledge. Our ignorance he finds to be infinitely larger than our knowledge. We have an intuitive knowledge of our own experience, a demonstrable knowledge of the existence of God, and sense knowledge of the existence of other things. But we do not know the nature of these "other things." A science of nature lies beyond our grasp (ibid., IV. iii. 26). We know only that other things exist *and* whether they cause us pain or pleasure. This is enough for Locke.

> Our faculties being suited not to the full extent of being, nor to a perfect, clear, comprehensive knowledge of things free from all doubt and scruple; but to the preservation of us, in whom they are; and accommodated to the use of life: they serve to our purpose well enough, if they will but give us certain notice of those things which are convenient or inconvenient to us. For he that sees a candle burning and hath experimented the force of its flame by putting his finger in it, will little doubt that this is something existing without him, which is assurance enough, when no man requires greater certainty to govern his actions by than what is certain as his actions themselves. . . . Such an assurance of the existence of things without us is sufficient to direct us in the attaining the good and avoiding the evil which is caused by them, which is the important concernment we have of being made acquainted with them'' (ibid., IV. xi. 8).

From this, Locke concludes that ''our proper employment lies in those inquiries and in that sort of knowledge which is most suited to our natural capacities and carries in it our greatest interest; i.e., the condition of our eternal estate. Hence . . . morality is the proper science and business of mankind in general'' (ibid., IV. xii. 11). So, rather than skepticism and despair, the discovery of the vastness of human ignorance led Locke to reverence. In the revealed knowledge of religion and the natural knowledge of morality, man can recognize the order, rationality, and goodness of God's creation, of which man is a part. Thus, man can recognize his calling, for ''besides his particular calling for the support of his life, everyone has a concern in a future life which he is bound to look after'' *(Of the Conduct of the Understanding,* no. 8).[7]

Locke insisted that man must be free to fulfill his calling. He must be secure, protected from interference and coercion. Each man must be free to think and reason about ''that noble study which is everyman's duty and everyone that can be called a rational creature is capable of'' (ibid., no. 23). This doctrine of ''the calling'' next led Locke from epistemology to political theory.

IV

The first political tract Locke published was the *Epistotles de Tolerantia.* Written in 1685, it appeared in print in 1889 as *A Letter concerning Toleration.* In it, Locke based his plea for tolerance on the doctrine of ''the calling'' and on his recognition of human ignorance.

Men, he writes, in response to their calling, join a church for ''the

---

7. The central significance of ''the calling'' in Locke's work is brilliantly analyzed by John Dunne, *The Political Thought of John Locke* (Cambridge: University Press, 1969).

public worshipping of God in such a manner as they judge acceptable to Him, and effectual to the salvation of their souls.'' Neither the church nor the state has the right to persecute or deprive a person of his ''civil enjoyments'' because of his religion. Each man is responsible for answering his calling in the way he sees as right. And ''if any man err from the right way, it is his own misfortune.'' [8] But, of course, man is ignorant of the truth, and so no one person, no church, or no state can claim to have certain knowledge of the true religion. Hence, toleration is the only course for all men, all churches, all states. Any attempt to ''invade the civil rights and worldly good of each other on pretense of religion . . . will sow a seed of discord and war . . . a provocation to endless hatreds, rapines, and slaughters'' (*A Letter,* p. 7). The peace and security man needs to fulfill his calling will be shattered. ''No peace and security, no, not so much as common friendship, can ever be established or preserved amongst men so long as this opinion prevails, that dominion is founded in grace and that religion is to be propagated by force of arms'' (ibid.).

The state, however, is not obliged to tolerate those who do positive harm to others or to the state. Atheists, not having a proper foundation for morality (i.e., belief in God) are not to be trusted. Nor should the state tolerate those who, like Roman Catholics, give allegiance to a foreign potentate. If the state does intervene and suppress or deprive these people of political rights, it does so on social and political grounds, not religious grounds. The state must protect and provide security for the people.

Within this notion of the protectionist role of governments lies a dilemma that Locke must ultimately confront. The state itself may be an oppressor. In the name of protection of the people, the state may take away their freedom, their very lives. How can the individual protect himself from the state? To answer this, Locke had to raise the question of the legitimacy of the state's power.

Locke first confronted this problem of the legitimacy of power in 1680 with the publication of Sir Robert Filmer's *Patriarcha: On the Natural Power of Kings*. In this much acclaimed book, Filmer argued that kings had absolute power inherited from Adam, who had received the power directly from God. Locke himself had, back in the 1660s, entertained the theory of divine right as one possible theory of the source of power of the civil magistrate. But he had never accepted the notion of absolute power.

The doctrine propounded by Filmer challenged Locke's firmly held beliefs about man's calling. To fulfill his calling, man needed the security and peace that the state or civil magistrate could guarantee, but he also needed to be protected *from* the civil magistrate—protected from any exercise of arbitrary or absolute power. All men needed to be free. Filmer had explicitly denied the equality and freedom of all men. Locke had to

---

8. ''A Letter Concerning Toleration'' in *Great Books of the Western World,* ed. Robert B. Hutchins (Chicago: Encyclopedia Britannica, 1952), 35:6.

refute him. More important, he had to offer an alternative theory that would account for the legitimacy of the authority of the state but a theory that, unlike Filmer's, would restrict or limit the authority of the state.

In 1690 Locke published his *Two Treatises on Civil Government*. In the long, repetitious, tedious *First Treatise,* he detected and overthrew "the false principles and foundations of Sir Robert Filmer and his followers." In the *Second Treatise,* he presents an essay concerning "the true original extent and end of Civil Government." Before determining the source and extent of the legitimate authority of the state, Locke carefully describes that authority in protectionist terms: it consists of "regulating and preserving property . . . the defense of the Commonwealth from foreign injury . . . for the public good."

Locke finds the source of the authority of the civil state in the original state of nature. There, he tells us, all men were equal in the eyes of God. They were equal and they were free. For then no man had the right to harm another in his life, health, liberty, or possessions (*Second Treatise,* par. 6). Men were free simply because they belonged to God alone; they were his property. No *man* had the right to appropriate what belonged to God alone.

In this state of nature, each man tried to protect himself, tried to secure his life, health, liberty and possessions from appropriation by others. This oftentimes led to violence. But God would never set up a mere man as an absolute monarch to establish order as some (Hobbes?) would have it. No, for any claim of any mere mortal to absolute power is a declaration of war. Thus, Locke explains in an aside, we have the right to kill a thief who places himself in absolute power over us: he has declared war on us.

After describing the state of nature with its condition of human freedom and equality, Locke contrasts this with civil liberty. When he has natural liberty, man is not under the power of any other man or group; when he enters civil society, man *consents* to place himself under a ruler or legislative and to obey the rules it sets forth. In both the natural and civil state, man is free from arbitrary and absolute power.

After insisting that man is free and equal in both the natural and civil state—he is the property of no other man or group—Locke takes up some counterarguments. What about property? Surely, some men have more than others. A few are rich; many are poor. How can Locke insist that all men are equal? In a long digression, Locke tries to answer this, explaining the origins of the unequal possession of wealth in terms of the emergence of money. Prior to the use of money, no man possessed or took more property than he could use. But, he argues, since men have consented to the use of money, they, in effect, have agreed to the "disproportionate and unequal possession of the earth." This inequality of wealth, like inequality of age or virtue, is perfectly consistent with his notion of the equality of all men. For, by the equality of all men, Locke means "that *Equal Right* that every Man hath, to his Natural Freedom, without being subjected to the will or authority of any other Man" (ibid., par. 54).

Another counterargument to the equality of all men is the power a father has over his children. But, Locke points out, this power is temporary, not absolute; nor is it a power over the life and property of the child. This temporary subjugation of all men while they are children is simply due to the absence of reason. So likewise with lunatics and idiots: they have not the right to that freedom shared by all rational adults.

What about the power husbands have over wives? Not an absolute power, says Locke. Servants? They suffer only a temporary and constricted power, he counters. And slaves, he argues, are not part of the civil society; hence, they do not share in the freedom from subjugation enjoyed by all citizens.

After meeting these objections to his claim that all men are equal and free in the state of nature and in civil society, Locke returns to his central theme: "the true original extent and end of civil government." The civil government originates, he claims, when every one of the members gives up his right of self-protection to the community itself. Men give up the right of self-protection they had in the state of nature because of the violence and inconveniences that followed from every man being judge in his own case.

> And thus all private judgment of every particular Member being excluded, the community comes to be Umpire by settled standing Rules, indifferent, and the same for all Parties; and by Men having Authority from the Community for the execution of those Rules, decides all the differences that may happen between any members of that Society concerning any matter of right; and punishes those Offences which any Member hath committed against the Society with such Penalties as the Law has established: Whereby it is easy to discern who are, and who are not, in Political Society together (ibid., par. 87).

Locke concludes that an absolute monarchy is inconsistent with civil society since it, unlike a (legitimate) civil society, has no known authority for people to appeal to for the decision of any differences between them and the monarch. Every absolute monarch is still in the state of nature "in respect to those who are under his *Dominion*" (ibid., par. 90). Absolute monarchy is not a legitimate civil government since it does not fulfill the end of civil society: protection of the natural rights of men.

After explaining the origins and ends of civil society in terms of man's quest for self-protection, Locke takes up the matter of the extent or limitations of the government or civil magistrate. The government or, as Locke now calls it, the legislative, is created by the consent of the people.

It is the supreme authority. Yet it cannot possibly be absolute nor arbitrary. For, in the first place, its power derives from the people who gave up their own power to it, and since "no body has an absolute Arbitrary Power over himself, or over any other," he cannot transfer such power. Second, since men enter civil society to protect their rights, the rule must be "by promulgated standing Laws and known authorized Judges. Otherwise, their Peace, Quiet, and Property will still be at the same uncertainty as it was in that state of nature" (ibid., par. 136). Third, since society presupposed that man has property (i.e., life, liberty, and possessions), nobody has the right to take it away without consent. "For I have truly no *Property* in that which another can by right take from me, who he pleases, against my consent" (ibid., par. 138). The final restriction Locke places on the government is that the power of making laws cannot be transferred to any other hands.

Locke next applies his theory of the limitations on government to such matters as prerogatives and conquest, to determine what acts are legitimate, what not. He also shows how his theory condemns usurpation and tyranny. Finally, he comes to the most important question: the dissolution of government. When the government does not perform its duties—the end for which it was created—of securing the rights of the citizens, the people have a right to dissolve it.

> The Reason why Men enter into Society is the preservation of their Property; and the end why they choose [*sic*] and authorize a Legislative is that there may be Laws made, and Rules set as Guards and Fences to the Properties of all the Members of the Society. . . . Whensoever therefore by the Legislative shall transgress this fundamental Rule of Society; and either by Ambition, Fear, Folly, or Corruption, endeavor to grasp themselves, or put into the hands of any other an Absolute Power over the Lives, Liberties, and Estates of the People; By this breach of Trust they forfeit the Power the People had put into their hands, for quite contrary ends, and it devolves to the People, who have a Right to resume their original Liberty, and by the Establishment of a new Legislative (such as they shall think of it) provide for their own safety and security, which is the end for which they are in Society (ibid., par. 222).

Although he began composing his treatises on government in 1680, Locke did not publish them until 1690, two years after the Glorious Revolution by which the people had removed King James II from the throne. In the preface, Locke writes that his book is a justification to the world of "the People of England, whose love of their Just and Natural Rights, with their Resolution to preserve them, saved the Nation when it was on the very brink of Slavery and Ruin." Locke indeed did justify the Glorious Revolution. He did it by justifying rebellion when the government does not fulfill the end for which it exists: the protection of the rights of its citizens. But, in justifying rebellion or revolution, Locke has opened the door to potential chaos and anarchy. In the last pages of the *Second Treatise,* he tries to quell the fears of anarchy. First, he says, his theory of government no more "lays a ferment for frequent Rebellion" than any other theory since it is not theories but ill treatment of people by the rulers that causes rebellions. Second, he avers that people will not break out in rebellion over every minor abuse, "every little mismanagement in public affairs" (ibid., par. 225). Third, he argues that his doctrine, which gives the explicit right to people to rebel, will in itself be a guarantee against frequent rebellion because rulers will now be more cautious, less arbitrary, and less prone to exercise absolute powers. Finally, Locke insists that tyranny must be resisted, men must protect their rights, even if this does lead to a revolution (ibid., pars. 228, 229).

In his lifelong pursuit of the peace and security necessary for man to pursue his calling, Locke moved from theology to epistemology to political theory. Ironically, his attempt to create a political theory of government that would guarantee peace and security for all led him to the brink of anarchy. One way to avoid anarchy and continual revolutions would be to create or mold leaders and rulers who would not knowingly transgress or interfere with the rights of people. In short, Locke now had to turn to the matter of the education of rulers. The Glorious Revolution made it clear that the reins of power rested in the hands of the upper classes, the gentry or gentlemen.

V

In 1693, three years after his *Treatises on Goverment* appeared, Locke published *Some Thoughts concerning Education.* What had started in 1684 as a series of letters to Edmund Clarke containing advice on the education of his young son now appeared in print at the persuasion, Locke tells us, of some who told him that they "might be of some use if made public." He agreed to publication because "it [is] every man's indispensable Duty to do all the Service he can to his Country. Later he adds: "The well Educating of their Children is so much the Duty and Concern of Parents and the Welfare and Prosperity of the Nation so much depends on it, that I would have everyone lay it seriously to heart. . . ." He concludes with the observation, "that most to be taken Care of, is the Gentleman's Calling. For if those of that Rank are by their Education once set right, they will quickly bring all the rest into Order" (*Thoughts,* The Epistle Dedicatory).

Consonant with his experience theory of knowledge, Locke claims in the first paragraph of the book "that of all the Men We meet with, Nine Parts of Ten are what they are, Good or Evil, useful or not, by their

Education.'' Our main care, he says, should be with the ''inside'' of the child—his mind. But, he adds, ''the clay cottage should not be neglected'' (*Thoughts*, par. 2).

In the education of the bodies of their sons, gentlemen should take yeomen as their model: avoid ''cockering'' and ''tenderness.'' The body must be disciplined: don't clad children in warm or tight-fitting clothing, winter or summer; shod them with thin shoes, ones that leak; keep them in the open air in all seasons and all kinds of weather; feed them plain and simple meals at irregular hours; permit them lots of sleep in a hard bed; accustom them to early rising. One more dictum, ''a great influence on the health: they should go to stool regularly.'' Here, as with all his precepts, Locke insists that ''the great Thing to be minded in Education is what Habits you settle'' (ibid., par. 18).

After explaining how the child's body is to be disciplined, Locke turns to the ''principal Business'': that of ''setting the mind right that on all Occasions it may be disposed to consent to nothing but what may be suitable to the Dignity and Excellence of a rational Creature'' (ibid., par. 31). To do this, to make the mind ''obedient to discipline and pliant to Reason,'' we must begin early, while the mind is ''most tender, most ready to be bound'' (ibid., par. 34). Unless we get the young child to submit his will to the reason of others, he will never be able to submit it to his own reason when he grows up. Therefore, Locke points out, liberty and indulgence can do no good for children. Lacking judgment of their own, they *need* restraint and discipline. So parents and tutors must establish their authority over them. Initially, they must secure this power through fear and awe; later, through love and friendship (ibid., par. 42).

After insisting that the first task is to ''curb'' and ''humble'' the child's mind, Locke adds a caution: the child's ''spirit'' must not be abused nor broken (''much''), else they lose all vigor and industry, becoming worse off than before. Thus he condemns corporal punishment except in cases of obstinance. He also rejects rewards: ''they serve but to increase and strengthen those inclinations which 'tis our Business to subdue and master'' (ibid., par. 55).

How then should education proceed? Locke suggests that parents and tutors use the strategy of esteem and disgrace. Of all possible stratagems, these, he says, are the most powerful: ''if you can once get into Children a Love of Credit, and an Apprehension of Shame and Disgrace, you have put into them the true Principle, which will constantly work and incline them to the right'' (ibid., par. 56). Rules and precepts are of little help here. Practice alone will get this love of reputation and fear of disgrace into the child. Practice begets habits, and habits are the stuff of education.

Once again Locke enters a caution. Although the educator's task is the inculcation of habits of body and mind, the learning of these habits ought not be a burden or a task. The tutor should heedfully lay hold of the favorable seasons of aptitude and inclination (ibid., par. 74).

In addition to working with the child's own dispositions and aptitudes, the tutor must instruct by example. The great danger to the child comes from servants and ill-ordered children who set before him undesirable patterns of behavior. For this reason, Locke advises parents to educate their children at home rather than send them to school.

After explaining in general terms his theory of how the gentleman must educate or discipline his son, Locke turns to the aims of education: "That which every Gentleman (that takes any care of his Education) desires for his Son, besides the Estate he Leaves him, is contained (I suppose) in these four Things: *Virtue, Wisdom, Breeding* and *Learning*" (ibid., par. 134).

Significantly, he places *Virtue* first as the most necessary endowment that belongs to a gentleman. The virtuous man is "valued and beloved by others." A virtuous ruling class will forestall frequent revolutions and anarchy. Similarly, a wise ruling class will stabilize the society, for by *wisdom* Locke means the prudential managing of private and public affairs. And *breeding,* too, is a requisite because the well-bred man will neither incur nor evince disrespect. The rule of good breeding is "Not to think meanly of ourselves, and not to think meanly of others" (ibid., par. 141).

Learning Locke considers of less importance than the other three aims. The sons of gentlemen ought not to be trained as scholars. To be sure, learning must be had, but it is not primary; indeed, learning is a matter of technique. Locke insists that it can be had easily and with dispatch. Reading, for example: the mother can teach the child how to read through using dice with letters pasted on them. Other games and playthings can be invented for learning language skills.

In addition to making learning more pleasant, Locke suggests discarding much of the traditional curriculum. The gentleman's son should learn French and Latin, but he need not learn grammar. Languages are to be learned naturally and directly through use. Nor should he waste time composing Latin themes, verses, and declamations. Locke proscribes the memorization of Latin passages and discounts the relevance of learning any Greek.

Having abolished much of the traditional schoolwork of his day, Locke proceeds to show how to expedite learning further by integrating the subjects studied. He suggests, for example, that Latin and French be the language of instruction for arithmetic, geography, chronology, and geometry. Moreover, by use of a globe the child can combine the study of geography and arithmetic, as well as chronology. Similarly, the study of Latin literature can be integrated with the study of ethics, and the history of the Bible with natural history.

After demonstrating how learning might be expedited by paring away irrelevant parts of the traditional curriculum and by then integrating the remaining parts, Locke advocates two studies he considered essential for the gentleman—studies not traditionally provided. The gentleman should study law, not for the purpose of becoming a lawyer but as preparation to fulfill the stations in life he may hold—"from a Justice of the Peace to a Minister of State. I know no place he can well fill without it" (ibid., par. 187). The gentleman must know the general part of civil law, including the ancient and modern interpretations of the English Constitution and government. Significantly, Locke stresses that these "are Studies which a Gentleman should not barely touch at, but constantly dwell upon, and never have done with" (ibid., par. 186). The other subject Locke holds of great importance for an English gentleman is the English language. He will constantly use this language, so he must learn to use it correctly and well—"labour to get a facility, clearness, and elegance to Express himself" (ibid., par. 190).

To round out his education, a gentleman must acquire certain skills like dancing, wrestling, and riding. And for recreational purposes he ought to learn a craft or trade—painting, gardening, woodwork, or metalwork. For practical reasons (the preservation of his estate) he should master "merchants' accounts." Locke agrees with the traditional practice of having a young gentleman make a Grand Tour, but he objects to the time this usually took place. Men are least suited for travel abroad between the ages of sixteen and twenty-one. Rather, he suggests, they might go abroad between the ages of seven and fourteen, when they could easily pick up a foreign language; or, better still, have them do it when they are older and less prone to corrupting influences.

At this point, Locke closes his essay on education. He reminds his reader that he has not presented a full treatise on education. He has merely presented some "thoughts" for those concerned with the education of a gentleman, for those especially who dare to follow reason, not custom, in the molding and fashioning of future gentlemen.

Summary and Evaluation

Locke's educational theory is of a piece with his abiding quest. From the beginnings of his intellectual career, Locke had sought a secure society: "I would be quiet and I would be safe." Secure so that he and all men could pursue the Divine Calling. The quest led him, initially, into the controversy over indifferent things. In his *Tracts on Government,* Locke put himself on the side of the government or the civil magistrate, justifying governmental imposition on political or social ground: it prevented chaos and anarchy.

Locke then sought justification for the authority of the civil magistrate in the doctrine of natural law. These theological speculations led him to epistemology, resulting in his monumental *Essay concerning Human Understanding*. Here he revealed the vastness of human ignorance, save for the certain knowledge of natural morality and religion, thereby vindicating his belief in the Divine Calling of all men.

To pursue the calling, men needed freedom. In his *Letter concerning Toleration,* Locke insists that the state must guarantee freedom to each man, providing him with security, protecting him from interference as he pursues, in his own way, the Divine Calling. Locke justified this protective function of the state in his *Treatise on Civil Government,* where he explains the purpose and the origin of the state. He argues that men create governments in order to protect themselves, to secure their natural rights. When the government does not protect them, men have the right to rebel and overthrow the government.

To quell the fears of continual anarchy and chaos presaged by his revolutionary doctrine, Locke published his *Thoughts concerning Education*. Approaching education in terms of its political function, he construed it as a bulwark against anarchy. A ruling class that was virtuous, wise, and wellbred would be the best guarantee against rebellion and revolt.[9]

By approaching education this way, Locke inevitably created an authoritarian educational theory. He openly admits this authoritarianism in his *Thoughts,* declaring that he has designed an education "for a Gentleman's son, who being then very little, I considered only as white Paper, or Wax, to be moulded and fashioned as one pleased" (*Thoughts,* par. 215).

The authoritarianism of his educational theory grows directly out of the inadequacy of Locke's protectionist theory of government. Locke saw, rightly I think, that the government existed to protect the people, and in addition that the people must be protected against the government. But Locke regarded revolution or the threat of revolution as the only way for people to protect themselves against government. Of necessity then, the stability of the society rested in the hands of the rulers. They, and they

9. Locke later displayed this safeguard or security conception of the political function of education in a memorandum he wrote in 1697 to the Board of Trade proposing a solution to the problem of unemployment and pauperism. Part of his "solution" lay in the creation of compulsory working schools "for the children of the poor." All those receiving poor benefits would be forced to send their children between the ages of three and fourteen to these schools where they would "be kept in much better order, be better provided for, and from infancy be inured to work." This last, he adds, "is of no small consequence to the making of them sober and industrious all their lives after." H. R. Bourne, *The Life of John Locke* (Oxford, 1894), 2:383–84.

alone, would either provoke the people to revolt or secure peace and tranquility. Herein lies the genesis of Locke's authoritarian educational theory. The miraculous power of education will make all sons of gentlemen into ideal rulers.

But education cannot make someone an ideal ruler. True, we should hope for the best rulers; but we should prepare for the worst, relying on built-in or institutionalized checks on the power of rulers, checks that hold them accountable. Such institutionalized arrangements must be manned, continually maintained and frequently renewed, which means that *all* citizens must be educated to know what their rights are and how well the existing institutions function to protect them. Such an education cannot be in the Lockean authoritarian mode; it must be in the critical mode.

Rousseau's *Emile*

One fine summer's day in 1749, a solitary walker on the road from Paris to Vincennes had, so the story goes, a vision. The solitary walker was Jean Jacques Rousseau. The vision occurred as he read a newspaper advertisement about an essay contest sponsored by the Academy of Dijon. The subject proposed for the essay was "Has the restoration of the sciences and arts tended to purify morals?"

"From the moment I read these words," Rousseau later wrote, "I beheld another world and became another man." He entered the competition, and his essay won first prize. In his discourse he took the negative side, or, as he expressed it, the side "which becomes an honest man who is sensible of his own ignorance, and thinks himself none the worse for it."

Progress in the arts and sciences, Rousseau argued, has added nothing to our real happiness, has corrupted our morals and vitiated our taste. Mankind, he claimed, should lift up hands to heaven and pray: "Almighty God! Thou who holdest in Thy hand the minds of men, deliver us from the fatal arts and sciences of our forefathers; give us back ignorance, innocence and poverty which alone can make us happy and are precious in Thy sight."

This sounds outlandish. Children of enlightenment, we tend to hold that the advancement of knowledge or the advancement in the arts and sciences is somehow connected with the advancement of happiness, morality, and taste. How could Rousseau have denied this?

Rather than trying to understand the force of Rousseau's thought through fascinating, but necessarily tenuous, biographical probings into the mind and heart of Jean Jacques, we can, I think, look to the logic of the situation in eighteenth century political theorizing and gain an understanding of his thought by seeing Rousseau's essay as an attack on the central doctrines of the philosophes. In fact, by seeing Rousseau in the context of a battle against the philosophes, the total fabric of his thought can be woven together, revealing his educational writings as tracts for political reconstruction.

I

For the philosophes, the most crucial problem of modern civilization was the problem of freedom. They proposed that man could be free only if he lived according to the laws of nature. Having witnessed the remarkable results of the work of Newton and the discoveries made by other scientists during the preceding century of genius, the philosophes argued: (1) that there were natural laws that regulated society; (2) that a free society was one that followed these natural laws; and (3) that reason could discover such natural laws, since they were in harmony with the canons of reason.

The philosophes used the concept of nature or of natural law as a weapon in assailing the vestiges of feudalism in France. These vestiges, which consisted of a plurality of autonomous powers and privileges—the powers and privileges of the nobility, the powers and privileges of the towns, and the powers and privileges of the church—all curtailed freedom. The philosophes argued that these vestiges must be eliminated because they were unreasonable, hence unnatural. Voltaire attacked the power and privileges of the Catholic church, seeking to replace what was unreasonable with deism—a natural religion.[1] Those philosophes who

1. Voltaire, *Poeme sur la loi naturelle* and his article, "Lois, civiles et ecclesiastiques," in his *Philosophical Dictionary,* trans. Peter Gay (New York: 1963).

were physiocrats, like Quesnay, attacked the contemporary economic structure with its antiquated privileges, its inconsistent systems of weights and measures, its frustrating trade barriers. They sought to replace what was unreasonable with laissez-faire—a natural economy.[2] Condorcet made a wholesale attack on the remnants of feudalism, arguing that only if these unreasonable vestiges were removed could the natural law take effect.[3]

The institution that had already done most in the way of eliminating the feudal society was the monarchy. It was to the monarch, then, that the philosophes turned as the despot to remove those vestiges that inhibited freedom. The monarch, of course, must know the natural laws in accordance with which society was to function: the despot must be enlightened. Once enlightened, the monarch would eliminate the plurality of autonomous powers in order to create a new society that would be natural, reasonable, and free.[4]

This rationalist approach to the problem of freedom allowed the philosophes to ignore the possibility that the enlightened despot might turn out to be a tyrant. The philosophes equated enlightenment with goodness and purity, so for them a *tyrannical* enlightened despot was a logical impossibility. Rousseau opened his attack against the philosophes' rationalist solution to the problem of freedom with a salvo against this equation of enlightment with goodness. He contended that, rather than moral improvement, progress of the arts and sciences contributed more to the corruption of morals.

II

"Before art had moulded our behavior and taught our passions to speak an artificial language, our morals were rude, but natural," Rousseau explains. Progress in the arts and sciences had made men artificial, corrupted them from their original innocence. Not that human nature was better before, but men were open, childlike, and ingenuous. They could see through one another so they had no need to dissemble, to conceal, to lie, or to cheat.

Starting from the same premise as the philosophes—to live according to nature is to live morally—Rousseau concludes that progress in the arts and sciences contributed to the corruption of morals simply because he

2. Francois Quesnay's *Tableau economique* (1758) is the principal manifesto of the physiocrats.

3. Marquis de Condorcet, *Esquisse d'un tableau historique des progrès de l'espirit humain* (*Sketch for a Historical Picture of the Progress of the Human Mind*) (1795).

4. See George Lefebvre, "Enlightened Despotism," in *The Development of the Modern State,* ed. Heinz Lubasz (New York: Macmillan, 1964).

rejected their second premise: to live according to nature is to live according to reason. Completely ignoring "natural law" and following Montaigne (whom he called "wise"), Rousseau equated "nature" with "primitivism," thus placing nature in direct opposition to civilization. By restricting "nature" to its factual or "primitive" use, he was able to argue that nature and reason were antithetical. The progress of reason, which advanced the arts and sciences, made society less natural. Once man had developed the cunning of reason, morals became corrupted.

In presenting his empirical or "primitive" conception of what it meant to live according to nature, Rousseau begins to unveil the sociological void in the thought of the philosophes. The philosophes believed eighteenth-century France could become a free society if it functioned according to natural laws knowable through reason. In focusing on the ideal, on what ought to be and not on what is, the philosophes ignored concrete society. They sought absolute freedom: dispelling the remaining, unnatural vestiges of feudalism would, they thought, usher in the totally free society. Dedication to the rational ideal of absolute freedom blinded them to the coercion implicit in every society. No real society can have absolute freedom. This is the message of Rousseau's second essay: *A Discourse on the Origins of Inequality.*

III

In order to know the origins of inequality, Rousseau says, we must know man. And in order to know man, he continues, we must know man as he came from the hands of nature. We must know man as he existed in his primitive state. It is difficult to do this, for every advance made by the human species removes it still farther from its primitive state. However difficult this task might be, we must, he insists, gain this information if we are to know man as he naturally is. "What experiments," he asks, "would have to be made to discover the natural man?"

Those philosophes who had inquired into the foundation of society had felt the necessity of going back to a state of nature, Rousseau points out. "But," he adds, "not one of them has got there." What, then, must man have been like as he came from the hands of nature? According to Rousseau, "We behold in him an animal weaker than some, and less agile than others, but taking him all around, the most advantageously organized of any." From the equation of "nature" with "primitive" it follows that man, natural man, is an animal—a happy animal and, above all, a free animal.

In his primitive state man does not fear nature because all that he perceives proceeds in a uniform, regular manner. Nor has he fear of savage animals, even those that exceed him in strength, because he is more adroit than all of them. He is less subject to sickness because the causes of illness (i.e., idleness, excessive fatigue, anxiety, gluttony) are foreign to him. Nor does he suffer from the quackery of physicians whose ministrations, more often than not, aggravate wounds and maladies. Primitive man *has* neither clothing nor shelter, it is true, but this means that he becomes hardened and inured to the inclemencies of weather and the rigors of the seasons.

Solitary, indolent, and perpetually accompanied by danger, his chief and almost sole concern is with self-preservation, which means that his senses of sight, hearing, and smell are developed to an exceedingly fine and subtle condition. Destitute of any species of intelligence, his passions spring from the simple impulse of nature. Primitive man is not evil, cannot be evil, because he is ignorant of vice. The only goods he recognizes in the universe are food, a female, and sleep; the only evils he fears are pain and hunger. He has no fear of death, for no animal (and primitive man is indeed an animal) can know what it is to die.

Because in this primitive state man's imagination paints no pictures, because his heart makes no demands on him, he does not want to change things. He lacks foresight and curiosity: "without any idea of the future . . . his projects, as limited as his views, hardly extend to the close of day."

But mankind did not remain in this happy and free state where desires never went beyond physical wants. Man's imagination, in time, conceived of new desires, desires for more than he actually needed. In this way, civil society was founded. "The first man is he [who], having enclosed a piece of ground, bethought himself of saying, 'This is mine,' and found people simple enough to believe him, was the real founder of civil society."

It is in the founding of society that Rousseau finds the answer to the search for the origins of inequality. With the founding of society, men become mutually dependent upon one another. It is in this mutual dependence and in the reciprocal needs that unite them that the bonds of servitude are formed.

With the founding of society, original man, natural man, vanishes; with him natural happiness and natural liberty disappear. Men, when they became civilized, when they came to live in society, all found themselves in some degree slaves: "if sick, they stood in need of the services of others; if poor, of their assistance; and even a middle condition did not enable them to do without one another."

Since society alters and transforms man from his natural inclinations, what is to be done? Something must be done because man is no longer happy, no longer free. Must societies be totally abolished? "Must we," Rousseau asks, "return again to the forests to live among bears?" For some men, Rousseau admits, retiring to the woods is about the best thing they could do. But most men "can no longer subsist on plants or acorns, or live without law and magistrates,'' and so man ''must remain in society and respect the sacred bonds of the community, loving his fellow citizens, obeying the laws, honoring wise and good princes.'' But, concludes Rousseau, the society must be based upon a constitution for which the people do not have contempt.

A Discourse on the Origins of Inequality was not well received by the philosophes. Rousseau had taken their weapon—that man should live according to nature—and look at the results! Taking ''nature'' in its purely primitive sense, Rousseau had shown what a life according to nature would be like. Voltaire's reaction was typical: ''I have received your book against the human race and thank you for it. Never was such cleverness used to make us all stupid. One longs on reading your book to walk on all fours.'' [5]

But Voltaire and other philosophes did not grasp the full significance of the discourse. Rousseau, it is clear, did not want men to return to nature, to a primitive existence. He wanted man to live in society. But in society, as he tried to show in the discourse, natural freedom simply could not exist.

''Natural'' freedom, as Rousseau has shown, is complete freedom: it is incompatible with society because coercion is the essence of society; without laws that impose restrictions on people, no society could exist. This being so, the problem Rousseau now confronts—since he does not want to return to living in a state of nature—is to find some suitable form of society in which these coercions could be made bearable, could be legitimatized. He attempted this in *The Social Contract*.

IV

''Man is born free; and everywhere he is in chains.'' With this dramatic paradox, Rousseau introduces his attempt to solve the problem he had set himself in the preceding discourse. How did this change come about? ''I do not know,'' he answers. What can make it legitimate? ''That question I think I can answer.''

The chains that bind men are the necessary coercions that exist in any society. Who rightfully or legitimately has the authority to impose these coercions? The philosophes had ceded the authority to an enlightened monarch who understood the natural laws according to which society ought to function. The authority of the monarch in their scheme of improvement would destroy the other authorities in the society: the authority of the towns, of the nobles, of the clergy. With all authority in his hands, the enlightened despot could create a free society.

---

5. Quoted in Bertrand Russell, *A History of Western Philosophy,* 14th ed. (New York: Simon and Schuster, 1964), p. 688.

Aware of the possibility that the monarch, however enlightened, might become a tyrant, Rousseau insists that no man has natural authority over his fellows. And if a man voluntarily subjects himself to a king, he alienates himself—he sells himself, and in return for what? Civil tranquility? Possibly; but the monarch's ambition, his insatiable avidity, and the vexatious conduct of his ministers are all more likely to bring war than peace (*Social Contract,* bk. 1, chap. 4).

To give increased power to the monarch, as the philosophes advocate, is to court tyranny. Therefore, a man who sells himself in return for this tyranny is out of his mind. And to say the same for a whole people is to suppose a people of madmen. A king has no right over other men, for "madness creates no right." Even if each man could alienate himself, Rousseau adds, he could not alienate his children. They are born free, their liberty belongs to them, and no one has the right to dispose of it.

Rousseau concludes that for a man to give up his liberty is to act against his nature; it is to act immorally. "To renounce liberty is to renounce being a man, to surrender the rights of humanity and even its duties. For him who renounces everything, no indemnity is possible. Such renunciation is incompatible with man's nature; to remove all liberty from his will is to remove all morality from his acts" (ibid.).

Instead of subjecting himself to a king, Rousseau argues that man must obey himself alone. The only legitimate source of coercion is from the wills of those coerced. His quest for legitimate authority has led Rousseau to the authority of the people. They must agree to the laws, the restrictions that bind them. Their agreement alone confers legitimacy on those laws. "Conventions form the basis of all legitimate authority among men."

Rousseau's problem now is to find some form of society wherein all men will agree to the laws and restrictions imposed on them. This requires some kind of compact, a "social contract." By engaging in the social contract man will give up his "natural freedom," his unlimited right to everything he tries to get and succeeds in getting. But in return he gains civil freedom, which is the freedom appropriate to man in society. Natural liberty, Rousseau explains, is bounded only by the strength of the individual, whereas civil liberty is limited by the general will. The general will is the cornerstone of society. It is the essence of the social contract: "Each of us puts his person and all his power in common under the supreme direction of the general will, and in our corporate capacity we receive each member as an indivisible part of the whole" (ibid., bk. 1, chaps. 6 and 8).

According to Rousseau, whenever people form a group, there emerges what he calls the general will. As the will of the individual seeks the individual (or private) good, so the general will of the group seeks the common or public good: what is good for the group or the society.

The general will is different from, and indeed superior to, the will of all, since the latter takes only private interests into account. Further, the general will is always right, although the deliberations of people are not always correct. Thus, if there is to be a social contract, people must overcome their private interests and look only to their common interests. They must subordinate private or individual goods to the public or common good. Rousseau insists that all people must do this if the social contract is to endure. Whoever refuses to obey the general will "shall be compelled to do so by the whole body." This compulsion is justified, Rousseau notes, because it "means nothing less than that he will be forced to be free" (ibid., bk. 1, chap. 7).

Of course, force will not be adequate to the social engineering task of getting people to place themselves under the general will. This is basically a task for education. Six months after the publication of *Social Contract,* Rousseau brought forth *Emile,* a treatise on social reconstruction through education.

V

Any suggestion that *Emile* be taken as a work of social reconstruction implies that in this work Rousseau was concerned with the education of citizens. Immediately a contradiction confronts us: Rousseau's declared intentions in the opening pages of *Emile* constitute an explicit rejection of the training of citizens. He says that "forced to combat either nature or society, you must make your choice between the man and the citizen; you cannot train both." He then declares his intention to educate not the citizen but the man: "When he leaves me, I grant you, he will be neither a magistrate, a soldier, nor a priest; he will be a man."

In dealing with this explicit refutation of my suggested interpretation, we must first note that—as others have pointed out (especially William Boyd)—Rousseau's disavowal of citizenship education in *Emile* is at odds with his other writings on education.[6] In an article on "Political Economy," for example, published in the *Encyclopedia* seven years before the publication of *Emile,* Rousseau emphatically emphasizes that the aim of education is the making of citizens:

> A real nation cannot exist without freedom any more than freedom can exist without virtue. Make the citizens good by proper training and everything else follows. Without that, there will only be a nation of slaves, including the rulers. Such a civil education is not the affair of a day. If from infancy children are led to think of their personal interests as com-

6. William Boyd, *The Emile of Jean Jacques Rousseau* (New York: Bureau of Publications, Teachers College, Columbia University, 1962), editor's Epilogue.

> pletely bound up with the interests of the state and never to regard their own existence as having any meaning apart from it, they will come in time to identify themselves in some measure with the grand *Whole* and become conscious of themselves as members of their country. . . . Public education regulated by the state, under magistrates appointed by the supreme authority, is an essential condition of popular government. If children are educated together as equals and have the laws of the state and the maxims of the general will instilled into them as worthy of respect above all else, they will assuredly learn to regard each other as brothers, and to desire only what the community desires. In course of time, they themselves will become the defenders and fathers of the country whose children they have been.

Again, in his "Memorandum on the Government of Poland," written eleven years after the publication of *Emile,* Rousseau stresses even more strongly the citizenship aim of education:

> It is education that should put the national stamp on men's minds and give the direction to their opinions and tastes which will make them patriots. From birth and all through life the child should only have eyes for his native country. It is love of country that makes a man what he is. By himself, he counts for nothing. If he loses his fatherland, life ends so far as he is concerned: if not dead, he is worse than dead.

How can these two strong pleas for education for citizenship, written before and after the publication of *Emile,* be reconciled with its disavowal in the book itself? Boyd explains the contradiction by distinguishing between Rousseau's concern with private education and his concern with public education. Thus, according to Boyd, when Rousseau wrote about private education (as in *Emile*), he took the self-realization of the individual as the aim of (that kind of) education, but when he wrote about public education (as in the article on "Political Economy" and the "Memorandum on the Government of Poland"), he took citizenship as the aim of (that kind of) education. Although we can view education for individuality and education for community as complementary, these two ideals, Boyd maintains, are never reconciled in the thought of Rousseau. "Rousseau's mistake was to stop at *either-or;* either education for individuality, or education for community. Faced with the problem of educating the individual for life in the community, Rousseau seems to have given two contradictory answers."

I do not happen to think that Rousseau was inconsistent in his views of the aim of education. To assume that he was, and then to use his advocacy of public education at one time and private education at another in an attempt to explain this supposed inconsistency, overlooks the fact that different means can be used to accomplish the same end. If we give Rousseau the benefit of the assumption of consistency in his views on the aims of education, then what needs explaining is his advocacy of public education in one place and his advocacy of private education in another. A clue to an explanation is contained in the early pages of *Emile:* "The public institute does not and cannot exist, for there is neither country nor patriot. The very words should be struck out of our language. The reason does not concern us at present, so that though I know it, I refrain from stating it" (*Emile,* bk. 1).

Although Rousseau refrains from stating why "the public institute does not exist," why "there is neither country nor patriot," from his earlier writings we already know: the existing state is not a legitimate state; it is not founded upon a social contract, which alone can make it legitimate. When Rousseau in *Emile* explicitly seeks to combat society, we must understand that he has a specific society in mind: eighteenth-century France. When he wrote the "Political Economy," Rousseau did not make this distinction between a legitimate and an illegitimate state. In that work he argued for a public education for citizenship, just as he did in the later "Memorandum on the Government of Poland," where he assumed an existing legitimate state. But in *Emile* he does not want his pupil educated for citizenship in the existing illegitimate state. Rather than conform to the existing state, he wants his pupils to reconstruct it. Rousseau had to shift from a public to a private form of education because the established institutions of what might be called public education in eighteenth-century France completely supported the (illegitimate) status quo.

If this interpretation is correct, Rousseau's advocacy of private education in *Emile* represents merely a change in strategy, or in means, not a change in aim. His educational aim was constant in all his works. The aim of education is citizenship, but citizenship in a legitimate society, a society based on the social contract.[7]

VI

"God makes all things good; man meddles with them and they become evil." In this opening sentence of *Emile,* Rousseau once again repeats his belief that natural man (primitive man) is much better off than modern, societal man because natural man is happy and free.

In *The Social Contract* Rousseau had stated his conviction that modern men could recapture the happy and free state of natural existence by

7. Further support for my interpretation of the *Emile* is found in a letter Rousseau sent to his publisher, Duchesne, on 23 May 1762: "this work, [*The Social Contract*] having been cited several times and even summarized in the treatise on education [*Emile*] should be considered as a kind of appendix to it. . . ." Quoted in Roger D. Masters, *The Political Philosophy of Rousseau* (Princeton: Princeton University Press, 1968), p. xiii.

placing themselves under the general will, thereby creating a society based on the social contract. Men must make a moral-social decision to place themselves under the general will. But Rousseau realized that rational as such a decision is, modern men would not make it because such decisions are a product of man's emotions, and in the existing society man's true emotions had been thwarted, dried up, in fact all but eradicated.

For this reason, Rousseau insists that his pupil, Emile, be taken away from, indeed, out of, the society—not, as he remarks, so that he may become a barbarian, but so that he may "see with his own eyes and feel with his own heart." Emile's bucolic surroundings are designed to free and preserve his natural emotions. Once the innocence of the natural state is recaptured and Emile is allowed to develop in such a way so that he does "feel with his own heart," then, Rousseau tells us, Emile will make the natural, moral decision—the right moral decision—to place himself under the general will and thus seek the common good.

At this point, it may be well to compare the views of Locke and Rousseau on freedom. Both Locke and Rousseau agreed that human beings are not, and cannot be, absolutely free: society imposes restrictions on the individual. Locke wanted to limit those restrictions. He tried to do this through the notion of natural rights; society (the state) should not restrict individuals from the enjoyment of their natural rights. Freedom for Locke is the absence of restraint or coercion. In Locke's world, one had limited freedom to enjoy one's natural rights, rights that no one was supposed to interfere with, contravene, or restrict.

Unlike Locke, who wanted to limit the restrictions on the individual, Rousseau wanted to legitimize the restrictions. The only source of legitimacy, he argued, was the will of those being restricted—they had voluntarily to accept the restrictions. Thus, a society with legitimate restrictions is one where the people themselves have agreed to those restrictions. And since such restrictions can, and usually do, interfere with the individual's pursuit of his own interests or goods, Rousseau argued, people will accept such restrictions only if they do place the common good above their own private good.

It is important to note that his quest for legitimate restrictions led Rousseau to a conception of freedom quite different from that of Locke. For Locke, freedom was the absence of coercion. This is sometimes called negative freedom. Rousseau, however, construed freedom as something positive: being able to do as one wishes. But since the power of being able to do as one wishes can never be absolute—there are always physical, social, and political restrictions—then, freedom in the real world, Rousseau somewhat paradoxically concludes, is the willing acceptance of restrictions. That is, to be free in the physical world, the social world, the civic world, one must voluntarily restrict what one wishes to do: a free person wants to do only what is possible to do in those worlds.

And this is what education is all about: getting people to accept voluntarily those necessary restrictions. "The true free man wants only what he can get, and does only what pleases him." This, Rousseau notes, is his "fundamental maxim." When we apply it to childhood, he explains, all the rules of education follow (*Emile,* bk. 2).

Through education, the child brings his desires and his powers into harmony. This harmony comes about as the child voluntarily agrees *not* to want anything that is proscribed by the physical, moral, or civic worlds in which he lives. This is, Rousseau assures us, a natural developmental process. The key to education consists in following nature. Little children are weak and dependent. When he is young, the child is not aware that he inhabits a moral world, a social world, a political world. The child is apolitical, asocial, and amoral. He is simply aware that he lives in a physical world, and therefore the only law he can recognize is the law of necessity. What the child gets, then, he should get because he needs it, not because he asks for it. Moreover, Rousseau adds, the child should never act from obedience but only from necessity. We must banish the words "obey" and "command" from our vocabulary when we speak to children. Nor should we use the words "duty" and "obligation." These words are meaningless to the child, who can only, at this stage, recognize the physical laws of necessity. The child is weak and the adult is strong. The child must know that he is at the mercy of the adult. In the physical world the weak are always at the mercy of the strong—this is the law of necessity.

Thus, to follow nature at this early stage of the child's development, we must make him dependent upon things only. His unreasonable wishes should meet with physical obstacles only, or with punishments that result from his own actions. From such experiences, the child will learn what is possible, what not. The law of necessity, the only law the child is able to recognize, will teach him to want only what he can get and do only what pleases him. Quite early, Rousseau suggests, the child should feel the

> . . . heavy yoke which nature imposes on man, the yoke of the necessity of things as opposed to human caprice. If there is anything he should not do, do not forbid him, but prevent him, without explanation or reasoning. Whatever you give, give at the first word without prayers or entreaty, and above all, without conditions. Give with pleasure, refuse with regret, but let your refusals be irrevocable. Your 'no' unuttered must be a wall of brass which the child will stop trying to batter down once he has exhausted his strength on it five or six times (ibid.).

Unlike Locke, Rousseau did not want the tutor to reason with the young child. "If children understood reason, they would not need education,'' he charges. Moreover, this early education should be negative, not positive. Instead of doing as Locke suggested—trying to inculcate virtuous habits into children—Rousseau would have the tutor simply preserve ''the heart from vices and the mind from error.'' No one should try to give the young child moral instruction. Nor, at this time, should he receive any instruction in subject matter: no language instruction, no geography, no history, or instruction in reading. Instead of fancy gadgets for teaching reading (Locke had suggested the use of dice with letters on them), Rousseau announces a better course is merely to create the desire to read, through letters and notes from friends and relatives, for example.

In this early education, the focus is on the body and the senses—their nurture and development through experience. Given such an education, the child by the age of twelve is strong, healthy, keen, eager, and full of life; free from gnawing cares and painful forebodings, the child is absorbed in his present state. Unlike the child raised by Locke's tutor, Rousseau's pupil, Emile, will not know the meaning of habit, routine, and custom. (''The only habit the child should be allowed to contract is that of having no habits.'') Rousseau offers a comparison between twelve-year-old Emile and a pupil of the same age, raised as Locke would do it:

> Your scholar is subject to a power which is constantly giving him instructions; he acts only at word of command; he does not eat when he is hungry, nor laugh when he is merry, nor weep when he is sad, nor offer one hand rather than the other, nor stir a foot unless he is told to do it! Before long, he will not venture to breathe without orders. What would you have him think about when you do all the thinking for him? He rests securely on your foresight; why should he think for himself? He knows you have undertaken to take care of him, to secure his welfare, and to feel himself freed from this responsibility.

But look at Emile, nature's pupil:

> . . . he has been trained from the outset to be as self-reliant as possible; he has not formed the habit of constantly seeking help from others, still less of displaying his store of learning. On the other hand, he exercises discrimination and forethought; he reasons about everything that concerns himself. He does not chatter; he acts. Not a word does he know of what is going on in the world at large, but he knows very thoroughly what affects himself. As he is always striving, he is compelled to notice many things, to recognize many effects; he soon acquires a good deal of experience. Nature, not man, is his schoolmaster, and he learns all the quicker because he is not aware that he has any lesson to learn.

Around the age of twelve, the child is ready for a new mode of instruction. Until now, he has recognized only the law of necessity. Now he can have regard for utility as well. The child of twelve is curious about the world in which he lives. He can and will learn geography, beginning with the place in which he lives. He can and will learn natural science—those things he needs to know, those things that interest him. "What is the use of that?" is the question always on the lips of both the tutor and the pupil. The education of this period focuses on those things recognized as useful: astronomy, physics, and chemistry—the useful parts thereof—are quickly and easily learned, as are industrial arts, agriculture, and applied mathematics.

Through the laws of necessity and utility, Emile learns how to live in the physical world, the world of nature and things. He now knows much about the relations between man and things, but nothing yet about the moral relations between man and man. Moral education cannot occur before adolescence, Rousseau insists. This is because learning to live in the moral world has its own law: the law of love. At the onset of adolescence, Emile is completely egocentric. He loves or cares for no one but himself; he seeks only his own self-interest. Until this time, Emile loves his sister like his watch and his friend like his dog. But during this adolescent period, the child becomes capable of loving others.

During this period, the tutor extends the child's love of self to the love of his fellowman. At this point Emile is made to witness the sufferings of humanity, with the caution that he, too, could likewise suffer. The enthusiasm of Emile's overflowing heart—the heart of the adolescent—identifies him with his fellow creatures. This empathy for his fellows leads him to resolve, a resolution of the heart, that he will not let them suffer lest he should suffer too. Emile has become aware of his moral nature. He is a man—he will not dishonor mankind.

Here, once again, we see a marked contrast between Locke and Rousseau; this time in their conceptions of moral education. Both viewed morality as restraint on behavior. Locke thought that the restraints must be imposed early, deliberately, and thoroughly—as habits. Later, when he grows older, the child would understand and appreciate the reasons for such restraints.

Rousseau claimed that moral restraints must be self-imposed, voluntarily, when the child reaches adolescence. The basis for such restraints, he held, is not reason but emotion: one refrains from actions that hurt another because one loves one's fellow humans. Such love of others is not possible until adolescence, when it emerges as a natural, spontaneous extension of one's natural love of self.

Rousseau charges that Locke's "imposed" morality prevents the child so educated from ever becoming morally autonomous. Moreover, the use of the tactic of self-esteem in dealing with young children, as Locke suggests, makes them, Rousseau says, perpetually dependent on what others think of them. Concern with reputation is the tomb of virtue, Rousseau insists.

By the age of eighteen, Emile has entered the moral world, but he is not yet ready to enter the social or civic world. He knows little about society, a world from which he has been so far isolated. The initial introduction comes through the study of history. Through history, man's social and political relations can be studied from afar. Through history, Rousseau can get Emile to project beyond himself even further. More important, through history, Emile can confront and assess alternatives of life and society. Ultimately, however, Emile must experience the world directly.

Before taking Emile away from his books and into society, Rousseau must prepare him for a most controversial aspect of that society—religion. Just as Rousseau views education in terms of the creation of a more perfect society, and just as he views psychology in the same context, so he also pictures religion. Rousseau's natural religion is designed to give sanction to all that he has been trying to teach Emile thus far. In essence, it is that God, the omnipotent, is in all men. God, therefore, is the basis of the self-love that all men feel. And when man extends this self-love to his fellow creatures, he is loving not only them but God as well. By loving God (and men), man will not only love the good; he will be good, he will be just. In this way, he and his fellow creatures will be happy. Since true religion is of the heart, then all religions, Rousseau says, must be equally of value. Armed with this knowledge of true natural religion, Emile is equipped to face the contending religious factions in society with equanimity. He will not be swayed by their prejudices.

Emile, predictably, is dismayed by his first contact with society, dismayed by Paris, where "the women have ceased to believe in honor, and the men in virtue." The reason for this trip to Paris was to find a wife for Emile. Not finding anyone suitable in Paris, Emile's tutor suggests they travel a distance away from Paris. Soon Sophy is found, and she and Emile fall deeply in love. But Rousseau has not yet finished Emile's education. Indeed, all he has taught him so far is merely preparatory for what is to come next. Although Emile wants to marry Sophy, Rousseau will have none of it, and for the first time, he speaks harshly to his pupil:

> You hope to be a husband and a father; have you seriously considered your duties? When you become the head of a family, you will become a citizen of your country. And what is the citizen of the state? What do you know about it? You have studied your duties as a man, but what do you know of the duties of a citizen? Do you know the meaning of such terms as government, laws, country? Do you know the price you must pay for life, and for what you must be prepared to die? You think you know everything, when you really know nothing at all. Before you take your place in the civil order, learn to perceive and know what is your proper place.
>
> Emile, you must leave Sophy . . . (ibid., bk. 5).

Emile has learned to consider himself in his moral relations with other men and in his physical relations with nature and things, but he must now consider his civil relations with his fellow citizens. He must leave Sophy because Rousseau proposes to teach him these duties through travel—not travel to observe foreign lands but to observe foreign nations. Emile is told that he must become aware of the existing alternatives so that he can choose what sort of man he wants to be; choose how he wants to spend his life and where he wants to live. Rousseau explains to the reader that in trying to answer these questions, Emile will gain "a full knowledge of questions of government, public morality, and political philosophy of every kind."

In a passage obviously referring to the lack of impact of his earlier works on political philosophy, Rousseau points out that "the chief difficulty" in getting people to consider the "is" and the "ought" of government is to induce an individual to discover and answer these two questions: "How does it concern me; and what can I do?" Rousseau notes that Emile's education has provided him with the freedom and the desire to decide for himself what he wants to do and where to live.

Before the journey, Emile is instructed in how government ought to be, which instruction turns out to be a synopsis of all that Rousseau had said in his *Social Contract*. The journey itself takes two years, and at the end, Rousseau asks Emile for his decision. He answers that the more he studies the works of men in their institutions, the more clearly he sees that in their efforts after independence, they become slaves, and that their very freedom is wasted in vain attempts to assure its continuance. Rousseau is pleased. "I knew what the results would be before our travels; I knew that when you saw our institutions you would be far from reposing a confidence in them which they do not deserve."

But what will Emile be? Where will he live? The answer he gives is that it doesn't matter.

> What matter it where I am? . . . . Rich or poor, I shall be free. I shall be free not merely in this country or in that; I shall be free in any part of the world. All the chains of prejudice are broken; as far as I am concerned, I know only the bonds of necessity. I have been trained to endure them from my childhood, and I shall endure them until death, for I am a man; and why should I not wear those chains as a free man, for I should have to wear them even if I were a slave, together with the additional fetters of slavery.

But is this all? Is this the culmination of Rousseau's battle with the problem of freedom? Is the answer of the Stoics the only answer after all? Not quite—and this I take to be the genius of Jean Jacques Rousseau. For the Emile that he has created is to be an apostle and an exemplar. Emile realizes that no existing society is based on a social contract, but *he* is devoted to the common good. Emile realizes that the existing laws are unjust, but *he* is just. Emile realizes that the existing laws have not made men free, but *he* is free; *he* can rule himself. Emile is the prototype of those who will place themselves under the general will—those who will make the social contract. For now he is to live, with Sophy, among his fellows as if there were a social contract. Rousseau, the tutor, explains this to Emile:

> Do not say therefore, 'what matter where I am?' It does matter that you should be where you can best do your duty; and one of these duties is to love your native land. Your countrymen protected you in childhood; you should love them in your manhood. You should live among them, or at least you should live where you can serve them to the best of your power, and where they know where to find you if ever they are in need of you. There are circumstances in which a man may be of more use to his fellow countrymen outside his country than within it. Then he should listen only to his own zeal and should bear his exile without a murmur; that exile is one of his duties. But you, dear Emile, you have not undertaken the painful task of telling men the truth; you must live in the midst of your fellow creatures, cultivating their friendship in pleasant intercourse; you must be their benefactor, their pattern; your example will do more than all our books, and the good they see you do will touch them more deeply than all our empty words (ibid.).

Emile will be a model for other men, teaching them by living what Rousseau had been trying to teach them by writing *A Discourse on the Moral Effects of the Arts and Sciences, A Discourse on the Origin of Inequality,* and *The Social Contract.*

Summary and Evaluation

Rousseau, more than any other thinker in modern times, confronted the problem of freedom and authority. Insisting (correctly, I think) that natural or complete freedom is not possible in society, he argued (incorrectly, I think) that a free society was one that had a legitimate authority. For him, the legitimate authority was the general will: men who followed the general will give up their natural freedom, but they secured civil freedom.

A search for a legitimate authority is a search for a final authority—an infallible authority. To search for the legitimate authority is to take seriously the question of sovereignty: "Who should rule?" Since Plato, political theorists had asked this question and had come up with a variety of answers: the wisest should rule, the bravest should do it, the holiest, the richest. Rousseau proposed that the "general will" of the society should rule, and he suggested that the will of the majority be taken as the expression of the general will. This answer is, of course, authoritarian, as are all answers to the question of sovereignty. The question "Who should rule?" demands an authoritarian answer.

Rousseau's proposals for education are in keeping with the tradition of political authoritarianism. He turns to education to secure acquiescence to the legitimate authority. Education will secure political socialization. Rousseau, however, like many of his interpreters, was blind to the authoritarianism of his total political-educational theoretical system because he believed that it was "natural" for civil men to obey the general will. That is, once man leaves the state of nature and lives in society, it is no longer "natural" to follow his individual will. Therefore, Rousseau insists that with the right kind of education—one that preserves the original innocent condition of children—men will "naturally" obey the general will; they will seek the common good.

Rousseau proposes a novel approach to the educator. No longer the imposer, the teacher is a guide—a preserver and guardian of the young. Nothing seems less authoritarian than this "natural education." Nevertheless, it is authoritarian. Rousseau uses his truly keen insights into human nature and human development to concoct an educational process that will control and manipulate the young. He counsels teachers to let the pupil "always think he is master, when you are really master." Then, in a relevant aside, he says, "There is no subjection so complete as that which preserves the forms of freedom" (*Emile,* bk. 2). When the child reaches adolescence and is stronger than the teacher, he is to be controlled through his emotions: "His first affections are the reigns by which you control his movements; he was free, and now I behold him in your power" (ibid., bk. 4). The tutor's function is to manipulate the young toward a preordained political end: acquiescence to the general will, in actual practice, acquiescence to a voluntary acceptance of the infallible authority of the majority.

Mill's Logic

Sometime during the winter of 1821–22, sixteen-year-old John Stuart Mill read Jeremy Bentham's *Treatise on Legislation*. "I felt taken up," he reports, "to an eminence from which I could survey a vast mental domain and see stretching out into the distance intellectual results beyond all computation." When he laid down the last volume, he had become a "different being." He was, he now confessed, a utilitarian. From this point on, the principle of utility became the keystone that held together his knowledge and his beliefs. "I now had opinions; a creed, a doctrine, a philosophy; in one of the best senses of the word, a religion, the inculcation and diffusion of which could be made the principal outward progress of a life." Perhaps most important, that doctrine of utility supplied "a grand conception . . . of changes to be effected in the condition of mankind." [1]

For five years, John Stuart Mill remained a true believer. He diligently diffused and logically inculcated the principle of utility in his untiring efforts to improve mankind and reform the world. Then, in the autumn of 1826, the keystone of his beliefs and actions crumbled. At the age of twenty-one, Mill underwent a "crisis" in his "mental history" that laid bare the inadequacy of that doctrine of utility. Raised to become the paramount "utilitarian" of his day, John Stuart Mill now confronted the debacle of his education. His desire to improve mankind never lagged, nor did he ever stop wanting to be a utilitarian. But before he could improve mankind, before he could again *be* a utilitarian, he had to reconstruct the doctrine, converting it into a theory of education that would guarantee the improvement of mankind.

I

Like most of us, utilitarians believed that everybody wants to be happy. But perfect happiness, Jeremy Bentham (1748–1832) believed, belonged to the imaginary realm of philosophers. Real men, in the real world, should strive for a more modest goal: the maximization of happiness.

How? Well, happiness, according to Bentham, is pleasure; and so to increase or maximize happiness, we simply increase pleasure and diminish pain. Bentham believed that human beings are selfish and egoistic: they seek their own happiness. We cannot change human natures, nor should we try. Rather, we should arrange things so that the greatest number of people can actually attain the happiness they seek. It is the environment or the society we must change (not the people); we must change it so that individuals, while seeking their own private happiness, will actually perform in ways that maximize the happiness for all in the society.

Yet, "society" is, in fact, a "fictitious body," having no existence apart from the individuals who make it up. So what we actually change are the laws. Through the science of legislation, society could discourage mischief, those antisocial acts that cause pain to others. The way to do this was to select in advance the appropriate punishment for each crime. But since the aim of legislation was to maximize the sum total of happiness, then the pain caused by a given punishment ought not to exceed the pain it prevented through deterrence. Bentham's "object all sublime," as

1. What Mill read in 1821 was Dumont's French redaction of Bentham's *Traite de Legislation*. Mill's recollection of this episode is in his *Autobiography* (New York: Columbia University Press, 1924), pp. 45–47.

Gilbert and Sullivan parodied it in *The Mikado,* was "to make the punishment fit the crime." Bentham went so far as to concoct a "felicific calculus," a moral arithmetic to measure pains and pleasures so that legislators could construct appropriate punishments to fit specific mischiefs.

What made Bentham's theory of morals and legislation appeal to John Mill and to others was how it made the task of human improvement so plain, so direct and simple. Laws, politics, and actions improved the human condition if they maximized happiness. Utilitarianism made it unnecessary to worry about abstractions like natural rights or the state of nature or the social contract. All that mattered were the consequences of human behavior: did it increase pleasures and diminish pain? or not?

The utilitarian philosophy supplied social reformers with a new weapon to assail authoritarianism, a new basis for pleas for liberty. It became the creed of many nineteenth-century liberal reformers, earning them the label "Benthamites" or, later, "philosophical radicals." As social reformers, they would imitate God. For just as God had created laws for the universal happiness of mankind, so now they would create laws for the happiness of their society.

II

Even before he had read the *Treatise on Legislation,* John Mill's education had been, in a certain sense, a course in Benthamism. He had taken that course at home under the tutelage of his father, James Mill, who was Bentham's most famous disciple. ("Bentham's prime minister," as some people called him.) During John's early years, Bentham took an active role in the supervision of the boy's education when the Mill family spent the summers on his estate. Together, James Mill and Jeremy Bentham set out to make John "a successor worthy of both of us." [2]

John Stuart Mill began the study of Greek at age three, Latin and arithmetic at eight, logic at twelve, and political economy at thirteen. James Mill had strongly held often ingenious theories about the instructional process. He introduced his three-year-old son to Greek with the help of cards containing common words together with their English meaning. The child learned to recognize them by association to the common objects they represented. Once he mastered the basic vocabulary, James Mill set young John to translating Aesop's fables, next Herodotus, and then on to Xenophon. Only later did the young scholar learn grammar—and only later still did he understand what he had read. In the evenings,

2. Élie Halévy, *The Growth of Philosophical Radicalism* (London: Faber and Faber, 1949), pt. 2, chap. 2, sec. 3.

his father taught him arithmetic. These two subjects—along with the reading and writing of English—were his sole studies until he was eight. At that age, he added Latin, algebra, and geometry. Latin he learned as he had learned Greek: reading Cicero straightaway. By the time he was twelve, he had read Ovid, Livy, Virgil, Horace, Lucretius, Tacitus, and Juvenal. In mathematics young Mill soon outstripped his father, who, rather than spare the time from his own work to keep ahead of his pupil, merely exhorted him to get on with it.

John Mill later described how he studied Latin and Greek at a table across from his father, who was engaged in writing his monumental *History of British India.* Since he had no lexicons for Latin and Greek, the boy had to ask his father the meaning of every word he did not know. Yet, John says, "This incessant interruption, he, one of the most impatient of men, submitted to, and wrote under that interruption several volumes of his *History* and all else that he had to write during those years."

Francis Place, a friend of James Mill, confirms reports of the severe dedication of James Mill to the education of his children. In a letter to his wife, Place wrote:

> . . . they have a hard time of it, learning their lessons every morning from eleven to one, and learning again in the afternoon—learning too, with a precision unknown to others. . . . [James Mill] is beyond comparison the most diligent fellow I ever knew or heard of; almost any other man would tire or give up teaching, but not so he; three hours every day, frequently more, are devoted to the children and there is not a moment's relaxation. His method is by far the best I have ever witnessed, and is infinitely precise; but he is excessively severe. No fault, however trivial, escapes his notice; none goes without reprehension or punishment of some sort.

When John had learned Latin, his father assigned him the task of teaching his younger brothers and sisters. This young Mill continued to do for over a decade, until he had educated all eight of them to his father's satisfaction. And his father held him strictly accountable. Here is an incident from one of Francis Place's letters:

> Lessons have not been well said this morning by Willie and Clara; there they are now, three o'clock, plodding over their books; their dinner, which they knew went up at one, brought down again; and John, who dines with them, has his books also, for having permitted them to pass when they could not say; and no dinner will any of them get until six o'clock. This has happened once before since I came. The fault today is a mistake in one word.[3]

---

3. Michael St. John Packe, *The Life of John Stuart Mill* (New York: Macmillan, 1954), p. 34.

Later, John Mill admitted that he considered this to have been an inefficient way to educate his brothers and sisters, although it greatly enhanced his own education: he learned more thoroughly and retained more lastingly those things he was set out to teach. "Perhaps too," he added, "the practice it afforded in explaining difficulties to others may even at that age have been useful."

Besides studying and teaching what his father assigned, John began writing histories at the age of eight—"for his own amusement." His father encouraged him, but with pedagogical sagacity judiciously never asked to see what his son wrote, so that John recounts he did not feel "the chilling sensation of being under a critical eye."

At the age of twelve, John was well beyond his father in mathematics and could understand both Greek and Latin as easily as English. He had composed verses in English and read some poets—Milton, Goldsmith, Burns, Gray, Spencer, and Dryden—but none of the Romantic poets of his own time. At this point he began the more advanced stage of his education, where the main object was thought itself. Logic became his principal study. Through his father's persevering drill, young Mill gained proficiency in dissecting bad arguments and uncovering fallacies. In his *Autobiography,* Mill strongly endorses the study of logic (over mathematics) as the way to train people to think. And more important: it teaches them how to engage in critical dialogue. Mill insists that logic be taught early so that people

> may become capable of disentangling the intricacies of confused and self-contradictory thought before their own thinking faculties are much advanced . . . a power which, for want of some such discipline, many otherwise able men altogether lack; and when they have to answer opponents, only endeavor, by such arguments as they can command, to support the opposite conclusion, scarcely even attempting to confute the reasonings of their antagonists; and therefore, at the utmost, leaving the question, as far as it depends on argument, a balanced one.

During this phase of his education, John continued reading Latin and Greek authors—Demosthenes, Tacitus, Juvenal, Quintilian, Plato—but now he did it to study their thought, not their language. He would read them aloud to his father, who made interpretive comments, asked questions, and corrected his elocution.

Between the ages of twelve and fourteen, much of Mill's education came through his serving as a research assistant to his father. First, he assisted him with proofreading the *History*—learning, John reported, much about the government and institutions of both India and England. (The acclaim James Mill gained from this book when it was finally published in 1818 led to his appointment by the government to a position in

India House, where he later rose to the position of chief examiner of Indian correspondence. In 1823 he secured an appointment there for John. John remained at India House for thirty years, eventually moving up to the same position his father had held.) John Mill also assisted his father in the preparation of *Elements of Political Economy*. Together they would take long walks while James Mill lectured on his friend Ricardo's recently published *Principles of Political Economy and Taxation* (1817). Each day the father expounded a portion of the subject, and the next day the son turned in a written account—often written over and over again until it was "clear, precise, and tolerably complete." Later, the elder Mill used his son's accounts to write his own treatise—a work he referred to as his "school book on Political Economy."

John Mill was brought up from the first without any religious belief. He believed he was one of the few examples in his own country of a person who didn't throw off religious belief because he never had any. Yet he did receive moral instruction in the moral virtues of the Greek philosophers. His father, Mill tells us, in brief sentences "of grave exhortation or stern reprobation," uttered as occasions arose, decisively conveyed the Greek "moralities": justice, temperance, veracity, perseverence, readiness to encounter pain and especially labor, regard for the public good, estimation of persons according to their intrinsic usefulness, and a life of exertion in contradiction to one of self-indulgent sloth. The effect produced in the son was all the more forceful because the father embodied all these virtues. As to standards of morality, John Mill learned from the first the utilitarian test for right and wrong: good acts produce pleasure; bad acts, pain. Acts, he learned, are deemed good or bad solely by their consequences, not by the motives of the actor. The guide to good action was the intellect; it could calculate the consequences of an action. Feelings were no guide at all, there being no feeling which may not lead, and does not frequently lead, "either to good or bad actions." For passionate emotions of all sort James Mill professed—and taught his son—nothing but contempt.

Thus, before he had reached fourteen years of age, John Stuart Mill had become a human calculating machine, judging human behavior by how much happiness (pleasure) it produced.

In 1820, just before John's fourteenth birthday, his father sent him to France where he spent a happy year living with Jeremy's brother, Samuel Bentham, and his family. There John had little time to pursue his studies in mathematics, classics, and logic, but he was very busy acquiring the skills of a gentleman: dancing, riding, fencing, piano playing, and French. During the winter, he did squeeze in some lectures at the University of Montpellier on chemistry, zoology, metaphysics, and the philosophy of science. He also arranged for some private tutoring in higher mathematics.

When he returned home from France, John began what he labeled in his *Autobiography* his "last stage of education and first stage of self-education"—two names for the same phenomenon. For during this last period of education, he discovered he could not intellectually accept becoming "a worthy successor" to his father and Bentham, at least not without making modifications in the role.

III

The final stage of John Mill's education lasted until 1829. It consisted of two parts: (1) an intensive study of the basic texts of the utilitarians, and (2) an application and testing of those fundamental doctrines through active involvement in the real world of political reform.

Immediately on his return from France, his father had him prepare the "marginal contents" (a short abstract of every paragraph) for his *Elements of Political Economy,* which was now ready for publication. Soon thereafter, he read Bentham's *Traite de Legislation* with the results described earlier. As Mill said later in his *Autobiography,* that book did nothing less than "light up my life, as well as to give a definite shape to my aspirations."

But the "foundational study" most important to the utilitarians—more important than economics and political theory—was psychology, associationist psychology. David Hartley (1707–57) had first formulated associationist psychology in his *Observations on Man.* Condillac (1715–80) later developed it in his *Traite des Sensations,* as did Helvetius in *De l'Espirit.* Associationist psychology was a consistent carrying out of the contact theory of mental life. The mind, according to it, received knowledge from sensations. And all complex beliefs and habits come from associating sensations contiguous in origin. This complete passivity of the mind in obtaining knowledge is reversed in acting; that is, all acts are the result of reason. And by reason, the associationist psychologist meant the foreseeing of consequent pleasures and pain. Men always act to produce pleasure and to avoid or reduce pain.

During this last period of his education, John Mill read Hartley and Condillac and Helvetius. Just at this time, his father began to write his own book on associationist psychology, *Analysis of the Phenomena of the Human Mind.* In this book, James Mill wrote to his friend Ricardo, he hoped to make the human mind "as plain as the road from Charing Cross to St. Paul's." It did, in fact, become the classic formulation of associationist psychology. Mill reports that his father worked on it over several years, up to 1829 when it was published. He allowed his son to read the manuscript, portion by portion, as it advanced.

Of all his father's doctrines, Mill claims, none was more important, and none needed more to be insisted upon, than that principle of association: the formation of all human character by association. This was the basis for believing in the unlimited possibility of improving the moral and intellectual condition of mankind. For if all knowledge comes from sensations, and if anticipated sensations (pleasures and pain) determine all human action, then the environment is omnipotent. To change people's behavior (not their human nature), you simply have to change the environment. Here, of course, is where Bentham enters with his proposals to create an appropriate legal environment, one that will maximize the happiness of the greatest number.

In addition to legislative reform, the crusade for human improvement based on associationist psychology also demanded educational reform because people had to learn to recognize what *would* bring them happiness. They had to learn to anticipate correctly the consequences of their actions, calculating the pleasures and pains they would bring.

Obviously, the utilitarians needed a theory of education—a foundational text. James Mill supplied it, when in 1818 he published *Education* in the form of an article for the *Encyclopaedia Britannica.* His son must have read it (although he never mentions doing so) along with all the other foundational texts he studied during this period.

IV

James Mill begins his treatise on education with a predictable declaration of the purpose of education: "to render the individual, as much as possible, an instrument of happiness, first to himself, and next to other beings." [4] How are people to be educated to attain this goal of happiness? Well, happiness is the result of human actions; so it is necessary to encourage, cultivate, or instill those actions that maximize the happiness of all. Which actions are they? Acts that we usually characterize as temperate, benevolent, generous, just, intelligent, knowledgeable, and sage. Mill construes all these characteristics—or virtues, as he calls them—in utilitarian terms: as ways of maximizing happiness. Thus temperance is the resisting of a present pleasure or happiness for the sake of greater happiness. Benevolence is producing the greatest possible quantity of happiness to others; one can do this in two ways: by abstaining from doing them harm (justice), or by doing them positive good (generosity). Intelligence consists of understanding our environments, understanding "the system in which we are placed" and anticipating the consequences of our acts within that system.

How do we instill, cultivate, and develop these behaviors? Mill's

---

4. "Education," in *James and John Stuart Mill On Education,* ed. F. A. Cavanagh (Cambridge: Cambridge University Press, 1931).

answer is that we so arrange the environment that the desired behavior produces pleasure for the actor, while its opposite produces pain.

There are, Mill points out, at least five different educative environments or "systems," that determine our behavior: the physical environment, the environment of the home and family, the "technical" environment of the schools, the society or social environment, and the government or political environment.

The physical environment affects behavior through both the condition of the body (the influence of a person's health, strength, temperament, age, sex) and the conditons external to the body (the influence of climate, food, the activities we engage in). As much as possible, we should construct physical environments that encourage the development of the desired behavior, or at least environments that do *not* encourage unwanted behavior.

The special educative function of the family and home environments, Mill says, is to nurture benevolence and temperance. The schools, too, have a special educative function: to cultivate intelligence. In schools, students should acquire (1) knowledge, by which Mill means understanding of the environments (or "systems") in which they live; and (2) sagacity, by which Mill means learning how to anticipate the consequences of one's action in those environments.

The physical environment, as well as the domestic and school environments, actually exist in and are part of a larger environment—the social environment, or society. This means, Mill says, that the educative force of society is greater than the other environments. The social environment determines behavior by providing models for imitation and bestowing favorable opinions on those who please it and withholding this from those who displease it.

Yet, Mill says the most influential environment, "the keystone" of education, is the political environment. This is so in part because the nature of the social environment depends on the political. Moreover, the most important part of the physical environment (the living and working conditions of all, especially of the lower classes) is "in the long-run determined by action of the political machines." But the basic reason for the supreme educative influence of the political environment is that it determines the means by which men attain the pleasures they desire. The political environment of government creates the laws and controls the system of rewards and punishments within which men act in society. "When the political machine is such," James Mill wrote, "that the grand objects of desire are seen to be the natural prizes of great and virtuous conduct—of high service to mankind and of the generous and amiable sentiments from which great endeavors in the service of mankind naturally proceed—it is natural to see diffused among mankind a generous ardour in the acquisition of all those admirable qualities which prepare a man for admirable actions; great intelligence, perfect self-command, and over-ruling benevolence."

But when the government is controlled by a ruling few, then people can gain happiness only by serving *them* and *their* interests, *not* the interests of mankind. And in their efforts to secure those desired and scarce favors from the ruling few, people become subservient and often resort to "intrigue, flattery, back-biting, treachery, etc."

Of the five environments James Mill identified, only two—schools and government—are susceptible to direct reform. Understandably, then, it was school and political reform that occupied the attention of the utilitarians.

As early as 1809, the year after its founding, James Mill lent his support to the Royal Lancasterian Society (later called the British and Foreign School Society), which sponsored a truly fantastic scheme to disseminate schools throughout the nation. According to this plan, each school would contain a thousand children who would receive, in squads of ten, instruction from a hundred monitors, at the cost of five shillings per head per year. Joseph Lancaster, a philanthropic Quaker, had set up such a school in London, and James Mill sketched a plan for a complete system of primary and secondary education for all of London. The plan called for dividing the city into school districts to be governed by independent school committees and turning Lancaster's original school into a training school for teachers.[5]

Bentham became involved in the scheme, offering his own garden as the site for a secondary school and writing a book, *Chrestomathia,* setting forth an architectural, administrative, and pedagogical plan for the institution. The curriculum was to be based on utilitarian principles: all subjects to be taught in order of their utility, thus suppressing the classics and justifying the sciences. The teaching methods were to be utilitarian, too: maximizing the pedagogic results by minimizing the amount of pain in the teaching process.

The grand plans of the Lancasterian Society soon met severe opposition from a rival organization founded in 1811, called the National Society for Promoting the Education of the Poor According to the Principles of the Established Church. The National Society disproved educating the poor in schools that admitted youths of different sects and objected to schools that provided no, little, or watered-down religious instruction. In 1812 James Mill defended the Lancasterian schools in a pamphlet titled *Schools for All; Not Schools for Churchmen Only,* arguing that the Anglican schools were financially extravagant, "exclusive," "restrictive," and conferred too much political power on the clergy.

More than the opposition of the Anglican church, however, it was the

---

5. W. Burston, *James Mill on Philosophy and Education* (London: Athlone, 1973), esp. chap. 3, "Practical Work in Education."

bitter dissension within the Lancasterian Society itself that curtailed its growth, at least its growth in the way Mill and the utilitarians had hoped for. The leadership of the Lancasterian Society consisted of an uneasy alliance of religious dissenters, political liberals, and freethinkers. In time, the religious dissenters, led by Joseph Lancaster, denounced the antireligious tendencies introduced by James Mill and his friend Francis Place. (Both Mill and Place had argued, successfully, to suppress the society's rule that made teachers take all children to places of worship every Sunday.) The proreligion faction ultimately gained the upper hand in the society, and both Place and James Mill resigned. In 1820 Bentham refused to give the society the site promised for the erection of a school.

In their attempts to secure school reform, the utilitarians next turned to a more direct approach: the education of the "middling classes." They took over a struggling Mechanics' Institute set up by London workmen for their own education. The utilitarians transformed it into their own institution to promote political and economic emancipation. To secure the books and pamphlets necessary for such popular instruction, they formed the Society for the Diffusion of Useful Knowledge, which published them "at a cheap price for the education of the people."

Perhaps the most impressive of the utilitarian school reforms was the creation in 1828 of the University of London. This third university—the first established in England in over five hundred years—made university education free from religious tests and accessible without scholarships to students of moderate means. James Mill insisted that the professor appointed to the chair of philosophy teach Hartley's psychology. He did.

Schools, of course, provide only what James Mill called "technical education." The most important education, he claimed, came from the political environment. Government alone could create the necessary system of rewards and punishments that could educate people to act in ways that would maximize the happiness of all. As the utilitarians saw it, government had the responsibility to improve the people so that they would be happy—which, after all, is what people want. Thus it was political reform that most exercised the utilitarians, and that finally organized them, in the 1820s, into a political party called the philosophical radicals.

V

Their efforts to get at the basic philosophical roots of the problem differentiated the philosophical radicals from other radicals of the day. They went beyond matters like high taxes, nepotism, and high prices to strike at the root of the problem: the ruling class's pursuit of its own selfish interests at the expense of the public good.

It was James Mill, not the aged and eccentric Bentham, who crystalized utilitarianism into a political movement. "It was my father's opinions," John Stuart Mill later wrote, "which gave the distinguishing character to the Benthamic or utilitarian propaganda of that time." His father, he added, was "as much the head and leader of the intellectual radicals in England as Voltaire was of the Philosophes of France." Or, as Halévy tersely expressed it: "Bentham gave Mill a doctrine, and Mill gave Bentham a school." [6]

James Mill saw, perhaps more clearly than the less practical Bentham, that the necessary legal reforms they both wanted could come about only by first reforming the government. As Mill viewed the task, reform consisted of combating the "sinister" interests of the ruling elite who sought private gains incompatible with the public good. Under the pretext of protecting the people, the ruling elite—the aristocracy—secured for itself sinecures, places, and money. As a utilitarian, Mill had to concede that this venality of the aristocracy was simply the product of "the steady operation of the law of human nature,"—the aristocracy was seeking its own happiness. Yet the result for society was unacceptable: the ruling elite corrupted the purpose of government. A change was needed, a radical change in the philosophy of government.

The philosophical radicals expected to protect people from the injuries inflicted by the ruling elite by changing the existing institutions in ways that would guarantee that rulers act for the public good. What changes? The principal one was representative government. Representatives of the people would check the abuses of power. And to watch the watchdogs, the philosophical radicals further proposed near universal suffrage, a secret ballot, and annual parliaments.

According to the theory James Mill put forth in his treatise *Essay on Government,* representative government will permit all (or nearly all) people to seek their own interests through their elected representatives and thus create an identity of interests between the ruled and the rulers. Since the common good is the sum total of individual goods, then representative government, through creating an identity of interests, will maximize happiness in the society.[7]

By the 1820s, many thought it possible to carry out the reforms James Mill called for. The lessening of governmental repression of criticism and harrassment of critics during this period made this an appropriate time for the launching of the movement to improve mankind. In 1823 Bentham put up the money to finance a new journal, *The Westminster Review,* to call for the creation of a new party—a people's party. Because of his government position at India House, James Mill could not become editor of such

---

6. Halévy, *Growth of Radicalism,* p. 251.

7. James Mill, *An Essay On Government* (Cambridge: Cambridge University Press, 1937). Originally written for the supplement to the fifth edition of the *Encyclopaedia Britannica,* which was completed in 1824.

an antiestablishment periodical; but he did write a spectacular article for the initial issue—a scathing criticism of a rival journal, *The Edinburgh Review*. Mill accused that journal of adroitly manipulating public opinion on every issue that touched the interests of the governing class. It was, he insisted, purely and simply, a political organ of the Whig party.

The excitement of being in the vanguard of a movement to improve mankind now enveloped young John Mill. Indeed, he soon experienced the heady delight—at the age of seventeen!—of being one of the leaders of the movement. After serving as his father's research assistant for the article lambasting the Whigs and their journal in the first issue of the *Westminster Review,* John himself received the assignment to compose a similar attack on the *Quarterly Review,* the "political organ" of the Tory party. The article was widely acclaimed, and over the next five years the *Westminster Review* published twelve more articles by the younger Mill. John's fame further soared when Bentham insisted that his name appear on the title page of the five volumes of *Rationale of Judicial Evidence* that the young man had spent over a year editing for him.

During this period of working for and within the movement, a period he labeled in his *Autobiography* "the period of youthful propagandiam," the young Mill helped form a political discussion group he dubbed the Utilitarian Society. He also helped found the London Debating Society, where he and other young disciples of his father did oratorical battle with the Tories and the Whigs.

John Mill's smashing debut into London intellectual life confirmed his father's observation that his mental age exceeded his chronological age by about a quarter of a century. For John found himself frequently in the role of teacher to a growing number of acquaintances attracted by his impressive intellectual attainments and his devotion to the cause of reform. Many of this coterie had recently come down from Cambridge, where, using the elder Mill's articles and tracts as textbooks, they had taken the side of reform in debates in the Cambridge Union. Contact with the disputatious young Mill turned their disposition toward reform to zeal for the program of philosophical radicalism.

The argumentative young utilitarian was no dogmatist. His father had trained him too well as a reasoning machine who prized critical analysis above all. And critical he was: of the Tories and the Whigs, but also, increasingly, of the basic ideas of the philosophical radicalism he had been educated to diffuse and inculcate.

During this period of his education—the beginning of his self-education—Mill founded a study group that set out to analyze critically the foundation texts of the movement. Starting off with James Mill's *Elements of Political Economy,* the group worked its way through Ricardo's *Principles of Political Economy and Taxation* then on to some books on logic as a preparation for Hartley's *Observations on Man,* and finally,

James Mill's *Analysis of the Human Mind.* "With this," Mill says, "our exercises ended," adding: "I have always dated from these conversations my own real inauguration as an original and independent thinker."

The group met twice a week. At each meeting, one of them read aloud a chapter or some smaller portion of the book under review. There followed a no-holds-barred critical discussion, with every objection, great or small, thoroughly examined until all were satisfied. They followed every topic the chapter or the conversation suggested, never leaving it until they had "untied every knot they had found."

Such freewheeling, wide-ranging, vigorous dialogue with the razor-sharp young intellects Mill had assembled naturally uncovered inadequacies in some of the doctrines of the philosophical radicals, leaving them unraveled. Sometime during these sessions, Mill resolved to write his own treatise on political economy and one on logic, too. He planned these works as emendations to the foundational doctrines. Only later, with the onset of his "mental crisis," did Mill discover that philosophical radicalism needed a totally new philosophical foundation—a philosophical foundation that led him to a new political theory *and* a new theory of education.

VI

It began in the autumn of 1826. Mill was twenty. He was, he tells us, "in a dull state of nerves, such as everybody is occasionally liable to; unsusceptible to enjoyment or pleasurable excitement." He goes on:

> In this frame of mind, it occurred to me to put the question directly to myself: "suppose that all your objects in life were realized, that all the changes in institutions and opinions which you are looking forward to could be completely effected at this very instant: would this be a great joy and happiness to you?" And an irrepressible self-consciousness distinctly answered, "No!" At this, my heart sank within me: the whole foundation on which my life was constructed fell down. All my happiness was to have been found in the continued pursuit of this end. The end had ceased to charm, and how could there ever again be any interest in the means? I seemed to have nothing to live for.[8]

His education had failed. Educated for happiness, he recognized he was neither happy nor had any expectations of ever being so. Taught that doing good is the source of human happiness, Mill still believed—but he did not feel happy.

The depression lasted for months. He mechanically carried on his

8. J. S. Mill, *Autobiography,* p. 94.

work at India House and even continued many of his activities among the philosophical radicals. But he did so without the same feeling, the same excitement as before. He had no one he could talk to. Above all, he could not even mention it to his father. His education had been the work of his father. The failure of that education lay beyond the power of *his* remedies.

His education, he now saw, had cultivated his intellect at the expense of his feelings. Having no feelings, he had no real desires; hence, no motivation to act for the general good, the improvement of mankind. Without feelings, he could not become a moral being. He was but half a man.

For a time, Mill feared himself incapable of any feelings. Then, sometime in the spring of 1827, while reading a passage in Marmontel's *Memories* that describes the feelings of Marmontel had upon the death of his father, Mill was overcome and moved to tears. At last he knew he could feel. Gradually he worked his way back to normalcy, finding pleasure in the ordinary conditions of life: sunshine and sky, books, conversation, public affairs, and even in exerting himself for the public good.

As a result of this experience, Mill learned not to make his own happiness the aim of his life, but to accept it as something that comes *en passant* from the pursuit of other objects: the happiness of others, the improvement of mankind, or art. This theory became the basis of his life. He never wavered in the utilitarian conviction that happiness is the end of life, but now he believed he could attain that end only by not making it the direct end.

Aside from this rule for living, Mill drew an educational lesson from his bout with mental depression: the necessity to cultivate feelings. Feelings, he now believed, were the springs of morality; without their cultivation, people would not become moral beings. Poetry and art he found the best means of cultivating the emotions. His first reading of the poetry of Wordsworth became an important event in his life. In Wordsworth, he found medicine for his state of mind, expressing "states of feeling and of thought covered by feeling under the excitement of beauty." He never turned against the culture of the intellect, but from this time forward, he actively sought to complement this aspect of his education with the cultivation of the emotions. The cultivation of both the intellect and the feeling led to what he now began calling—to differentiate it from the hedonism of the vulgar utilitarians—the "higher happiness."

Yet, what Mill calls his "mental crisis"—actually the "crisis in my mental history"—lasted until the early 1830s. The psychological depression of 1826–27 was but a symptom of the crisis he endured. This crisis in his mental history was at root an epistemological crisis. The utilitarian doctrine on which John Mill had been raised was false—at least it had a false conception of how we acquire knowledge. This false epistemology had led James Mill to provide his son with an inadequate education.

Stressing cognitive development alone, James Mill, in his educational program for his son had overlooked the necessity of emotional cultivation. John Mill now came to see that his father had overlooked the importance of feelings to human nature and to human morality simply because James Mill's approach to knowledge systematically excluded them. And in that chapter in his *Autobiography* when he describes the crisis in his mental history, John identified what had brought on the crisis in his mental history: Thomas Macaulay's slashing critique of James Mill's *Essay on Government,* a critique that laid bare the epistemological inadequacy of utilitarianism.

VII

Macaulay begins his essay, which appeared in the *Edinburgh Review* in 1829, with a graceful tribute to James Mill: "Of all the philosophers who call themselves Utilitarians, and whom others generally call Benthamites, Mr. Mill is, with the exception of the illustrious founder of the sect, by far the most distinguished." Continuing in the same respectful tone, Macaulay turns to the *Essay on Government,* "perhaps the most remarkable of the works to which Mr. Mill owes his fame." The members of Mill's sect, he notes, consider it "perfect and unanswerable"—no man, they mantain, can read this masterpiece of reasoning and remain unconvinced.[9]

"We have," Macaulay counters, "formed a very different opinion of this work."

With verve and audacity, the twenty-nine-year-old Whig proceeds to take on the whole utilitarian movement—a movement he tells us, made up of ordinary men with narrow understandings and little information, "whose attainments just suffice to elevate them from the insignificance of dunces to the dignity of bores."

With unerring accuracy, Macaulay zeroes in on the crucial point in the *Essay on Government:* the notion of "identity of interests." The only way to prevent rulers from seeking their own selfish interests, Mill had argued, was through a representative government elected by the people so that the rulers would have an identity of interests with the entire society and thus seek the happiness of all. But, Macaulay points out, those representatives, once elected, will become an aristocracy, an elite, who, according to the basic doctrine of the utilitarians themselves, will seek their own happiness. Thus, according to the utilitarians' very philosophy of human nature, an identity of interests is not possible. Of course, Mill had suggested annual parliaments as a further mechanism to secure an identity of interests. But, Macaulay counters, the elected rulers can seek their

9. Thomas B. Macaulay, "Mill on Government," in Macaulay's *Prose and Poetry,* ed. G. M. Young (Cambridge, Mass.: Harvard University Press, 1952).

own interest by simply changing the laws—to make themselves rulers for life, if they so choose. Moreover, Macaulay continues, Mill's plan of a limited universal suffrage further obviates the possibility of an identity of interest between rulers and ruled. For Mill denies the right to vote to women, to the very poor, and to the young—not to mention denying it to those generations yet unborn. How could Mill assume that elected representatives would ever have an identity of interest with all those excluded from the franchise? Here again, Macaulay reveals, the very utilitarian doctrine that man is a pleasure-seeking organism contradicts the possibility of there ever being an identity of interest between rulers and ruled.

But, logical contradictions aside, suppose the utilitarians got their dream, and a representative government came about. What then? Would this result in the maximization of happiness for the greatest numbers? Not likely, Macaulay sniffs. It will usher in raping and plundering—of the rich—resulting in chaos and, ultimately, barbarism. Why? Once again, because, according to the utilitarians, men are selfish and seek only their own pleasure.

If James Mill is correct, Macaulay concludes, then *all* rulers would always plunder and terrorize the people. Mill himself had argued that this is exactly what happened under monarchy and under aristocracy. Now Macaulay has simply turned the same criticism back on representative government.

But, to be sure, this is all nonsense! Macaulay cries. In the real world, rulers simply do not behave the way James Mill says they do. We have not, Macaulay insists, suffered unceasing oppression and terror: "During the past two centuries, some hundreds of absolute princes have ruled in Europe. Is it true that their cruelty has kept in existence the most intense degree of terror, that their rapacity has left no more than the bare means of subsistence to any of their subjects, their ministers and soldiers excepted? Is it true of all of them? Of one-half of them? Of one-tenth part of them? Of a single one? Is it true, in the full extent, even of Philip the Second, Lewis the Fifteenth, and the Emperor Paul?"

Yet, why refer to history? Macaulay shrugs: no man of common sense can live among his fellow countrymen a day without seeing innumerable facts that contradict Mill's claim about government.

But why does James Mill propound such nonsense about governments? In part, Macaulay explains, this is because Mill takes an admittedly true proposition about human nature and interprets it too narrowly. It is, Macaulay agrees, absolutely and universally true that men always act from self-interest. But Mill interprets this to mean that men have no desires but those which can be gratified only by spoliation and oppression. This is assuredly false; men, Macaulay reminds us, certainly have some desires that they can gratify only by pleasing others. And this fits rulers, too.

James Mill had looked at only one half of human nature and he had based his deductions about government on this narrow, and therefore false, premise. Therefore, his conclusions about governments—existing and proposed—were absolutely false.

But Mill's perversion of an absolutely true proposition about human nature is understandable, Macaulay explains. For only by making such a narrow interpretation could he draw any deductions from the proposition. This is because the proposition "man always acts for self-interest" is what Macaulay calls an "identical" proposition: we can deduce nothing from it. Macaulay illustrates: "One man goes without a dinner that he may add a shilling to a hundred thousand pounds; another runs into debt to give balls and masquerades. One man cuts his father's throat to get possession of his clothes; another hazards his own life to save that of an enemy." Each of these men, Macaulay agrees, has acted from self-interest. But in no case could we have reasoned with certainty from what we might have taken his interest to be, to those actions. The doctrine of self-interest means only that men, if they can, will do as they choose. Only when we see the action of a man, Macaulay concludes, do we know with certainty what he thinks his interest to be.

Here we reach Macaulay's "fundamental objection" to Mill's approach to government. For, since there is but one absolutely and universally true proposition about human nature, but a proposition from which it is impossible to deduce any proposition about human behavior (except by misconstruing and falsifying that proposition, as Mill had done), then, Macaulay argues, "it is utterly impossible to deduce the science of government from the principles of human nature." Mill's attempt to approach government in this way marks him "an Aristotelian of the fifteenth century, born out of due season." What Mill gives us, Macaulay quips, is an elaborate treatise from which "but for two or three passing allusions, it would not appear that the author was aware that any governments actually existed among men."

Instead of this a priori approach of Mill, the only way to develop a science of government, Macaulay insists, is through the method of induction: "by observing the present state of the world,—by assiduously studying the history of past ages,—by shifting the evidence of facts,—by carefully combining and contradicting those which are authentic,—by generalizing with judgment and diffidence,—by perpetually bringing the theory which we have constructed to the tests of new facts,—by correcting, or altogether abandoning it, according as those new facts prove it to be partially or fundamentally unsound."

This "inductive" approach, Macaulay declares, is a reasonable, healthful, and generous way to approach the science of politics. As for the utilitarians' quibbling about self-interest, motives, objects of desire, and the greatest happiness of the greatest number—well, this is a "poor employment for a grown man." And yet, Macaulay finishes, "it certainly hurts the health less than hard drinking, and the fortune less than high play: it is not much more laughable than phrenology, and is immeasurably more humane than cock-fighting."

John Stuart Mill never forgave Macaulay. His father did, even going so far as to help Macaulay secure a position with the government in India a few years later. But not John. Here is the younger Mill's appraisal of Macaulay in 1855: "He is what all cockneys are, an intellectual dwarf—rounded off and stunted, full grown, broad and short, without a germ of principle of further growth in his whole being." [10]

Yet, it is to Macaulay that John Mill owes his own intellectual odyssey. For Macaulay had crystalized Mill's mental crisis, making clear why the famous educational experiment had failed. It had failed because his father, James Mill, had approached education the same way he had approached government, the same way he had approached all matters: deducing proposals from a fundamental theory about human nature. But that theory of human nature was too limited and inadequate. He, John Stuart Mill, was living proof of its inadequacy. An education deduced from that theory of human nature had created but half a man—a human reasoning machine that could not feel. John Mill never abandoned utilitarianism. He never rejected associationist psychology. Above all, he never gave up his faith and hope in the improvement of mankind. But he now saw—and this was his "mental crisis"—that the enterprise of human improvement required a firmer epistemological foundation than his father and Bentham had given it. Nor could he accept Macaulay's proposal for an "inductive" approach. (Mill insisted Macaulay never understood what induction was, and he relabeled Macaulay's approach, calling it "empirical.")

What was needed, Mill realized, was a new approach to knowing: a method through which we can attain true propositions about human nature, propositions that have empirical content. The quest resulted in his greatest intellectual production, *A System of Logic, Ratiocinative and Inductive,* a work Mill was to spend over ten years completing.

In the meantime, during the 1830s, John tried to salvage what he could of the utilitarian philosophy and the program of the philosophical radicals. After 1829, the year Macaulay's article appeared, Mill says he withdrew from the debating society. Actually, as many commentators have noted, after 1829 John Mill seemingly all but abandoned the philosophical radicals, remaining aloof from politics at the very moment popular demand for universal suffrage had become so great that Parliament finally passed the Reform Bill in 1832. He played no role in agitation for the bill and took no great joy in its passage into law. He had had "enough of speechmaking," he later explained and was glad to carry on his private studies and meditations.[11]

10. F. A. Hayek, *John Stuart Mill and Harriet Taylor, Their Correspondence and Subsequent Marriage* (London: Routledge and Kegan Paul, 1951), p. 155.

11. Joseph Hamburger, *Intellectuals in Politics: John Stuart Mill and the Philosophical Radicals* (New Haven: Yale University Press, 1965), chap. 3, "John Stuart Mill as a Philosophical Radical."

And well he might. For, during this period, he found the fabric of his ideas and opinions—taught him by his father and Bentham—giving way "in many fresh places." He never allowed it to fall into tatters, but he found himself "incessantly occupied" with weaving it anew. The first public display of the new pattern John was weaving in his efforts to patch up the fabric of utilitarianism appeared in a series of essays published in 1833. He called them "The Spirit of the Age."

Macaulay's devastating critique had convinced John Mill that good government could not be based—as James Mill had based it—on the creation of an identity of interest between rulers and ruled. On what then could it be based? At this juncture, John Mill found an answer in the theories of Auguste Comte (1798–1857). Good government, according to Comte, is the independent product of a specially educated few. In a passage (later discarded) in an early draft of his *Autobiography,* Mill wrote:

> I no longer believed that the fate of mankind depended on the possibility of making all of them competent judges of questions of government and legislation. From this time, my hopes of improvement rested less on the reason of the multitude than on the possibility of effecting such an improvement in the methods of political and social philosophy as should enable all thinking and interested persons who have no sinister interest to be so nearly of one mind on these subjects as to carry the multitude with them by their united authority.[12]

This was the message he tried to express in "The Spirit of the Age" in 1833. Adopting one of Comte's concepts, Mill claims that the spirit of the age is one of transition. People now perceive the inadequacies of the old doctrine, the old institutions, the old leaders. But newer, more adequate ones have not yet appeared: we are living in an age of transition. How can we move into something more stable? [13]

Widespread critical discussion, Mill points out, has led to the uncovering of the inadequacies of the old ways. But criticism will not lead us to the new answers, the new doctrines, and the new institutions society needs. It is right that men should follow their reason and cultivate that faculty as highly as possible, Mill notes, but, he adds, reason itself will teach men that they must, in the last resort, fall back on the authority of still more cultivated minds as the ultimate sanction of their own motives. The "more cultivated minds" he had in mind, Mill tells us, were "those who have made moral and social philosophy their peculiar study." Unfortunately, he admits, we do not yet possess the wisdom necessary to create

---

12. John Stuart Mill, *The Early Draft of John Stuart Mill's Autobiography,* ed. Jack Stillinger (Urbana: University of Illinois Press, 1961), pp. 188–89.

13. John Stuart Mill, "The Spirit of the Age," in *Essays on Politics and Culture,* ed. Gertrude Himmelfarb (Garden City, N.Y.: Doubleday, 1962).

the new age. What we now require in the moral and social sciences, he says, are methods of inquiry like those already developed in the physical and mathematical sciences. Only then will we be able to find the political and moral truths the society needs; only then will we have the real moral and social authorities we need. Mill's efforts to develop such methods took him longer than anticipated, but in 1843 *The System of Logic* appeared.

VIII

Mill's problem in the *Logic* was to determine what is science, what is not. Once he did this, he could establish a science of society, a science that would serve as the basis for rational governmental legislation. Mill realized that the principle of utility could not serve as the basis of such a science. Not that he rejected utility, but rather that he now saw that utility must be viewed as the end or aim of government, not as the premise from which legislation could be deduced. Moreover, lest anyone confuse his notion of utility with the hedonism of Bentham, Mill explains in the *Logic* that it is the "higher happiness" that he had in mind: "the cultivation of an ideal nobleness of will and conduct." This nobleness of character, he concludes, "will go farther than all things else towards making human life happy—both in the comparatively humble sense of pleasure and freedom from pain, and in the higher meaning of rendering life not what it now is almost universally—servile and insignificant, but such as human beings with highly developed faculties can care to have." [14]

The principle of utility supplied the end of government: the government was to promote happiness (higher happiness). However, no rule or plan of action follows from an aim. His father had mistakenly thought it did and had tried to deduce a science of government from the principle of utility. Macaulay had shown how wrongheaded this geometrical approach was. But Macaulay's empirical approach would not do either. For you cannot create a science of government from gross empirical facts. In any science, Mill insists, empirical observation has to be incorporated into a body of tested theory. This is the key point in Mill's criterion for science.

According to Mill, science consists of causal claims or propositions (*X* causes *Y*) that are proven. Logic Mill takes as the method of proof. Therefore, only logically derived causal propositions are to be called scientific. It is true that the causal propositions come from experience, but gross experience—such as Macaulay advocated—could not itself provide

14. John Stuart Mill, *A System of Logic, Ratiocinative and Inductive: Being a Connected View of the Principles of Evidence and the Methods of Scientific Investigation,* vol. 7 and 8 of the *Collected Works of John Stuart Mill,* ed. J. M. Robson (Toronto: University of Toronto Press, 1973).

scientific propositions. We can obtain truly scientific propositions, Mill tells us, in the following way: first, we infer (induce) general laws from particular evidence; next, we infer (deduce) particular cases from the general laws; and finally, we verify the cases by experience (experiment).

Mill spent much of the first five books of *Logic* presenting his analysis of the nature of logic (induction and deduction) and the nature of scientific experiment. Only in the sixth book does he finally come to what he calls the moral sciences, among which is the science of society. This, Mill, following Comte, calls "sociology." But at this point, Mill admits that sociology, like all the moral sciences, is different from the physical sciences. The inductive-deductive-experimental scientific method that characterizes the natural or physical sciences simply cannot be used in social matters. For, he points out, we cannot induce causal propositions in social matters because causes are too complex and effects are not easily distinguished. Moreover, in social matters, we cannot perform experiments to ascertain either causes or effects. Therefore, instead of the method used in the physical sciences, sociology must use inverse deduction, which Mill calls the historical method.

From history, we can ascertain (induce) social uniformities and social correlations that are not causal propositions but simply "trends." Yet trends can, Mill insists, provide the basis for a science of society. To render them "scientific" we must verify the trends we induce, and we do this by independently deducing them from the established laws of psychology. Thus, "inverse deduction" consists of deducing from the established laws of associationist psychology those trends we have inductively obtained from history. It is an imperative rule, Mill declared, "never to introduce any generalization from history into the social sciences unless sufficient ground can be pointed out for it in human nature" (psychology). For Mill, a science of society is only possible by reducing sociology to psychology, incorporating historical trends into the theoretical framework of associationist psychology.

After having explained the historical or inverse deductive method of sociology, Mill goes on to describe some of the laws of this science. Following Auguste Comte, Mill divides the laws of sociology into two kinds: social statics and social dynamics. Social statics consists of those laws essential for "a stable political union." The first law of social statics Mill identifies as "obedience to a government," subordinating personal impulses and aims to what are considered "the aims of society." The other two laws for social stability Mill mentions are loyalty and nationalism. Loyalty consists of a feeling that something in society is permanent, unquestionable, and certain. Nationalism, he says, creates a coherence through a feeling of common interest.

The laws of social statics we discover by analyzing and comparing different states of society, paying no heed to the order of their succession.

But in the second branch of sociology, social dynamics, we focus on those laws of succession. In other words, social dynamics reveals the laws of social progress. Here, Mill explains, one cause is paramount: social progress is the result of the advancement of human knowledge. Mill admits that only exceptional individuals are committed to the pursuit of truth; nevertheless, it is obvious that the progress of industry, for example, rests on the progress of knowledge, as does progress in the arts, in morality, and in politics.

At this point, John Mill uses the science of sociology to overthrow one of the basic tenets of utilitarianism as professed by his father and Bentham. For if, Mill argues, both stability and progress depend on the intellectual condition of the members of society, then each individual cannot be permitted to pursue willy-nilly his own self interests. So, with the aid of science, and in the name of a "higher utilitarianism," Mill now opposes the vulgar utilitarian acceptance of self-interest as the basic principle of social science. Selfishness, Mill insists, "decimates mankind." The propensity to selfishness must be submitted to a common system of opinions.

With the *Logic,* Mill has supplied the scientific basis for the task of social improvement. The historical method of sociology reveals the laws of society: the laws of social stability and the laws of social progress. We can make use of these laws in fulfilling the end of government: the promotion of happiness (the higher happiness). To promote happiness, the people must be educated. Human opinions must be transformed, diverted from the pursuit of selfish interests to a pursuit of common interests, thus creating an improved, more advanced, and stable social union where all can enjoy the higher happiness.

IX

How is mankind to be educated so that all might attain the higher happiness? Recall that James Mill had identified five educative environments: the physical, the domestic, the technical (schools), the societal, and the governmental. Of them, he held that the most influential were the social and the governmental environments. Not unexpectedly, his son now composed a treatise called *Principles of Political Economy,* which explained just how the government could create an educative environment that could help people attain higher happiness.

From the point of view of political economy, social improvement consists of improvement in the production and in the distribution of wealth. From Mill's point of view, improvement in the production and distribution of wealth was not social improvement but would lead to social improvement: by liberating people from economic worries so that they could pursue the "higher happiness." "There would be," Mill wrote, "as much scope as ever for all kinds of mental culture and moral and social progress; as much room for improving the Art of Living, and much more likelihood of its being improved when minds ceased to be engrossed by the art of getting-on." As Mill saw it, the government can improve both production and distribution through education; that is, through the adoption of policies or practices that create an educative environment that will change the behavior of people.

Yet, before Mill can get on with telling us how to improve production and distribution he must confront the Malthusian problem of overpopulation. Thomas Malthus (1766–1834) had demonstrated that improved or increased production leads to increased population, and this population must then "work harder or eat less." Ultimately, then, one had to face the dismal conclusion: increased production has always led to a deterioration in the condition of the producers. But, Mill insists there is a way to solve the Malthusian problem: population control. One of nine children, and a supporter of female emancipation, Mill was throughout his life obsessed with the absolute necessity of control over population growth. Thus, right at the outset Mill puts forth education of the people through governmental policies as the key to social improvement.

By the time he wrote his *Principles of Political Economy,* John Mill was, he tells us, very much influenced by the view of his long-time constant companion and future wife, Harriet Taylor. An ardent feminist, Harriet had not only heightened his concern with population control, but in addition, Mill tells us in his *Autobiography,* she had made him realize that the *real* problem of political economy was the distribution of wealth, not its production. For the laws of distribution are of human design; hence they are more open to modification and change than the laws of production. Under Harriet's influence, Mill has become a socialist: only through socialism can the inequitable distribution of wealth be overcome.

With regard to production, however, the government can do some things to create an environment that will increase productivity. For, in those countries where there is little or no spirit of industry or desire of accumulation, like the "Asiatic countries" and the "less civilized" parts of Europe, the government can do the following: it can provide more security of property, it can moderate taxes, and it can adopt more advantageous land tenure policies to guarantee profits to owners and cultivators. Another step is to introduce foreign arts as an example to the people. Most important, the government can directly improve the public intelligence by destroying usages or superstitions that interfere with the effective employment of industry, and by stimulating the people to seek "new objects of desire."

Another way the government could improve production, Mill suggested, was to promote economic competition. How could a self-proclaimed "socialist" support economic competition? The answer lies in his conception of government as first and foremost an educational agency. His is an educational socialism. This is why he argues against economic protectionism: "to be protected against competition is to be protected against idleness and mental dullness; to be saved the necessity of being as active and as intelligent as other people." Mill actually opposed governmental interference in the economy and advocated a policy of laissez-faire. A strange sort of socialist indeed! Yet, once again he does this on educational grounds.

> A people who look habitually to their government to command or prompt them in all matters of joint concern, who expect to have everything done for them except what can be made an affair of mere habit and routine have their faculties only half developed; their education is defective in one of its most important branches.[15]

Mill's socialism was simply a means to free people from poverty so that they could better pursue the higher happiness. Hence Mill explicitly repudiated "with the greatest energy" that tyranny over the individual common to most socialist systems. As he saw it, the real social problem of the future was "to unite the greatest individual liberty of action with a common ownership in the raw material of the globe, and an equal participation of all in the benefits of combined labor."

As a solution to this problem of combining equality with freedom, Mill proposes the stationary state. In a stationary, no-growth society, attention will shift from economic striving for the sake of striving. In a stationary state, he goes on, "there would be a well-paid and affluent body of laborers, no enormous fortunes, except what were earned and accumulated during a single lifetime; but a much larger body of persons than at present not only exempt from coarser toils, but with sufficient leisure, both physical and mental, from mechanical details, to cultivate freely the graces of life, and afford examples of them to the classes less favorably circumstanced for their growth."

All these seemingly contradictory economic proposals Mill makes in his *Principles of Political Economy* cohere and make sense when they are construed as an educational program. The equal distribution of wealth, the stationary state, open competition, laissez-faire—all will create an educational environment to make it possible for more people to pursue the higher happiness. Thus, the equal distribution of wealth and the stationary state would free people from economic worries: minds would cease to be engrossed with the problem of "getting-on." At the same time, an environment of laissez-faire competition would stimulate and help develop the intellectual faculties of all people.

---

15. John Stuart Mill, *Principles of Political Economy with Some of Their Applications to Social Philosophy,* vols. 1, 2, and 3 in the *Collected Works,* bk. 5, chap. 11, par. 6.

But when people no longer worried about "getting-on," would they actually pursue the higher happiness? They would, Mill argues, if they were properly guided and educated. He illustrates how this guidance and education might come about in a chapter called "On the Probable Future of the Labouring Class."

In the past, Mill says, employers held down the laboring classes, controlling the economic, political, social, and religious conditions of their lives. But this has now changed. An ever-more educative social environment had liberated the laboring classes from this domination. The penny press, institutes for lectures and discussions, collective deliberations on questions of common interest, the trade unions, political agitation—not to mention increased possibilities for schooling—all these had served to awaken the public spirit and diffuse a variety of ideas among the masses, exciting thought and reflection among the most intelligent. As a result, Mill warns, the old paternalism of the employers will no longer do: the laboring classes will become "even less willing than at present to be led and governed, and directed into the way they should go by the mere authority and *prestige* of superiors." Yet they will, Mill insists, feel respect for superiority of intellect and knowledge and will defer to *true* experts.

So far, the emancipation of laboring classes has come about because they have sought their own self-interest. Now, Mill says, the truly superior intellects—those who know the basic scientific laws of social stability and social progress—must guide and direct the laboring class so that they will develop public spirit and generous sentiments, and so that they will become concerned with the common good, the public interest. Mill advocates various forms of cooperative associations to accomplish this education: profit-sharing, collective ownership, workers' cooperatives, and wholesale societies. These associations, Mill claims, will be a course in moral and social education, transforming social life "from a conflict of classes struggling for opposite interests to a friendly rivalry in the pursuit of a good common to all. . . ."

In *The Principles of Political Economy* Mill has outlined how government can create an environment that will free people from worries about getting-on and induce them to pursue the higher happiness—the higher happiness of all. Of critical importance to these grand educational enterprises is the role of the intellectual elite, those knowledgeable in the scientific laws of social stability and social progress who must guide and direct the rest of society toward improvement. Because the improvement of society depends ultimately upon this elite, it must be protected. Mill attempted to provide such protection in his next work, *Essay on Liberty*.

X

Ever since he had read Tocqueville's *Democracy in America,* John Mill had had deep fears of what the French author had identified as "the tyranny of the majority." The greatest dangers to mankind, Mill wrote, were "not of too great liberty, but of too ready submission; not of anarchy, but of servility; not of too rapid change, but of Chinese stationariness." In two long essay reviews of *Democracy in America* published in 1835 and 1840, Mill had traced the repression and conformity Tocqueville warned about to the rise of the "commercial spirit" rather than to democracy itself. England, for example, did not have democratic equality, but all could witness there the growing insignificance of the individual. This was due, Mill argues, to the fact that the "commercial spirit" had swelled the middle class to such proportions that it was a mass, a mass so immense in size that individuals were powerless in the face of it. In England, the middle class had become an all-powerful class. (America, Mill notes, is all middle class.[16])

Those of "generous and cultivated minds" must see, Mill then warned, that "the most serious danger to the future prospect of mankind is in the unbalanced influences of the commercial spirit." They must, therefore, nourish and strengthen those other tendencies within mankind that will check that commercial spirit. Indeed, he suggests that this should become the main purpose of national education.

Now, if the intellectual elite is going to serve as a countervailing force to the burgeoning commercial spirit in society, then it will become suspect and regarded as an adversary by many. Hence the intellectual elite must be protected so that it can fulfill its function of guiding and directing the rest of mankind toward the higher happiness. In *On Liberty* Mill attempted to do this by proposing "one very simple principle"—a principle, he argues, that should govern absolutely the dealings of the society with the individual. "That principle is that the sole end for which mankind are warranted, individually or collectively, in interfering with the liberty of action of any of their number, is self-protection." This means, Mill explains, that power can be rightfully exercised over anyone *only* in order to prevent harm to others. "Over himself, over his own body and mind, the individual is sovereign." Here was a very simple principle indeed! From it, Mill concluded that all members of society should have freedom to think, feel, speak, and act without impediment from their fellow creatures "so long as what one does does not harm others." [17]

These freedoms, Mill insisted, must be absolute and unqualified because complete freedom is necessary in order to ensure human progress

16. John Stuart Mill, "De Tocqueville on Democracy in America," in *Essays on Politics and Culture*.

17. John Stuart Mill, *On Liberty,* in vol. 17 of the *Collected Works*.

and improvement. Without freedom, knowledge cannot advance and improve. Efforts to stamp out "error" may end up stamping out truth or a part of truth. Men are fallible, Mill insists, so that they never possess the whole truth; therefore, unity of opinion, unless resulting from "the fullest and freest comparison of opposite opinions," is not desirable. To foster such a critical, open outlook among people, Mill advocates that formal education adopt the mode of socratic dialectics, or even the scholastic disputations of the Middle Ages, in place of the didactic mode commonly used in schools, which simply reinforces dogmatism.

If the advancement of knowledge requires absolute freedom of thought and opinion, then the fullest development of the individual requires freedom of action. Each should be able to develop as fully as possible because in so doing, each person becomes more valuable to himself and therefore capable of being more valuable to others—as exemplars of new practices, more enlightened conduct, and better taste. Not everyone, of course, is capable of developing into becoming an exemplar for others. But exceptional people will, Mill maintains. Such genius needs freedom. Mill here "emphatically" insists on "the importance of genius and the necessity of allowing it to unfold itself freely both in thought and in practice."

The trouble, he recognizes, is that most people are simply average—moderate in intellect, moderate in inclinations. So they have no tastes or wishes strong enough to incline them to do anything unusual, and they class all who do as "wild" and "intemperate." Thus they are indifferent, even hostile, to the need for liberty and freedom. This despotism of custom, Mill concluded, is an obstacle to the improvement of mankind. And this is precisely why an ever-improving society *must* be a free society, where everyone is free to think, speak, and act as he wishes, as long as he harms no one else. Mill admits that not everyone recognizes that the spirit of liberty is the spirit of improvement; many would-be reformers seek to improve society in imposing "truth" on people and forcing them to act in predetermined ways. But, in *On Liberty* Mill has presented a nonimpositional approach to improvement: through freedom of thought, speech, and action, mankind will be able to advance toward truth, goodness, and beauty. Or at least the intellectual elite will be able to do so, and they in turn can guide and direct the rest toward this higher happiness.

XI

After having presented "one very simple principle" that would protect and secure those of "generous and cultivated minds" from the tyranny of the majority, Mill next turned to the matter of guaranteeing the intellectual elite an institutionalized role in the government itself, a place where they could actively work for human improvement. In 1861 he published his proposals under the title *Considerations on Representative Government.*

Anxious to avoid his father's mistake of deducing the correct form of government from a single principle, Mill begins by agreeing with a point made by Macaulay: each age demands a different form of government. Thus Mill suggests that people in a state of savage indolence require some form of despotic government—one that can make itself obeyed. Nevertheless, in spite of such seeming relativism, Mill insists that all governments can be judged on the same two criteria: (1) the degree to which they promote the virtue and intelligence of the people; and (2) the degree to which they organize and use the moral, intellectual, and active "worth" already existing in the society. This means, Mill explains, that a government is to be judged on how well it is adapted to the present and the future. The ideal form of government—the one that best educates the people and best utilizes educated people—is, Mill concludes, a representative government.[18]

Representative government educates people through their participation in the governmental process: it engenders public feelings, practical discipline, and moral virtue. And representative government, Mill further argues, allows people to use their own intelligence to act as wisely and as morally as they at present are. A representative government, Mill claims, frees each individual to protect his own rights and interests and to improve his own condition.

Having justified representative government on educational grounds, Mill somewhat surprisingly turns around and makes proposals to curtail the functions of the representative assembly. But he does this to ensure that the actual running of the government is in the elite hands of those already best educated.

The assembly of representatives, as Mill here construes it, is simply a debating society. He notes that many have taunted representative assemblies for being places of "mere talk and *bavardage.*" But, he replies, such derision is misplaced: "I know not how a representative assembly can more usefully employ itself than in talk, when the subject of talk is the great public interests of the country, and every sentence of it represents the opinion either of some important body of persons in the nation, or of an individual in whom some such body had reposed their confidence."

The representative assembly should not attempt to govern, Mill cautions. That is the task of the executive branch, the cabinet—those members of the body or the party "most fit" to govern. Moreover, he suggests that the representatives ought not to legislate, either. The writing of laws should be left to "professional legislators." For this, Mill proposes the

18. John Stuart Mill, *Considerations on Representative Government* (Chicago: Regnery, 1962), chaps. 2, 3. This is a reprinting of the original edition of 1861.

establishment of a Commission on Legislation composed of intelligent experts. The representative assembly would determine what laws were needed, the Commission on Legislation would compose them, and then the representatives could enact or reject them. Mill even prohibited the representatives from amending the legislation. (They could remit a law to the commission if they merely partially disapproved it, Mill advises.)

The basic reason a representative assembly cannot legislate, Mill argues, is that "they are not a selection of the greatest political minds of the country. . . ." They are, at best, "a fair sample of every grade of intellect among the people." Hence his conclusion that the proper function of a representative assembly is to initiate demands, criticize all opinions on public matters, and check the administration of the government.

But will a representative assembly, a democratic representative assembly, be able to carry out even these admittedly curtailed functions? Isn't there a danger that the representative body will have too low a grade of intelligence? And isn't there a related danger that the numerical majority will generate legislation solely favorable to its own class interests?

Mill sees the problems, and he has the solution. If the assembly has in it some, if only a few, "of the best minds in the country," then those "leading spirits," by their presence, will influence the direction *and* the level of general deliberation. "I am unable to conceive of any mode by which the presence of such minds can be so positively insured," Mill says, "as by that proposed by Mr. Hare." Thomas Hare, a barrister, had sent Mill a pamphlet expounding a system of proportional representation that, as Mill viewed it, would permit "instructed minds" scattered throughout the country to unite and elect a number—"proportional to their own numbers"—of "the very ablest men the country contains."

Even in a system of proportional representation, those of superior intellect and character will, of course, still be outnumbered. But they will be heard. In debate the others would have to meet the arguments of the "instructed few" by cogent responses. If we assume, Mill adds, that the others are well meaning, then such interchange will surely educate them: "their own minds would be insensibly raised by the influences of the minds with which they were in contact." Furthermore, Mill suggests, the members of this "instructed minority" will probably more often than others be selected to become cabinet officers, thus providing a democratic people with leaders "of a higher grade of intellect and character than itself."

Through his proposal for a Commission on Legislation and the one for proportional representation, Mill has tried to guarantee that the "instructed few" will have considerable influence in a democratic representative assembly. There remains the problem that the numerical majority has absolute power, which it can, and will, exercise in its own class interests. What is to be done? To restrict or limit suffrage is, for Mill, unthinkable for practical, as well as educational, reasons. (Mill does insist, however, on literacy qualifications for voting.) The only way Mill sees to counteract the absolute power of the numerical majority is the device of "plural voting." All should have a voice, he agrees, but not an equal voice. The "better" or "more intelligent" should have more of a voice. Thus Mill would grant a plural number of votes to university graduates and any others who could bring forth some credentials or some evidence of being "more intelligent."

The details of plural voting Mill does not go into; he merely presents it as the direction toward the "true ideal" of representative government: "It is not useful, but hurtful, that the constitution of the country should declare ignorance to be entitled to as much political power as knowledge." Everyone, of course, is entitled to some influence, but "the better" and "the wiser" are entitled to more than others. This doctrine, Mill insists, the state must profess and embody in the national institution.

John Stuart Mill's *Considerations on Representative Government* is quite different from his father's *Essay on Government.* But the son's book springs directly from his earlier *Logic,* which he composed in order to defend or rescue his father's endorsement of representative government from Thomas Macaulay's slashing attack. In the *Logic,* John Mill had fashioned a scientific approach to government (i.e., he argued that government ought to be based on the sociological laws of stability and progress). Progress consisted in enjoyment of the higher happiness, a happiness toward which all could tend provided they had the guidance of cultivated and generous minds—the instructed few. Now Mill has argued that such progress best takes place under representative government: it best promotes virtue and intelligence among the people and best utilizes those already educated. To ensure that a representative government will actually do this, however, Mill has recommended certain modifications so that the "instructed few" really can guide and direct the work of government, to wit: proportional representation, plural voting, and a Commission on Legislation.

John Stuart Mill was now fifty-five years of age. He had all but completed his appointed task of constructing a program for the improvement of mankind. All that remained was to tie it together and say a few words about the proper preparation of cultivated and generous minds—the intellectual elite who were to guide and direct the improvement of mankind. This he did in his *Address* to the students of Saint Andrew's and in the *Autobiography* that had occupied him for many years.

XII

By the mid-1860s, John Stuart Mill had become the most famous philosopher in England. His *Logic* had gone through five editions (it was to go through a total of eight editions before his death). The demand for his other books, now published (at Mill's request) in cheap "working-class editions," increased every year. The *Principle of Political Economy* alone sold over ten thousand copies in five years. Yet the great fame and bit of fortune that befell him could never offset the loss of his beloved Harriet. When, after Harriet's husband, John Taylor, had died and Mill and she married, who could have foreseen that they were to have but seven short years together as husband and wife? In 1858 Harriet had died from consumption. She had been his collaborator in all his writings since the *Political Economy*. *On Liberty,* Mill revealed, was a totally "joint production"; they had together gone over every sentence of that monograph. After Harriet's death, Mill had thrown himself more energetically than ever into his writing, completing *Representative Government* in two years while also working on his treatise, *The Subjection of Women,* which was published posthumously. This was followed by publication in 1863 of the essay *Utilitarianism* and then, while preparing the sixth edition of the *Logic* and writing a small volume, *Auguste Comte and Positivism,* Mill wrote his biggest (and least read) philosophical work, *Examination of Sir William Hamilton,* which he published in 1865.[19]

In that year, Mill was invited to run for Parliament. In spite of the severe conditions he laid down—he would not canvass for financial support, he refused to incur any personal expenses for his campaign, and he declared that if elected he would not give any time or labor to the local interests of his constituents (conditions under which someone noted the Almighty himself could not be elected)—Mill was elected. As a representative of those generous and cultivated minds, Mill spent most of his term in Parliament promoting and defending the principles of "advanced liberalism": woman's suffrage, civil liberties, proportional representation, parliamentary reform, and electoral reform—all causes he had justified in his writings as ways to improve humankind.

In the same year Mill entered Parliament, the students of Saint Andrew's University (without consulting him) elected him their rector. The following year, Mill delivered his inaugural lecture, taking the opportunity to summarize the work of his career, giving expression "to many thoughts and opinions which had been accumulating in me through life." The specific topic of the address was the central theme of Mill's life: the proper education of the intellectual elite and its role in the improvement of mankind.

Education, Mill begins, "is one of the most inexhaustible topics." This is so for Mill in large part because he had adopted his father's broad construction of educational environments; thus: "in its largest acceptation, it [education] comprehends even the indirect effects produced on

19. During this period, Mill also published several long essay book reviews and an article on the American Civil War, "The Contest in America."

character and on the human faculties, by things of which the direct purposes are quite different, by laws, by forms of government, by the industrial arts, by modes of social life; nay, even by physical facts not dependent on human will, by climate, soil, and local position.''[20]

But here Mill wants to talk about education in the narrow sense, what his father before him called technical education—the education given in schools, especially university education. Here is how Mill defines formal education: ''the culture which each generation properly gives to those who are to be its successors in order to qualify them for at least keeping up, and if possible, for raising, the level of improvement which has been attained.'' Mill's concern with human improvement leads him to exclude professional education as an essential part of the curriculum. Not that he would exclude schools of law, medicine, engineering, and the like; but such institutions, he says, are for the comparatively few (at their own expense, and after they receive their *real* education). Professional education is simply ''no part of what every generation owes to the next, as that on which its civilization and worth will principally depend.''

The aim of higher education, Mill proposes, is to provide a comprehensive and connected view of things the student has already learned. Mill calls this the philosophy of knowledge: ''the methods of science, the modes in which the human intellect proceeds from the known to the unknown.'' (One would probably not be too amiss in interpreting Mill's conception of higher education as a course of study in his *A System of Logic, Ratiocinative and Inductive*.)

Thus, for Mill, the university is no place for elementary instruction. Yet he does realize that students often lack that elementary instruction they should have obtained before coming to the university. Therefore, the university must provide it. Specifically, it must include instruction in both ancient languages and arts, *and* modern sciences and arts: a scientific education teaches us to think, a literary one to express our thoughts; ergo ''we require both.''

To those who argue that time is too short to study both, Mill replies that they simply do not realize how much conscientious and intelligent teaching can accomplish. (One of the reasons Mill wrote his *Autobiography* was to demonstrate ''how much more than is commonly supposed may be taught, and taught well.'') As Mill sees it, the possibility of future human improvement rests on the utilization of ever better teaching methods. He feared that the continuous rapid expansion of information in each generation would result in narrow educational specialization ''until each man's position, the district which he thoroughly knows, bears about the same ratio to the whole range of useful knowledge that the art of

20. John Stuart Mill, ''Inaugural Address at St. Andrew's'' in *James and John Stuart Mill on Education*.

putting on a pin's head does to the field of human industry.'' From Mill's point of view, specialization narrows and perverts the mind, breeding prejudices favorable to that pursuit and antagonistic to larger views. Through its very proficiency in small things, specialization dwarfs human nature and unfits it for great thoughts and deeds.

The cultivated intellect Mill envisions is neither a superficial generalist nor an expert. He is one who knows the ''leading truths'' and the ''great features'' of a subject; one who knows enough in all subjects ''to be able to discover who are those who know them better.'' The general diffusion of this amount of knowledge—an amount not to be lightly estimated, Mill avers—will render those so educated capable of appreciating the superiority of the experts and willing to follow their lead. Thus, in Mill's scheme for the course of human improvement, the university graduates will form a bridge between the intellectual elite and the rest of the society by ''guiding and improving public opinion.''

Turning to the nitty-gritty of what should and what should not be included in the school curriculum, Mill excludes modern languages, history, and geography—all subjects, he claims, better learned on one's own, outside the school. But the languages and literatures of the ancients are a must. The literature of antiquity helps us learn how to express our thoughts because, as Swift so felicitously put it, those writers invariably used ''the right word in the right place.'' But in addition to this traditional argument for the study of the ancients, Mill argues that such studies help us to think: they make us more critical of our present, contemporary theories, ideas, and motives. ''Since we cannot divest ourselves of our preconceived notions, there is no known means of eliminating their influence, but by frequently using the differently coloured glasses of other people: and those of the other nations, as the most different, are the best.'' And to use the ancients in this way, as another set of glasses to help us become more self-critical, it is not enough to read modern interpretations of the ancients, nor even translations of their works—one must encounter their writings in the original language. Mill argues similarly about the study of history: we should read the actual documents and writings from the past, ''the original sources,'' rather than interpretations of those documents made by historians of our own time.

In addition to teaching us to be more self-critical, the literatures of antiquity provide examples of practical wisdom and demonstrations of the methods of pursuing truth in all nonempirical questions: ''To question all things; never to turn away from any difficulty; to accept no doctrine either from ourselves or from other people without a rigid scrutiny by negative criticism, letting no fallacy, or incoherence, or confusion of thought, slip by unperceived; above all, to insist upon hearing the meaning of a proposition before using it; these are the lessons we learned from the ancient dialecticians.''

Turning to science, Mill announces that universal instruction in it is indispensable; for "unless an elementary knowledge of scientific truths is diffused among the public, they never know what is certain and what is not, or who are entitled to speak with authority and who are not: they either have no faith at all in the testimony of science, or are the ready dupes of charlatans and imposters." But, as important as is the information that scientific instruction supplies, of far greater worth is the training and discipline of the intellect it provides. Sciences exhibit the most perfect examples of the art of thinking: mathematics demonstrates how to discover truths through reasoning; experimental science their discovery by direct observation, including experimentation.

Yet the study of mathematics and science is not enough for Mill; we must go beyond practice to theory. And, for him, the theory of science is contained in logic ("ratiocinative and inductive"), for it "lays down the general principles and laws of the search after truth, the conditions which, whether recognized or not, must actually have been observed if the mind has done its work rightly." Here John Stuart Mill returns to the theme introduced earlier in his address, that logic, the method of science, fulfills the highest aim of education: "it helps us develop a comprehensive and connected view of things already learnt before."

What about the actual improvement of mankind? Is there a science to guide us? There is, Mill admits, in our present state of knowledge, no generally accepted science of politics or ethics. Nevertheless, there is what he calls a "scientific politics." This is not a science in which we have a set of ready-made conclusions that we can apply indiscriminately, but a science that sets the mind to work "in a scientific spirit to discover in each instance the truth applicable to the given case." Such a scientific spirit is engendered through the study of history. It is not the place of the professor of history to dispense facts (students can obtain these from their private reading), but it is his role to teach the meaning of the facts: to help students perceive what is stable or static throughout different stages of human development, and what is dynamic or progressive. Such an approach to history (an approach Mill had earlier advocated in his *Logic*) would, Mill claims, infuse in students a sense of responsibility for the improvement of mankind by leading them to construe the past, present, and future as "an unremitting conflict between good and evil powers, of which every act done by any of us, insignificant as we are, forms one of the incidents; a conflict in which even the smallest of us cannot escape from taking part, in which whoever does not help the right side is helping the wrong, and for our share in which, whether it be greater or smaller, and let its actual consequences be visible or in the main invisible, no one of us can escape the responsibility."

There are, Mill points out, the beginnings of a science of politics—collections of facts or thoughts "sufficiently sifted and methodized" to be taught *ex professo*. He has in mind political economy, which, he claims, approaches "nearer the rank of a science" than anything else connected with politics. Political economy (as demonstrated in his own *Principles of Political Economy*) provides guidance for life, supplies standards for judging laws and institutions and contains plans for improving them.

Of no less importance than political economy is the study of jurisprudence: the general principles of law, the social necessities laws are required to meet, the requisites of good legislation, and the modes of legal procedures. Knowledge of all this is necessary for those "ambitious of contributing toward the better condition of the human race." To obtain such knowledge, Mill refers his listeners to the works of the utilitarians, including Jeremy Bentham and John Austin.

For Mill, of course, the educated man is not merely one who contemplates truth; he is active, a doer of good deeds. Hence the will, as well as the intelligence, requires education. Moral education is beyond the provinces of school and university, however, because moral (and religious) education consists of training the feelings and daily habits, both of which are beyond the sphere of public education. Our direct moral education comes from the home, the family, and then is modified by society itself. The only moral influence a university can exercise, Mill suggests, is in the pervading tone of the place. "Whatever it teaches, it should teach as penetrated by a sense of duty: it should present all knowledge as chiefly a means to worthiness of life, given for the double purpose of making each of us practically useful to his fellow creatures, and of elevating the character of the species itself; exalting and dignifying our nature."

Another way the university can influence the moral education of its students (a way in keeping with the principles Mill laid down in *On Liberty*) is to maintain academic freedom on moral issues—presenting, analyzing and criticizing all the systems of moral philosophy that have been operative among mankind. And here, as always, the task of the teacher is not to impose his own judgment but "to inform and discipline that of his pupil." The same is true with the teaching of religion: it should not be in the spirit of dogmatism, but in that of inquiry, addressing the student not as if his religion had been chosen for him but as "one who will have to choose it for himself."

On the matter of academic freedom for the student, Mill says that while a university ought to be a place for speculation, there are limits. Where there is a "united authority" (i.e., unanimity among the experts) then student deference, "at least provisional," is called for. When such united authority does not exist, then all should keep their minds open. For if, and only if, we eschew dogmatism on these unsettled questions can we expect to improve our knowledge and approach greater certainty.

In the last section of his *Address*, after having presented his views on intellectual and moral education, Mill takes up the matter of aesthetic education, which he defines as the education of the feelings and the cultivation of the beautiful. England, he notes, has not given much attention to the aesthetic function of education in the past because of the countervailing influences of both commercial money-getting and religious puritanism. These two historical influences have long shaped the Englishman's conscience, chiefly in the way of restraint: restraint of impulses, desires, and feelings. As a result, Mill observes, the average Englishman is solely self-regarding, with no understanding of the possibility of higher happiness: someone "who has no higher purpose in life than to enrich or raise in the world himself and his family; who never dreams of making the good of his fellow creatures of his country an habitual object." True, he is oftentimes philanthropic, giving away sums for charity; and he has a conscience, scrupulously avoiding any "very illegitimate means for attaining his self-interested objects." But this is not enough. More desirable are human beings who have both conscience and sentiments. Here Mill, as he did in his own life during his mental crisis, casts aesthetic education as a propaedeutic to moral education: poetry and all literature that is poetical and artistic cultivate the feelings and elevates the tone of the mind. If we wish men to practice virtue, we should make them love virtue. Literature, all the arts of expression, can do this. Art elevates us to the higher life; it takes us beyond our selfish concerns and leads us to identify our joy and grief with the good or ill of the system of which we form a part. Such tone of mind as the arts cultivate can infuse our daily work and ennoble it as a public function; for no matter how humble our work may be, it is never mean, save when it is meanly done, and when it is done from mean motives.

Finally, through art we come to regard our selves as works of art to be continually improved and perpetuated. For he who has learned what beauty is will desire to realize it in his own life: he "will keep before him a type of perfect beauty in human character, to light his attempts at self culture."

In concluding his long address to the students of Saint Andrew's, Mill reminds them that the function of a university is to prepare people "for the higher uses of life." The university helps develop that facility of using the mind on all that concerns the higher interests of man (rather than the minutiae of a business or profession). Once acquired in school, this habit or tone of mind will dominate even the busiest afterschool life. The chief value of a university education, Mill tells the students, is "that of making you more effective combatants in the great fight which never ceases to rage between Good and Evil, and more equal to coping with the ever new problems which the changing course of human nature and human society present to be resolved."

Summary and Evaluation

John Stuart Mill died on May 7, 1873. Later that year, his *Autobiography* appeared, edited by his stepdaughter, Helen Taylor. The first part of that work was devoted to his early years: his education and the educational influences on his life. In the opening paragraphs Mill explained that he had written it to serve an educational purpose: to show "how much more than is commonly supposed may be taught, and well taught in those early years." In the second half of the *Autobiography,* called "A General View of My Life," Mill begins with his *Logic* and then ties together all his subsequent works to make clear his continual and interrelated endeavors to improve humankind. On the day he died, John Stuart Mill's final words, uttered to Helen Taylor were: "You know I have done my work."

Gladstone, who was prime minister during the time Mill served in Parliament, dubbed him "the saint of rationalism." A good title for one who believed, like Plato, that intellectuals should rule. Like Plato, Mill believed he had discovered *the* method whereby men of talent could ascertain truth. His *Logic,* he thought, laid out the method for demonstrating or justifying true claims about the world and man. Once they had secured these truths, the educated few could and should direct the course of human affairs. The rational saints would lead the rest into the promised land of the higher happiness.

This conceit of the intellectual, once again, as it did with Plato, gave birth to an authoritarian political and social theory called liberalism. Yet, for all that it was authoritarian, it was not usually perceived as oppressive (1) because it was rational and the established educational arrangements encouraged all to accept rationality as the criterion for leadership; and (2) because liberalism devoted itself to the improvement of mankind, as dictated by rational leaders. But this justificatory construction of human rationality—a construction Mill long labored to set forth in his *Logic*—is, itself, authoritarian.

Dewey's Democracy

In his essay "The Influence of Darwin on Philosophy" John Dewey announced that Darwin's great work, *Origin of Species,* introduced a mode of thinking that transformed the logic of knowledge. Darwin had applied the scientific method to the study of plants and animals, thereby clearing the way to apply it to life, mind, and politics. With one stroke, Darwin had eliminated the need to search for first and final causes. Philosophers henceforth could look "the facts of experience in the face." Through the application of the scientific method, Dewey argued, philosophy could become a method of locating and interpreting the more serious moral, social, and political conflicts, and a method of projecting ways for dealing with them—a method of moral and political prognosis, of directing development and growth.[1]

Dewey spent his entire philosophical career applying the scientific method to life, morals, politics, and education. Yet, as his essay on Darwin makes clear, he valued the form of Darwin's contributions to philosophy, not its substance. He capitalized on the influence of Darwin's theory of evolution and development but did not incorporate that theory into his own philosophy. Instead, Dewey, as we shall see, came up with a theory of social and political growth that was markedly Lamarckian, not Darwinian. And Dewey's educational theory, which was of a piece with his political and social theory, was also pre-Darwinian.

I

In a series of lectures delivered in 1899 and later published under the title *The School and Society,* John Dewey tried to explain the transformations then taking place in American schools. They were, he claimed, simply a part of "social evolution." The new education people wondered about had a developmental connection to the larger changes taking place in society. These were changes, Dewey tells us, writ so large that "he who runs may read." [2]

The single most important change he had in mind was industrialization, which he defined as "the application of science resulting in the great inventions that have utilized the forces of nature on a vast and inexpensive scale." Industrialization had stimulated and facilitated the search for the truth of nature, thereby making the application to life both practicable and commercially necessary. Nevertheless, as a result of industrialization, Dewey notes, we find habits of life abruptly and thoroughly altered: political boundaries wiped out, huge populations gathered into cities, and moral and religious ideas and interests threatened and eclipsed. In the face of such sweeping social changes, Dewey explains, it is no wonder that schools of the late nineteenth century had begun to change.

Yet, Dewey claims, most observers of the changing schools had failed to understand what was really afoot in education. Worried adults saw the school curriculum being "watered down" through the introduction of new subjects like cooking, woodworking, and sewing; they saw discipline growing more relaxed as students freely moved about the classroom and talked to one another with impunity; they saw lowered standards of excellence as schools became more and more places to play, not

1. John Dewey, *The Influence of Darwin on Philosophy and Other Essays in Contemporary Thought* (New York: Holt, 1910). See also Philip P. Wiener, *Evolution and the Founders of Pragmatism* (Cambridge, Mass.: Harvard University Press, 1949).
2. John Dewey, *The School and Society* (Chicago: University of Chicago Press, 1906).

work. Adults saw all this, and they lamented the decline of the American school.

John Dewey wanted to put these changes into proper perspective, as part of the progressive evolution of the school. For, beneath the superficial changes so many lamented—the new curriculum, the informal discipline, the changed climate of the classroom—Dewey explained, there lay a totally new conception of what schools are for.

In the past, people had viewed schools as places set apart in which to learn lessons. There, young people had learned how to read and write, how to speak properly, and perhaps some arithmetic and history. Schooling had been important; but the child's "real" education, Dewey insisted, had come from outside the school. At home, on the farm, and in the village, the child had learned how people lived and solved their problems of survival. He had learned how people secured the food they ate, got the clothing they wore and built the houses that sheltered them. Outside school, the child had learned how things worked and how to repair and mend them when they broke. In learning how to solve the problems of existence, the child had also come to see the connectedness of things—he learned that human actions have consequences, some of which he learned to predict. Growing up in the preindustrial world had also developed character. For the child on the farm had jobs to do, chores that were not trivial but essential to the continued survival of the group.

With industrialization, this educative environment had begun to disappear. In the city the child grew up alienated from the world of work. In the industrial society, ways of securing food, clothing, and shelter had become very complex: the division of labor, the specialization of tasks, the introduction of machinery, and the creation of large mills and factories, all made it difficult, perhaps impossible, for children (and adults) to recognize the interconnectedness of things, the interdependence of people on one another. Deprived of this lost educative world of farm and village, people in this industrialized, urbanized society seemed less self-reliant, less able to solve their problems. More important, they had lost the spirit of cooperation, that sense of responsibility to the group that had characterized the preindustrial world.

Industrialization was a result of social evolution—the result of the application of man's intelligence to the problems of existence—and so it behooved us, Dewey argued, to use that intelligence to reconstruct necessary educative experiences for the young that industrialization had destroyed. This, Dewey explained, was what was going on in schools.

This is why schools had begun to change the curriculum, why they had introduced manual training, shop work, and household arts. Yet, not everyone realized the true reasons for curriculum changes. If we asked those favorably disposed to this new education what it was good for, we would find, Dewey suggested, that they thought that the practical subjects engaged the interest and attention of children and prepared students for their future vocations. This is important, but it is too narrow an understanding, Dewey cautioned. As he saw it, working in wood and metal, and weaving, cooking, and sewing, are methods of living, not simply studies. "We must conceive of them in their social significance," Dewey wrote, "as types of the process by which society keeps itself going, as agencies for bringing home to the child some of the primal necessities of community life, and as ways in which these needs have been met by the growing insight and ingenuity of man; in short, as instrumentalities through which the school itself shall be made a genuine form of active community life, instead of a place set apart in which to learn lessons."

When we construe the school this way (i.e., as a social unit, a community), Dewey tells us, the students come alive. No longer passive and inert recipients, children become creatively engaged in the life of the school. Inevitably the old discipline breaks down, but in its place we find a new discipline. The teacher was the authority for the old discipline; the teacher determined what behavior was proper, correct, and acceptable. But with the new discipline the task at hand, the project, the exercise, the activity, determined what is proper or correct behavior. The confusion, bustle, and noise that results from activity shocked many adult observers of the new education. But such activity, Dewey points out, confers an infinitely wider discipline on students: the discipline that emerges from having a part to play in an ongoing activity, the discipline that comes from contributing to a result commonly sought.

Thus, what looks like play to the casual observer is really the creation of a new social spirit in the school. In the old days, when schoolwork consisted solely of learning lessons, mutual assistance was unheard of. Teachers insisted on strict competition, which, of course, often passed over into selfishness. But when schoolwork becomes active, then free communication and interaction become common and desirable. For here, in this embryonic community, a social spirit is fostered; children learn social responsibility through participation.

Yet, Dewey points out, even though this new education is superior to the old, there are still people who complain about it. It is narrow, they say; it will simply produce specialists instead of liberally cultivated people. Dewey retorts that it is the old "liberal" education that was narrow and specialist. It appealed simply to the intellectual part of our nature, not to our impulse to make, to do, to create, to produce. The simple facts of the case are that in the great majority of human beings, the distinctly intellectual instinct "is not dominant." When we direct education simply to intellectual pursuits, Dewey explained, most students leave school as quickly as they can.

Restricting education solely to intellectual pursuits was a legacy from a social world that no longer existed. In the past, an intellectual education served the existing social structures. It provided the symbols by which the upper class preserved power and privilege. Now, Dewey announces, the industrial revolution has broken the monopoly of learning. Printing, the telegraph, and the locomotive have brought information and knowledge to many more people. Knowledge has become liquefied, actively running in all the currents of society. As a result of this knowledge explosion, Dewey finds that a strictly intellectual education is no longer socially functional: it can no longer be used to secure and ensure class privilege. Nor is a strictly intellectual education functional for the mass of people who must now learn in school what they previously learned on the farm and in the village: intelligence, social competence, and responsibility.

The changes afoot in the schools are desirable, Dewey concludes. The introduction of active occupations, which carries with it changes in the school atmosphere and school discipline, are all a "necessity of the larger social evolution." We should go about this transformation of our schools consciously and deliberately, making each of them an "embryonic community life, active with types of occupations that reflect the life of the larger society, and permeated throughout with the spirit of art, history, and science."

Why should we do this to our schools? Why does the school have to become an embryonic community? Dewey's answer is that through the school's becoming a community, we can restore that larger community outside the school, the community industrialization shattered. Why must the eclipsed community be restored? Perhaps social evolution was such that the emerging civilization had no need for community? Dewey thought otherwise. Without community, he argued, there could be no democracy. And democracy was an essential part of the civilization that was now emerging.

II

Industrialization, Dewey believed, had made the evolution of democracy possible. The development of modes of manufacture and commerce, travel, navigation, and water communication, all of which flowed from the command of science over natural energy, had widened "the area of shared concerns" among people and liberated a greater diversity of their personal capacities. This increased liberation and this broadened community of interest are the hallmarks of democracy: in a democracy, all members participate in solving their shared problems.[3]

Now that these characteristics have emerged, Dewey argues in *Democracy and Education* (1916), we must deliberately and consciously sustain and extend them. This means educating all members of society to

3. John Dewey, *Democracy and Education* (New York: Macmillan, 1916).

personal initiative and adaptability. Otherwise, changes will overwhelm them as they fail to perceive their significance and connections. Indeed, without such an education, Dewey warns, we will never have a truly democratic society, but instead, a society where "a few will appropriate to themselves the results of the blind and externally directed activities of others."

As Dewey saw it, the emerging democratic society required more than simply taking the traditional education previously given to the few and extending it to the many. That traditional education, he argued, had grown out of a nondemocratic social order. A democratic social order stood in need of a new kind of education, a democratic education.

This is exactly what earlier philosophers of democracy had not understood—Mill, for example . . . and Rousseau. Mill had tried to incorporate democracy into a predemocratic social order and wound up with a severely restricted version of democracy, a so-called representative democracy where an intellectual elite guided and directed the rest of the people toward what *it* determined was good for society. Rousseau, unlike Mill, recognized that in a democracy all must participate in determining the common good, but he failed to supply any method by which all could ascertain just what the common good was. His romantic belief in the natural goodness of man led him to assume that, if protected and preserved, natural goodness would blossom into a love of one's fellows that would lead one to pursue the common good. Although Rousseau prescribed a novel kind of education, neither he nor Mill recognized the need for a truly democratic education.

What are the ingredients of a democratic education? First, the school itself, Dewey insisted, must be a democratic school. Neither private tutors (as Rousseau advocated) nor separate schools for different social classes (as Mill accepted) will sustain or extend a democratic society. Democratic schools are schools for all the people—common schools, as they were called in America. A school was a simplified, selective environment set apart from the hurly-burly of the real world, where the young could learn. A democratic school was this, but it had to be more; it had to be a broad social environment, broader than any child could experience in his home, through his family, or in his immediate neighborhood. This intermingling in the school of youth of different races, different religions, and unlike customs creates the possibility for a broad community to which the child must adjust. Contact with this new community liberates new powers from each individual, powers that may have been suppressed without this school experience. At the same time, each student comes to recognize a widening of the area of shared concerns as each learns to refer his own actions to that of others and to consider the actions of others to give point and direction to his own.

Now this does not just happen by itself. The mere coming together of people from different backgrounds does not automatically create a democratic community. Here we come to a second ingredient of democratic education: the development of social intelligence. In a democratic society, Dewey points out, each person must understand the meanings that things have in the society of which he is a part. Each must understand objects, events, and acts in ways that enable him to participate effectively in associated activities. Dewey calls this "social intelligence."

Some educators try to secure social intelligence through external direction. They try to control and guide their students toward "proper conduct." But, Dewey insists, modern psychology makes clear that such external direction is impossible. According to modern psychology, he continues, human beings makes responses in the face of stimuli, and their responses "proceed from tendencies already possessed by the individual." Teachers can do no more than furnish stimuli that evoke activities: they cannot force anything on or into students. The teacher can only *re*direct students, shift the activities already going on into another channel.

Thus, in addition to being a simplified, selective, broad social environment, a school must be an educative environment. It must present stimuli that evoke or promote social intelligence. This will be an environment different from the traditional school. The traditional school often secured technical, specialized ability in algebra, Latin, or botany, Dewey admits, but not the intelligence that directs ability to useful social ends. The new democratic school does this by engaging students in "joint activity." The stimuli that provoke this joint activity are problems, shared problems, real problems that human beings have always had to solve in order to survive and develop, like those problems people confront in securing food, clothing, and shelter.

In the Laboratory School he established at the University of Chicago in the 1890s, Dewey had young children work in "kitchen laboratories" where they helped to prepare food. This led to joint activities like building miniature farms, planting gardens where they grew their own "crops," and writing and performing plays and skits where they acted out the transporting and processing of goods and their delivery to stores. In this way the children came to understand the meaning of objects, events, and actions they experienced—they saw their social significance. In this way, beginning with the household occupations of cooking, sewing, and carpentry, the children learned about the world they lived in. By the time they were thirteen or fourteen, they had experimented and observed in many fields: horticulture, ecology, zoology, geology, physiography, astronomy, physical and commercial geography, physics, chemistry, biology, and physiology.[4]

---

4. Katherine Camp Mayhew and Anna Camp Edwards, *The Dewey School* (New York: Appleton, 1936).

This study of occupations not only led children into, and made them at home in the world of scientific knowledge, but it also led them into the social world, making them at ease in the world of social life. For, in the Laboratory School, students came to see the relationships and connections, the interdependencies among human beings, occupations, and roles. Even more important, the activities students participated in at the school were joint activities directed at solving shared problems. The children learned how to think, plan, and act—as a group.

Through his proposal to make social intelligence the focus of the school, Dewey sought to overcome many of the educational problems inherited from a preindustrial, predemocratic tradition. Dewey construed these problems as dualisms.

First, there was the problem of differential education according to social class or status: one kind of education for the leaders and bosses, another for the followers and workers. In a predemocratic society, the ruling classes did not labor or engage in practical activity. The lower classes performed these roles, while their "superiors" enjoyed leisure and engaged in intellectual activity. In keeping with the social order of that time, and its supporting philosophy, the ruling classes received a cultural education, one intended to develop their intelligence and character and thereby render them fit to rule and equipped to pursue worthy leisure-time activities. The lower classes received a vocational education or vocational training to prepare them to perform the work of that society. To counteract this dualistic, predemocratic construction of education, Dewey would have students of all social classes study occupations, with the focus on what he called the "realization of the activity," not the external product. That is, schooling was not to be a preparation for a job or a vocation, but rather a redirection or reformulation of the material dispositions of the young to cooperative social living through participation in joint activities.

Because we live in an industrial world, Dewey points out, the intellectual content inherent in the study of occupations overcomes a second educational dualism inherited from the predemocratic past: the dualism of practical versus intellectual studies. Our present industrial world uses machinery, materials, and techniques based on discoveries in mathematics, physics, chemistry, bacteriology, and so forth. Industrial occupations, Dewey insisted, "have infinitely greater intellectual content and infinitely larger cultural possibilities than they used to possess." Moreover, he warned, unless people are educated in a way to acquaint them with the scientific and social bases and bearings of their occupations, they will sink to the role of "appendages to the machines they operate."

Here we can see that although Dewey argued that industrialization created the conditions for the emergence of a democratic society, he recognized that democracy was not inevitable. Industrialization had widened the area of common concern among people and liberated the power and talents of many individuals. But there was always the danger that the masses would be excluded from the sphere of common concern and denied liberation. Industrialization, Dewey realized, could lead to greater oppression and victimization of the masses. To prevent this, the masses needed education, not training. Only education could bring the masses into the sphere of common concern. Only education could liberate them to participate in the joint activity to solve shared problems. Only education, Dewey held, could create a democratic society.

Ironically, industrial society was an obstacle to the education needed. For, although an industrial society has inherently more educative possibilities within it, industrialization creates arrangements that are much less educational resources than the arrangements that existed in the days of local production and local markets. Today, people, especially children, could not learn through direct experience with the industry going on in the world about them. This is precisely why we must transform the schools, Dewey insisted. For, in schools, the intellectual content and the social meanings inherent in industrial occupations can be laid bare and perceived by students free from the economic pressures of the actual industrial world.

Moreover, as an added bonus, as it were, transforming schools in this way overcomes another dualism inherited from the predemocratic society: the dualism between the school and the real world. In the earlier, predemocratic society when schooling was limited to the upper classes, formal education developed social habits, skills, and manners that distinguished the ruling classes from the rest. They became cultured. Yet, although schooling had relevance to the social order within that society, the content of that schooling had no relevance or meaning apart from that social order. What was learned in school did not enhance the power to control the environment, to guide and direct the course of progress: it did not ameliorate man's estate. It was only with the advent of modern science that mankind obtained real knowledge, knowledge that made a difference, knowledge that supplied power to control and direct the course of events. But when they had introduced modern science into the school curriculum, teachers treated it simply as a subject containing technical information. They made no attempt to relate it to the real world, no attempt to use it to increase the student's understanding of, and power over, the world he lived in. Although science had become a "school subject," it had not bridged the dualism or the gap between the school and the real world.

The way to bridge that gap and overcome that dualism, Dewey suggested, was to teach science as it had actually evolved, through the continued efforts of human beings to solve their real problems of survival.

Here, once again, teachers should begin with what is familiar to the students—the occupations and activities current in the real world. "The obvious pedagogical starting point of scientific instruction," Dewey wrote, "is not to teach things labelled science, but to utilize the familiar occupations and appliances to direct observation and experiment until pupils have arrived at a knowledge of some fundamental principles by understanding them in their natural practical workings."

By teaching science in this way, Dewey claims, teachers can, at the same time, overcome still another dualism: the dualism between scientific studies and the humanities. The traditional humanistic studies served a moral and intellectual function, Dewey admits. But they were narrow in scope: they served solely the interests of the aristocratic classes. Whereas the study of science, as he construed it, is, Dewey argues, humanistic: it will extend the range of culture to all, serving the common moral and intellectual interests of all classes.

Once again Dewey returns to his theme of developing social intelligence among all people, the social intelligence necessary to create and sustain a democracy. Yet, one might ask, Why? Why is it necessary to create and sustain a democracy? Dewey has so far argued that the changes taking place in the schools were part of social evolution. The schools, he said, were becoming embryonic communities in an attempt to recapture the lost educative community of the farm and village that industrialization shattered. We needed to restore and expand that community, infusing social intelligence throughout all the members of society, he argued, because only by doing this will we create the truly democratic society that industrialization has made possible. One can repeat, why? Why do we need a democracy? What is the justification for a democracy? Here we come to the core of Dewey's philosophy: his theory of growth.

III

The ultimate reason we prefer democracy, Dewey wrote in *Experience and Education* (1938) is because it promotes a better quality of human experience; one, he adds, which is more widely accessible and enjoyed than is possible in nondemocratic and antidemocratic forms of social life. In short, democracy provides the opportunity for the maximum amount of growth for the maximum number of people. In a democracy, he wrote in *Reconstruction in Philosophy* (1920), the "supreme test" of all political institutions and industrial arrangements is the "contributions they make to the all-round growth of every member of society." [5]

---

5. John Dewey, *Experience and Education* (New York: Macmillan, 1938); and idem, *Reconstruction in Philosophy* (New York: Holt, 1920).

By growth, Dewey meant the power to control the environment, power to control the means for achieving ends. Thus, we say a child has grown when he is able to do it by himself, whatever "it" may be: feeding himself, going to the bathroom, tying his shoelaces, crossing the street. In each of these instances of growth, the child is able to control his environment, is able to achieve his ends by himself.

Dewey believed that just about everyone was capable of growth. As he construed it, growth takes place through the solving of problems that emerge because people have needs, or aims, or ends in view. The environment often presents obstacles to the attainment of an end in view, thereby creating a problem situation. Solving problems creates knowledge, and knowledge is power—an expression of growth.

Here we begin to understand Dewey's justification of democracy. For, if growth comes about through problem solving, then democratic groups provide greater opportunities for growth than do nondemocratic societies, simply because in democratic societies the concern is with shared or common problems. In a democracy, decision making is not the prerogative of a ruling class but of all people. Moreover, to solve their shared problems, the members of a democratic society engage in what Dewey has called "joint activities." Through such participation, members of a democratic society grow; they develop skills, habits, and conduct that allow them better to control their environment, better to achieve their ends in view.

This, then, is Dewey's argument: The school must restore community because community is a necessary condition for a democratic society, and democracy is the best form of social arrangement because it provides the opportunity for the greatest growth for the greatest number of people. The conclusion, therefore, is that the goal of education is human growth.

But, if the end of education is growth, then what kind of growth? Growth in what direction? Dewey dismissed all requests to specify the kinds of growth or the direction that growth should take. He did not deny that someone may grow in efficiency as a burglar or as a corrupt politician, for example; but, he explained, from the standpoint of education as growth, the question is whether growth in this direction promotes or retards growth in general. "Does this form of growth create conditions for future growth, or does it set up conditions that shut off the person who has grown in this particular direction from the occasions, stimuli, and opportunities for continuing growth in new directions?" He concluded that there was nothing to which growth is relative, save more growth, and so "there is nothing to which education is subordinate save more education." (By taking growth as the end of education, Dewey made sense of that commonplace that says that education should not cease when one leaves school. For now we can see that this means that the purpose of school education is to ensure the continuation of education by organizing the powers that ensure growth.)

If growth is the end of education (indeed, growth is the only moral end of life, Dewey says in *Reconstruction in Philosophy*), how can schools promote growth? We already have Dewey's preliminary answer, but let me review it: The school must provide children with educative environments—simplified, selective, rich environments that stimulate children to joint activity through confronting them with shared problems. But to create such environments, as Dewey (and others) discovered, is no easy task.

To pull it off, teachers must know both the students and the subject matter. They must know the needs, interests, capabilities, ends, aptitudes, and so on, of all their students. Some of this teachers can obtain from the study of child psychology and sociology, and perhaps from economics and history; but the concrete details must come from a thorough study of the actual children they expect to educate. In addition, teachers must have a thorough understanding of the subject matter—a sophisticated, deep understanding so that they can package or repackage it in ways appropriate for their students. The teacher's task is to construct for the students real problems, meaningful problems, problems that will provoke interest and activity from the students; they must construct problems for which students are ready, and perhaps most important, significant problems that will promote student growth.

The key to creating an educative environment, Dewey tells us in *Experience and Education,* is the principle of the continuum of experience. That is, teachers should provide students with in-school experiences that have continuity with their experiences outside school as well as continuity with their past experiences and their future experiences. Furthermore, any specific in-school experience should have continuity with other experiences in school.

But this is still not enough. A simplified, selective, rich environment, replete with problems set forth in accord with the principle of continuity of experience—all this will not promote growth unless, in addition, students interact with the problems intelligently.

Intelligence Dewey defines in *Reconstruction in Philosophy* as "a shorthand designation for great and ever-growing methods of observation, experiment and reflective reasoning." He then adds that intelligence is a recent development in the history of mankind. He is talking about the scientific method. This, he notes, came into being in the sixteenth and seventeenth centuries and has become universally recognized as the basis for all progress. Mankind has so far applied the scientific method to physical nature, but not, Dewey complains, to human and social problems. With the scientific method, we can, he promises, reconstruct philosophy, democracy, and education.

When he talks about the scientific method, Dewey, of course, is not referring to the special techniques of laboratory research conducted by specialists. The scientific method is not a specialized technique but a method, a means, "the only authentic means at our command for getting at the significance of the everyday experiences in the world in which we live." The scientific method, he concludes, provides "a working pattern of the way in which, and the conditions under which, experiences are used to lead ever onward and outward" (*Experience and Education*).

The essence of the scientific method, Dewey held, was experimentation, the careful formulation of hypotheses or tentative solutions to problems which were then subjected to experimental testing. Thus, when Dewey says that growth depends upon the exercise of intelligence, he means that problem solving will promote growth only if problems are solved through the method of experimentation, not through blind reaction. And in his Laboratory School in Chicago, learning the experimental method was the primary lesson for all students.

Beginning with present needs, interests, and capabilities, teachers in the Laboratory School built meaningful experiences on the past experiences of the children and led them through a "continuum of experiences" into situations where the children could conduct and direct their own activities. They solved problems through experimenting. The children "worked things out"; they examined problems carefully, formulating hypotheses and testing them by experiment. Once students had learned the scientific method, they had learned how to solve problems, they had learned how to learn. Converting experiences into experimentation ensures continuing growth. Through experimentation, people can reconstruct or reorganize their experience. This, Dewey says, adds to the meaning of experiences and increases the possibility of directing the course of future experience. And this is what education is all about.

IV

With experimentation, we have reached the heart of Dewey's philosophy. For experimentation, he held, is *the* method of growth. Because human beings continually confront problems, "every idea and human act is an experiment in fact," Dewey points out in *Experience and Nature* (1929). To be consciously experimental enables us to profit by experience instead of being at its mercy. That is, through experimentation human beings can consciously and deliberately grow, they can gain greater control of life, mitigate accidents, turn contingency to account, and generally raise the quality of experience.[6] Since education, knowl-

6. John Dewey, *Experience and Nature* (Chicago: Open Court, 1929).

edge, and democracy are all modes of growth, Dewey's message is that all should be experimental.

He construed democracy as a form of social arrangement whereby all participated in joint activity to solve shared problems: for democracy to work, such joint activity was to be marked by social intelligence, which meant experimentation. The traditional democratic methods of discussion and dialogue must give way to organized cooperative inquiry, he argued in *Liberalism and Social Action* (1935). Only through experimental inquiry can conflicting claims be appraised and judged openly. "Democracy demands the substitution of the intelligence that is exemplified in scientific procedure for the kind of intelligence that is now accepted." [7]

In his attempt to reconstruct philosophy to experimentalism, Dewey makes inquiry, not truth or knowledge, the essence of logic. In *Logic, the Theory of Inquiring* (1938), he defined inquiry as "the controlled or directed transformation of an indeterminate situation into one that is so determinate in its constituent distinctions and relations as to convert the elements of the original situations into a unified whole." And the way to conduct such inquiry is the experimental method of science: "The demand for reform of logic is the demand for a unified theory of inquiry through which the authentic pattern of experimental and operational inquiry of science shall become available for regulation of the habitual methods by which inquiries in the field of common sense are carried on; by which conclusions are reached and beliefs are formed and tested." [8]

In his efforts to infuse experimentalism into educational practice, Dewey tried to replace the conception of education as a process of transmission with a conception of it as a process of discovery. Instead of transmitting "ready-made information" supplied in isolation from the students' own experience, the Deweyan teacher was to create educative environments where, through scientifically controlled experiments, students would discover solutions to problems of interest to them. Every lesson was to be taught, Dewey wrote in 1938, "in connection with its bearing upon creation and growth of the kind of power of observation, inquiry, reflection and testing that are the heart of scientific intelligence." [9]

Dewey supplied no blueprints for the teacher, no cookbook recipes, no formulas for creating educative environments. For teaching, too, was to be experimental. Creating educative environments was the teacher's problem, one the teacher should approach experimentally—observing, formulating hypotheses and testing them. By construing the work experimentally, the teacher, too, could continually grow.

---

7. John Dewey, *Liberalism and Social Action* (New York: Capricorn, 1935).
8. John Dewey, *Logic: The Theory of Inquiry* (New York: Holt, 1938), pp. 97–98.
9. John Dewey, "The Relation of Science and Philosophy as the Basis of Education," in *John Dewey on Education*, ed. Reginald D. Archambault (New York: Modern Library, 1964).

Summary and Evaluation

Although John Dewey believed he had resolved the dualism between the theory and the practice of education, he had, in fact, deepened the chasm between them. The most frequent reaction teachers and would-be teachers have to Dewey's educational proposals is that they are fine in theory but not so fine in practice.

Dewey thought he had related theory to practice in education by having practice serve as the instrument for theoretical instruction. In his Laboratory School in Chicago, future teachers learned, through practical experience, what schools were for, what was worth knowing, and how teachers ought to conduct themselves. There was no attempt to teach them the "tricks of the trade" then current in most existing schools. Once they understood that education was growth and that growth came about through experimentation, they were ready to become professional educators. The rest was up to them—and "the rest" consisted of conducting experiments in the classroom to discover truly educative environments.

The trouble is, as teachers to this day complain, it is difficult, if not impossible, for most teachers to conduct those experiments. They haven't the time, energy, imagination, intelligence, or patience; even if they do, they lack the freedom, the opportunity, the resources, and the support necessary to conduct such experiments. Dewey, teachers complain, had an unrealistic conception of the real situation in an ongoing educational system. Yet, they concede, his proposals are great—in theory.

But are they? His proposals for education demand highly imaginative, intelligent, sophisticated teachers—superteachers; and highly imaginative, intelligent, sophisticated students—superstudents. They also demand ideal schools with administrators and parents who are understanding, supportive and enabling. These fanciful expectations belie the notion that Dewey's proposals constitute a good theory for education. Its impracticability, on such a large scale, suggests theoretical inadequacy.

The inadequacy of Dewey's theory of education inheres, I think, in his conception of the scientific method: he believed that the scientific method supplies solutions to problems, the best possible solutions. But the scientific method, as most scientists view it, is not a method for discovering solutions to problems; it is a method for testing solutions, a method for finding out what is wrong with proposed solutions—how inadequate they are, what limitations they have. (Of course, experimentation can decide, between two proposed answers or solutions to a problem, which one is the better answer; but this simply means that, so far, we have discovered fewer or less significant inadequacies in one than in the other.)

This belief that experimentation or the scientific method provided answers—the best possible answers or solutions to problems—led Dewey to (1) an inadequate conception of democracy, (2) an absurd notion of growth, and (3) an authoritarian construction of education.

Dewey's conception of democracy rested on his belief that the scientific method can give the answers to problems, in this case, social problems—problems about what is good for the society, the common good. He recognized that the traditional democratic theories for ascertaining the common good were authoritarian. Thus, Rousseau insisted that the infallible "general will" determined what the common good was, but this was knowable only through the will of the majority (who had to be properly educated). In place of Rousseau's "authoritarianism of the majority," John Stuart Mill proposed that an intellectual elite should determine what the common good was. Dewey, in contrast to both, would have a democracy where the common good was determined through the exercise of social intelligence, through the scientific method. This, he believed, would result in answers to our social problems that are not authoritarian but that do have authority—the authority that adheres to results obtained through objective, free, and open inquiry and rigorous experimentation. In the *Problems of Men,* Dewey wrote: "the very foundation of the democratic procedure is dependence upon experimental production of social change; an experimentation directed by working principles that are tested and developed in the very process of being tried out in action." [10]

By attempting to create a democracy based on the scientific method, which was supposed to give us the answers to our social problems, Dewey actually curtailed democracy. For now those in power can use the scientific method or experimentation to demonstrate that their favored solutions are the correct ones. (Given sufficient skill and power, one can always arrange or interpret social experiments so that they confirm what one favors.) For if everyone accepts Dewey's claim that the scientific method is the best way of obtaining answers, then when they are presented with an answer obtained by the scientific method, people can do nothing but accept it.

By reducing democracy to the scientific method, Dewey wound up (unwittingly, to be sure) reenforcing the existing social power arrangements he had hoped to abolish. Now, those in power could (and do) use "experimentation" to confer a "scientific" legitimacy on their favored solutions to social problems.

Dewey had planned for something entirely different. He had envisioned a participatory democracy wherein all people participated in joint activity in solving their school problems. The basis for his vision was his belief that the scientific method, the method of experimentation, could be transmitted by school instruction to all members of society. Even

10. John Dewey, *Problems of Men* (New York: Philosophical Library, 1946), p. 157.

under the best of circumstances, however, most people simply do not participate in the social decisions that affect them. They do not have the time, energy, patience, or interest; the concern of most people is with their individual private good, not the common good. Moreover, Dewey, by reducing democracy to the scientific method, actually played a part in heightening public withdrawal from participating in solving the problems of society. For, according to Dewey, if these problems are solved scientifically, they will be solved in ways that serve the common good. Thus, when those in power claimed to have solved problems experimentally, those who had listened to Dewey—and to their schoolteachers—believed that those in power were acting in the public interest.

In the last third of the twentieth century, many Americans have become increasingly suspicious that those in power in politics, business, industry, the military, and in education itself are solving public problems in ways that serve their own private interests; even though those in power use the scientific method to come up with "the best possible answer." These suspicions have erupted into cynicism about the possibility of democracy. The source of this current malaise, I suggest, lies in an inadequate conception of democracy, which follows from the erroneous belief that the scientific method can give us answers to our problems.

Dewey justified his advocacy of democracy, you recall, by claiming that democratic arrangements promoted the greatest growth. Yet, just as his belief that science provided solutions to problems led him to formulate an inadequate conception of democracy, the same belief led him to accept an absurd notion of growth. The trouble with Dewey's notion of growth is with his criterion for growth, which is, we saw, further growth. That is, any change or modification in human behavior is to count as an instance of growth only if it promotes future growth. But we can never apply such a criterion because it refers to what does not exist: the future. We cannot tell if a specific change in behavior is real growth until we see if it promotes future growth, but that future growth is itself certifiable as real growth only if *it* promotes future growth, and *that* future growth is likewise certifiable as real growth only if it . . . and so on . . . into infinity.

Dewey's way out of this infinite regress was the scientific method. Because he believed that the scientific method could give us the best possible answers, provide the best possible solutions, he thought that experimentation could ascertain what behaviors, what actions, will promote future growth. He argued that behaviors or actions that had worked for us in controlling our environment in the past, behaviors and actions the consequences of which had been confirmed by rigorous experimentation, would likely work for us in the future.

Obviously this is not so. There is no way for us to predict the future. We have no empirical or logical basis for making claims about what will work in the future. Past results or past consequences, no matter how carefully or "scientifically" gathered, cannot justify such predictions. Therefore, Dewey's criterion for growth is inoperable: because we can never know what will promote future growth and development, we can never ascertain whether a specific, present change in behavior is an instance of growth.

Dewey's theory of growth or development was Lamarckian rather than Darwinian. This is not to say that Dewey believed in the biological transmission of acquired characteristics, but simply that, like Lamarck, Dewey (perhaps under the influence of Lester Frank Ward), construed human evolution as a telic process. Here is how he put it in *The Quest for Certainty:*

> Intelligence is a quality of some acts, those which are directed, and directed action is an achievement, not an original endowment. The history of human progress is the story of the transformation of acts which, like the interactions of inanimate things, takes place unknowingly to actions qualified by understanding of what they are about; from actions controlled by external conditions to actions having guidance through their intent:—their insight into their own consequences. Instruction, information, knowledge, is the only way in which this property of intelligence comes to qualify acts originally blind.[11]

Prior to the emergence of intelligence, by which Dewey meant the scientific method, human actions to solve problems were no more than blind trial and error. Prior to the development of intelligence, human beings relied on tradition, habit, instinct, impulse to solve their problems of survival. Once equipped with the scientific method, human beings, Dewey argued, had the power to solve their problems intelligently.

Now, according to Lamarck, once organisms discovered successful solutions to their problems, they transmitted them to their progeny. Lamarck thought that evolution took place through the biological transmission of acquired characteristics. His successor, Darwin, argued, to the contrary, that the environment was the operative factor in evolution: organisms produced offspring of different variations and the environment eliminated those offspring that were inadequate. Darwin called this "natural selection." Dewey's theory of human growth was decidedly Lamarckian. He, too, believed in the transmission of acquired characteristics—not a biological transmission but a transmission through instruction; and not, as we saw, the transmission of ideas or facts or subject matter, but the transmission of the method, the scientific method. Human progress or growth, Dewey believed, rested on the instructional

---

11. John Dewey, *The Quest for Certainty* (New York: Putnam's, 1929), p.249. See also David W. Marcell, *Progress and Pragmatism* (Westport, Conn.: Greenwood, 1974).

transmission of the method of experimentation. Once they had acquired this method, human beings would know how to learn, how to grow.

It is at this point that we can see Dewey's educational authoritarianism. It sounds shocking to accuse Dewey of educational authoritarianism because all his life he battled against teaching methods that imposed knowledge and predetermined answers and solutions on the young. He never recognized his own authoritarianism, his methodological authoritarianism. He believed: "The value of any cognitive conclusion is dependent on the *method* by which it is reached" (*The Quest for Certainty*). And since he thought it was the best method he would have teachers impose the scientific method on the young. This doesn't sound like authoritarianism, especially since Dewey defined this method as the method of intelligence. But it is authoritarianism. It is presented as the ultimate justification for all answers to all problems.

Popper's Fallibilism

Sir Karl Popper has written no books on education. He did publish a few, long-forgotten articles in Austrian educational journals early in his career. But he neither thinks of himself as, nor do others consider him, an educational theorist. Universally, his philosophic depth and breadth is acknowledged: as an epistemologist, a social and political philosopher, and, above all, as a philosopher of science. A recent biographer reports that he is "considered by many to be the greatest philosopher of science that has ever been." Popper's philosophy has influenced physical and biological scientists, statesmen, historians, psychologists, physiologists, anthropologists, economists . . . but no educationists. Yet his philosophy does have profound implications for this field too. It offers the theoretical basis for a nonauthoritarian approach to education—the first such approach since Socrates.[1]

I

Karl Popper grew up in the heady intellectual milieu of Vienna in the early twentieth century. He tells how, while still in his teens, he participated in discussions and arguments about the theories of Marx, of Freud, of Adler, and of Einstein. One problem that particularly fascinated young Popper was the question of the scientific validity of these different theories, or, as he phrased it, the problem of demarcation between science and nonscience.[2]

What are the criteria for a scientific theory? Popper noted that many of his friends who admired Marx, Freud, and Adler were impressed by the explanatory power of their theories.

> These theories appeared to be able to explain practically anything that happened within the field to which they referred. The study of any of them seemed to have the effect of an intellectual conversion or revelation, opening your eyes to a new truth hidden from those not yet initiated. Once your eyes were thus opened, you saw confirming instances everywhere: the world was full of verifications of the theory. What happened always confirmed it. Thus, its truth appeared manifest; and unbelievers were clearly people who did not want to see the manifest truth; who refused to see it, either because it was against their class interest or because of the repressions which were still "unanalyzed" and crying aloud for treatment.

His Marxist friends, Popper reports, could not open a newspaper without finding a news story (or the *way* a news story was presented) that confirmed their theory; and Freudians, or Adlerians, found their theories confirmed by each and every clinical observation that came up. But all these endless confirmations, Popper argues, only meant that one can interpret phenomena in the light of those theories; and since every conceivable phenomena could be interpreted in the light of these theories, then these confirming instances meant little.

But with Einstein, Popper realized, the situation was different. Einstein's theory about the universe led to making predictions; predictions that, if they did not hold up, would prove his theory wrong. Einstein's gravitational theory, for example, led to a prediction about "shifts" in the

---

1. Bryan Magee, *Karl Popper,* Modern Masters Series, ed. Frank Kermode (New York: Viking, 1973), Introduction.

2. Karl Popper, "Science: Conjectures and Refutations," in *Conjectures and Refutations* (London: Routledge and Kegan Paul, 1963).

position of stars. Careful, experimental observation corroborated these predictions. But it was not the fact that the prediction held up that made Einstein's theory a scientific one. It was the fact that it *could have been shown to be false*. The theory was falsifiable.

What made Einstein's theory scientific—and different from those of Marx, Freud, and Adler—was that it was incompatible with certain possible results of observation. In short, Popper concludes, the criterion of the scientific status of a theory is its falsifiability, or refutability, or testability.

II

With this criterion of falsifiability, Popper not only made it possible to demarcate science from nonscience, but he also solved a problem central to the philosophy of science. Science, most everyone agrees, consists of lawlike general descriptive statements (e.g., "All stars, except planets, move in circles," or "All swans are white"). Prior to Popper, the traditional question that had troubled scientists and philosophers of science was how to make these general statements certain. (The problem John Stuart Mill had wrestled with in his *Logic*.)

The answer proposed ever since the time of Francis Bacon was: induction. That is, through careful observation of a number of individual cases, the scientist could "induce" a general (universal) statement about all cases. After careful observation of a number of white swans, for example, the scientist could induce "All swans are white."

But induction was a totally unsatisfactory answer. It was, one philosopher noted, the skeleton in the closet. David Hume (1711–66) had conclusively demonstrated that induction is not valid—empirically or logically. The empirical objection is that universal statements refer to the future as well as to the past and present. But it is impossible to observe the future. Thus, "all swans are white" says that swans not yet born will be white. This is something we cannot observe, hence cannot claim for empirical reasons. The logical objection to induction is that one cannot infer a universal statement from a singular statement, nor from any number of singular statements. Thus, "this swan is white," and "this second swan is white," and "this third swan is white" . . . can never, logically, lead to the conclusion that "All swans are white."

Bertrand Russell succinctly summed up the difficulty confronting science: "Induction is an independent, logical principle, incapable of being inferred either from experiences or from other logical principles . . . [but] . . . without this principle science is impossible." [3]

The only way science was possible, it seemed, was the way pointed

3. Bertrand Russell, *A History of Western Philosophy* (14th ed.; New York: Simon and Schuster, 1964), p. 674.

out by Hume, who, after demonstrating the logical and empirical invalidity of induction, suggested that induction was a psychological process. That is, repeated instances of a phenomenon (e.g., white swans) induce us to *believe* that all future instances will be like those observed so far. (We are led to believe that "All swans are white.")

To accept this psychological basis for induction is to admit that a scientific theory can never be absolutely certain: a scientific theory is only tentatively held (believed) on the basis of past confirmations. Thus, we *believe* that all swans are white because all the swans we have observed so far have been white. One difficulty with this psychological conception of induction is that it reduces science to belief and commitment, making it impossible to demarcate science from nonscience. For, according to this construction of a scientific theory, the theories of Freud, Marx, and Adler were no different from that of Einstein: so far past experience has confirmed them—as Popper's friends in Vienna had argued. But this also means that *all* these theories were on a par with those of astrology, phrenology, and alchemy, since the validity of a theory was a simple matter of belief. Bertrand Russell dramatically stated this difficulty with Hume's widely accepted psychological interpretation of induction when he wrote, "It is, therefore, important to discover whether there is any answer to Hume within a philosophy that is wholly or mainly *empirical*. If not, *there is no intellectual difference between sanity and insanity*. The lunatic who believes that he is a poached egg is to be condemned solely on the ground that he is in a minority. . . ."

By introducing falsifiability as the criterion for demarcating science from nonscience, Popper provided a solution to the problem of how to validate scientific theories.

According to Popper, science is still made up of general statements or theories. And these theories are tentative, never certain. (Popper lumps scientific "hypotheses," scientific "theories," and scientific "laws" all together and terms them all "theories.") But the tentativeness of scientific theories lies, he says, in the fact that they have not yet been falsified or refuted. Scientists use tests or experiments to establish the worth of a theory. Yet, in spite of what many people think, a scientific experiment does *not* confirm a theory; it merely tests it and determines how well the theory holds up. A worthwhile theory, Popper concludes, is one that has been well tested and has survived, a theory that has not yet been falsified.[4]

To sum up: Scientific theories are not provable, but they are testable. For, whereas billions and billions of confirming instances will not prove a universal statement, one counter-instance will falsify or refute a universal

---

4. Karl Popper, *The Logic of Scientific Discovery* (New York: Science Editions, 1961), English translation of *Logik der Forschung* (1935).

statement. For example, the observation of billions of white swans will not prove the universal statement that all swans are white, but observing one black swan will refute it.

III

Popper's notion of falsifiability is surprisingly fruitful. Falsifiability allows us to demarcate science from nonscience and to weed out worthwhile theories from false ones; it also explains how scientific knowledge grows.

Prior to Popper, those who addressed themselves to the question of how science grows usually tried to explain it as the result of the accumulation of observations. That is, the story went, as scientists gathered more and more data that confirmed the theories we hold about the universe, our scientific knowledge expanded.

But the problem with this explanation, as Popper pointed out, is that we can always, if we are clever enough, find confirmations of our theories. But such observed confirmations do not advance knowledge. They simply reinforce our belief in our theories. Centuries of observation, for example, had at one time "confirmed" the theory that the world was flat. Our scientific knowledge of the world did not advance, however, until explorers like Columbus falsified that theory. Falsification, Popper argues, is the key to the growth of science. Scientific knowledge grows through "the repeated overthrow of scientific theories and their replacement by better or more satisfactory ones." [5]

A better theory is one that is not subject to the same refutations as the theory it replaces. It is closer to the truth, or as Popper sometimes puts it, a better theory has a greater degree of verisimilitude. Also, of course, a better theory must have greater content—it must tell us more than the theory it replaces. And the more a theory says, then the more it excludes or forbids, and the greater the opportunities for falsifying it.

One can see this relation between greater content and higher falsifiability by comparing the following two sentences:

A. Friday it will rain.
B. Friday and Saturday it will rain.

1. the content of *B* is greater than *A:* it provides us with more information.
2. But *B* excludes more than *A:* it prohibits two consecutive days of sunshine.
3. Hence, *B* is less likely than *A* to hold up: it has more opportunity to be falsified.

---

5. "Truth, Rationality and the Growth of Scientific Knowledge," in *Conjectures and Refutations*.

So, if the growth of science consists, as it must, of the continual replacement of theories with ones that tell us more, then, Popper argues, this process is one of replacing any given theory with a more risky theory—one less likely to hold up to experiments or tests.

Popper's explanation of how scientific knowledge grows has obvious dramatic implications for the method of science. Instead of looking for theories likely to be confirmed by tests and trying to verify them, scientists should take a bolder approach: look for theories of high content—risky theories, theories that forbid much, theories with greater opportunities for falsification, theories less likely to be confirmed—and subject those theories to severe tests and experiments. This is what scientists must do, Popper argues, if scientific knowledge is to advance, if we are to replace our present theories with ones that tell us more.

IV

Popper's contention that science grows through falsification of theories and their replacement by better ones is clearly borne out by the history of science, for surely we have better theories about the world than our ancestors. But if falsification does lead to their replacement by better ones, then the question arises: where, or how, do scientists discover these better theories?

The traditional answer to this question is a psychological one. That is, scientists discover new and better theories by observation—the observation of numerous instances of a given phenomenon leads them to discover a theory about that phenomenon. Now, this psychology of discovery is simply a rendition of logical "induction." But, induction, we saw above, is not valid. Observations, however repetitious, of white swans cannot logically or empirically allow us to come up with the general (universal) statement "All swans are white." Therefore, Popper concludes, theories do not emerge from observation, neither directly nor indirectly. Psychology cannot explain how new theories come into being. In place of a psychology of discovery (an area in which he himself worked many years), we must turn, Popper insists, to a logic of discovery.[6]

Although many people believe that science begins with observations, this is, Popper insists, logically impossible. He has repeatedly demonstrated the point in articles and lectures by challenging people: "Observe!" No one, he maintains, starts to observe without first having a definite question in mind, a question which might be decided by observations. So when told to observe, most people respond by asking, "What do

6. Karl Popper, "Autobiography," in *The Philosophy of Karl Popper,* ed. Paul A. Schlipp (LaSalle, Ill.: Open Court, 1974), sec. 12.

you want me to observe?'' Observation, Popper argues, comes *after* expectations. But expectations themselves are, or are derived from, theories (or hypotheses). So theories must, logically, precede observation. Every observation we make is made in light of a theory.

And theories? Where do they come from? Theories, Popper says, come from us, from human beings; we create them as conjectures. These conjectures are triggered by problems. And the problem itself comes into being only because of logical prior expectations, which means that every problem is logically related to a prior theory. A problem logically implies a prior inadequate theory. Thus, if we have a practical problem, say, with our car, this logically indicates we have an inadequate theory about the car—about its maintenance, its operations, or whatever.

This practical problem with our car leads us to create or conjecture a new theory about its maintenance, its operation, or wherever the problem lies. When our conjectured theory solves the problem, this means we have improved the original theory—the theory that generated the problem to begin with.

Popper has expressed all of this by saying all knowledge is theory-impregnated, including our observations. Accordingly, all improvements in knowledge consist of the modification, possibly the rejection, of previous knowledge. This means that we must begin our lives with inborn theories, which is precisely what Popper concludes:

> I assert that every animal is born with expectations or anticipations, which could be framed as hypotheses; a kind of hypothetical knowledge. And I assert that we have, in this sense, some degree of inborn knowledge from which we may begin, even though it may be quite unreliable. This inborn knowledge, these inborn expectations, will, if disappointed, create *our first* problems; and the ensuing growth of our knowledge may, therefore, be described as consisting throughout of corrections and modifications of previous knowledge.[7]

It is important to note that Popper comes to this conclusion about inborn knowledge because of the logical necessity for *theories* to exist before having problems, or observations.

V

If the advancement of knowledge consists of the modification of previous knowledge, then those who would advance knowledge, must, logically, begin with problems inherent in the existing knowledge or theories.

---

7. Karl Popper, ''Evolution and the Tree of Knowledge,'' in *Objective Knowledge* (Oxford: Oxford University Press, 1972), p. 258.

These problems trigger the creation of better theories, theories that are closer to the truth, theories that tell us more. Now, if the growth of science begins with problems, then it behooves those who want to contribute to its growth to search out and discover problems. To do this means to criticize the existing theories, to try to find what is wrong with them, to try to falsify them.

So, once again, Popper reveals the fantastic fruitfulness of his falsificationist approach. Earlier, we saw that he used falsifiability to demarcate science from nonscience: only those theories that can be falsified are scientific ones. In addition, he used falsification to weed out worthwhile theories: a worthwhile theory is one that survives attempts to falsify it. He has also used falsification to explain how knowledge grows, describing this process as the replacement of falsified theories by better ones. We advance knowledge through the falsification of existing theories, by discovering problems inherent in them. This triggers the creation of new theories or conjectures, and we ascertain how much better the new theory is by seeing if it has a higher information content (which means that there will be more opportunities to falsify it) and by seeing if it can better withstand attempts to falsify it.

On this matter of growth of scientific knowledge, Popper makes one last important point. If growth is to be continued, then continual criticism is called for. That is, continual attempts to falsify our theories will yield new problems that will trigger new conjectures or theories. The growth of science, then, is one of continual trial-and-error elimination, of conjecture followed by refutation which leads to new conjecture followed by refutation . . . and so it goes . . . resulting in ever better theories. One must not forget, however, that criticism presupposes existing theories, accepted theories. These theories usually come to us from tradition. Without tradition, knowledge would be impossible. But every bit of traditional knowledge is open to critical examination. "Thus, we might say," Popper writes, "that the most lasting contribution to the growth of scientific knowledge that a theory can make are the new problems which it raises, so that we are led back to the view of science and of the growth of knowledge as always starting from, and always ending with, problems—problems of ever increasing depth, and an ever increasing fertility in suggesting new problems."

Popper has schematically presented this conception of the growth of scientific knowledge in the following diagram—where P is the problem, TT the tentative theory, and EE error elimination or criticism: [8]

$$P_1 \rightarrow TT \rightarrow EE \rightarrow P_2$$

8. Karl Popper, "On the Sources of Knowledge and Ignorance" and "Truth, Rationality and the Growth of Scientific Knowledge," in *Conjectures and Refutations;* and "Epistemology without a Knowing Subject," in *Objective Knowledge*.

VI

In placing the responsibility for the growth of science on man himself, the responsibility to be critical, we come to what I consider the heart of Popper's philosophy, his conception of human beings as fallible creators.

As Popper construes him, man is like God, a Creator, but unlike God, what man creates, including his own knowledge, is never perfect. This means, however, that what he creates can always be improved. And the responsibility for improving it rests with man himself. He must assume what Popper calls a critical approach, or a critical attitude. Through a critical approach to his knowledge, man can uncover the problems inherent in it and trigger his own new, better conjectures.

It is this conception of man as a fallible creator that helps explain Popper's emphasis on falsification. Man creates his knowledge, so it is never perfect; hence, he can never justify it. But he can improve it; by approaching it critically, he can discover when and how it is false. *Because* man is fallible, the knowledge he creates can grow—not by the accumulation of "justified" knowledge but through falsification or error elimination. And *because* he is fallible, he can identify which of the knowledge he creates is worthwhile—not by trying to justify or prove it, but by trying to falsify it, trying to eliminate its errors. And *because* he is fallible, he can demarcate scientific knowledge from nonscientific—not by verification, but by seeing if it is falsifiable.

Popper has identified the critical approach as the basic theme in his philosophy and has tried to use it to fashion a new concept of human rationality, called critical rationality, to replace what he calls justificatory rationality.

According to justificatory rationality, human rationality consists in accepting only that knowledge or those theories we have justified (i.e., proven). But, as we saw, no number of confirmations can ever prove or justify a theory. Induction is not valid, therefore, justification is not possible.

What is possible is critical rationality. This consists in accepting only those theories that have withstood severe criticisms. Here we must note an important distinction Popper makes between logic and methodology. Logically, a single counterexample refutes a theory. But in practice or at the methodological level, complete falsification is not possible—for one can always doubt a statement, or make a mistake in observation, or escape refutation by definition. In short, we can always refuse to accept a contradiction.

But what this means, methodologically, Popper insists, is that we should assume a critical approach toward our theories, trying neither to immunize them from all falsification, nor accept falsification too readily. Only such a comprehensively critical approach will provide vigorous and severe testing of our theories.

VII

It should now be clear how revolutionary Karl Popper's philosophy is. At the center of this intellectual revolution is his total repudiation of induction:

> I hold that neither animals nor men use any procedure like induction, or any argument based on the repetition of instances. The belief that we use induction is simply a mistake. It is a kind of optical illusion.[9]

Popper goes beyond David Hume, who first pointed out the logical and empirical arguments against induction but ended up interpreting induction psychologically. Popper maintains that induction does not ever occur. The method we—animals and human beings—use, he claims, is the method of trial-and-error elimination. We are misled because this method looks like induction. But the logic of trial-and-error elimination is totally different, and avoids all the difficulties traditionally connected to induction.

Prior to Popper, people had unsuccessfully tried to use induction to solve the problems about scientific knowledge already discussed. That is, they had tried to use induction to demarcate science from nonscience, to weed out worthwhile theories, and to explain the growth of scientific knowledge. In each case, the story went, the method of induction produced true, justified, and accumulative knowledge. But this is a myth: induction is not valid, not justified; it does not exist; hence it explains nothing.

Most people find it very difficult to accept this. Induction, they say, is part of common sense. Everyone knows that we learn from experience. If we see a number of white swans and never a nonwhite one, we are led to generalize, or to conclude (to induce) that all swans are white. This, so the story goes, is how learning takes place. Yet Popper insists that this common-sense notion of how we learn is mistaken, like an optical illusion. Popper bases his argument against the existence of induction on what he calls the principle of transference or the principle of the primacy of the logical situation. That is, if induction cannot occur logically, then it cannot occur psychologically. What really takes place, he says, is that we make observations in light of our theories and then modify these theories when they are falsified by experience. Now, this *looks like* induction. It looks as if we are learning, or *receiving,* knowledge from the outside world through our observations or experiences. But in reality, it is we who create our theories (and in the first instance are born with theories), which we then modify when we discover, through observations or experiences, that these theories do not hold up.

9. Karl Popper, "Replies to My Critics," in *The Philosophy of Karl Popper,* sec. 13.

As Popper views learning, we can learn from experience, but for him this means that our experiences can, if we are sufficiently critical and lucky, reveal to us the inadequacy or falsity of our theories, triggering us to create better ones.

VIII

In construing human beings as fallible creators, Popper credits us with creating more than knowledge. Human beings create society too. The society we create, like our knowledge, is never perfect, but, like our knowledge, it can be improved—through criticism.

Here his model is Socrates, who sought to improve Athens through criticism. But to improve society through criticism, we must have what Socrates had not: an open society—a society wherein the policies, practices, rules, and laws are open to criticism and where critics are taken seriously, not squelched and censured, or killed. The creation of an open society is up to us. We have to fashion institutions that hold society's decision makers open and responsive to criticisms—institutions that hold them accountable to those affected by their decisions.

Instead of worrying about who should rule or who should make decisions in our social and political institutions, our social and political scientists should try to help people protect themselves against incompetent rulers and decision makers, and against those who would abuse their powers. And the way to do this, Popper suggests, is to trace the actual consequences of the present social and political arrangements, uncovering the evils these arrangements generate. Social and political scientists thus take on the role of critics of society—the socratic role, if you will. Such criticism, when taken seriously, leads to critical dialogue or discussion, and then the modification or refinement of the existing arrangements in light of the unrefuted criticism. This improves the society through the elimination or diminution of the specific evils uncovered.[10]

Popper's view of social improvement emerges directly from his epistemological theory. Knowledge grows through trial-and-error elimination, and so the growth of scientific knowledge depends on the deliberate adoption of a critical approach. Here, in his social and political philosophy, he extends the critical approach to society. Of course, the critical approach cannot give us a perfect society any more than the critical approach can give us a perfect science. Society will always be imperfect because it is created by fallible beings and because there will always exist irreconcilable clashes of values. But society can always be improved. We can always reduce the existing suffering and pain.

---

10. Karl Popper, *The Open Society and Its Enemies* (4th ed.; London: Routledge and Kegan Paul, 1962), esp. vol. 1, chap. 10.

IX

In recent years, Popper has characterized his theory of growth of knowledge as a Darwinian theory. According to Darwin's theory of natural selection, the environment eliminated those organisms that were unfit or inadequate. Evolution or growth occurred when those organisms that did survive produced offspring that varied slightly from themselves, organisms that also survived and had progeny of their own. The crucial factor in evolution is the action of the environment as a critic—a critic that eliminates inadequate or unfit progeny.

Popper says this is also true in the evolution of our knowledge. It grows and evolves through criticism—the elimination of recognized errors from our theories. Confronted with these discovered inadequacies or problems, we create new, and better, theories.

This Darwinian explanation of the growth of knowledge is meant to explain how knowledge really grows. It is not meant metaphorically: "The theory of knowledge which I wish to propose is a largely Darwinian theory of the growth of knowledge. From the amoeba to Einstein, the growth of knowledge is always the same: we try to solve our problems, and to obtain by a process of elimination something approaching adequacy in our tentative solutions." [11]

X

The Popper-Darwinian construction of improvement is directly applicable to the process of education and provides what has been missing since Socrates: a nonauthoritarian conception of that process. (Here I must repeat that Karl Popper has not applied his theories to education. What follows is my own extrapolation, or adaptation, of his work.)

Most contemporary educators actually do construe the process of education as the process of promoting student growth: intellectual or cognitive growth, as well as moral, aesthetic, social, and—perhaps—emotional growth. Teachers try to improve or advance their students' theories, skills, dispositions. Yet few educators employ a Darwinian approach to the task. In fact, it is not unjust to characterize the approach commonly used by most teachers as Lamarckian.

Lamarck, a predecessor of Darwin, thought evolution took place through the transmission of acquired characteristics. He would explain the giraffe's long neck, for example, as an instance of the transmission of acquired characteristics. In order to adapt to changing environmental conditions, Lamarck's giraffe had to grow a long neck so as to eat the

---

11. Popper, "Evolution and the Tree of Knowledge," p. 261.

leaves off the topmost branches. This newly acquired characteristic was then transmitted to the giraffe's progeny.

As with Lamarckian giraffes, so with Lamarckian teachers. They transmit knowledge, or learning (acquired characteristics of the human species) to each generation of students. But such Lamarckian transmission never occurs, neither in biology nor in education. Of course, teachers—some teachers, at any rate—can point to what they take to be successful transmission of skills or theories or dispositions. The students—some students, at any rate—learned what was transmitted, didn't they? The answer to this, if the Popper-Darwinian theory of growth is correct, is that, yes, these students did grow or learn, but this did not come about through transmission—any more than did the long neck of the giraffe. What really takes place is growth through selection.

All learning, all growth of knowledge, according to the Popper-Darwinian theory, consists of the modification or rejection of some form of knowledge that was there previously. And such modification results from the observed inadequacies of the previously held knowledge. Thus, anyone who learns something new—whether it is Boyle's law or how to kick a football or how to save money—is simply modifying a theory, a skill, or a disposition he already had, even if in some gross, vague, or unarticulated form. And he modified this knowledge in light of its observed inadequacies.

Now, what deceives us is that this process of learning through selection (i.e., through the elimination of inadequacies in our existing knowledge), *looks* like a process of transmission. For what we see is a teacher telling students, say, how to spell the word *cat;* and later we see the students correctly spelling the word *cat*. This looks like transmission. But what is really happening is that the learner is going through the process of trial-and-error elimination. The learner already can speak, perhaps write as well, has seen cats, understands the sound *cat*, and has some understanding of the relation of letters to sounds, letters to words, and so on. Invited to demonstrate what he knows, the learner goes through a process of trial-and-error elimination, sometimes correctly, sometimes with the help of the teacher or the help of models. No transmission takes place. The learner has just modified the knowledge he already possesses through trial-and-error elimination.

The trouble with the transmission conception of the educational process, which has reigned since Aristotle, is not simply that it is wrong but that it results in an authoritarian construction of education.

Construing education as a process of transmission converts it into imposition. The teacher's task is to impose knowledge, or learning, on the students. The knowledge transmitted is the acquired (justified? proven?) wisdom of society. Teachers who try to transmit usually employ many different tactics and strategems to pull this off in a benign way. They try to "motivate" students to want to learn what they are supposed to learn. They try to match the materials to be learned to the learner—to his "needs," "interests," "abilities," "aptitude," and "capabilities." But the process is still one of imposition.

The argument against imposition is that it prevents growth. Here is the argument. If the Popper-Darwinian theory of growth is correct, then in all cases the student learns through trial-and-error elimination. Therefore, when teachers and schools try to impose learning, they are simply coercing students to adopt *their* criteria for identifying errors. They are saying, in effect, "All knowledge that is contrary to this knowledge we present to you is false." This prevents growth.

Here is another argument. Suppose teachers completely succeeded in imposing knowledge on the young and completely succeeded in "proving" that this knowledge was true. It is patently clear that for those students so taught (indoctrinated?) that the advancement of that knowledge would cease. Because, you see, these students would "know" the truth. So we are led to conclude that the growth of knowledge has occurred and will continue to occur *only* because teachers *failed* to impose knowledge on the young.

To sum up: construing the process of education as one of transmission is logically incompatible with the aim of promoting the growth of knowledge.

One reason why educators have not confronted the fact that the transmission conception of the educational process is inimical to growth is that there seemed to be no other way for education to take place except through transmission. But the Popper-Darwinian theory of growth offers an alternative conception to the educational process, and thus an alternative conception of the functions of the teacher and the school.

Summary and Evaluation

In adapting the Popper-Darwinian construction of growth, a teacher assumes that the student already possesses knowledge and also assumes that the student is the source of growth. Rather than an imposer of knowledge, the teacher tries to create a critical environment, an environment responsive to the knowledge the student has, an environment that will help the student discover the inadequacy of that knowledge and encourage him to modify it. (It is important to note that such a critical environment presupposes that the student does have knowledge. As Popper has put it: "There can be no critical phase without a preceding dogmatic phase, a phase in which something—an expectation, a regularity of behavior—is formed, so that error elimination can begin to work on it.") The teacher, of course, is a central part of that critical environment, trying, like Socrates, to take seriously the student's knowledge and help him become critical of it. The subject matter here becomes the material with which to elicit the student's knowledge and something against which he can test his knowledge. The teacher does not ask the student to accept the subject matter, but rather to encounter it—critically.

Now, much of this is not new, of course. One finds it adumbrated in twentieth-century educational theorists such as Maria Montessori, A. S. Neill, Jean Piaget, and Carl Rogers. All these theorists in one way or another advise educators to create a supportive, responsive environment, an environment that permits students to interact freely with one another, with the teacher, and with the subject matter. They all insist that given this kind of an environment, children will need no extensive rewards or punishments—they will learn naturally, through their own activity. Learners, these theorists all claim, do not require teachers.

In Popper's philosophy, we find a rigorous philosophical defense of this twentieth century theory of education. He provides a theory that explains why the educational practices of Montessori, of Neill, of Rogers, and yes, of Piaget, work. All these pedagogical geniuses were groping toward a nonauthoritarian construction of education—a construction in keeping with human fallibility.

Karl Popper was himself a teacher in the Vienna schools for seven years before migrating to New Zealand when Hitler came to power. In his "Autobiography," he tells how as a college student he had dreamed of creating the kind of school that those twentieth-century educational theorists later prescribed: "I dreamt of one day founding a school in which young people could learn without boredom, and would be stimulated to pose problems and discuss them; a school in which no unwanted answers to unasked questions would have to be listened to; in which one did not study for the sake of passing examinations."

Karl Popper never carried out that dream, never founded a school—but he did create the philosophy for the founding of such a school of his dreams.

Index